THE DARK SIDE OF BEHAVIOUR AT WORK

The Dark Side of Behaviour at Work

Understanding and avoiding employees leaving, thieving and deceiving

Adrian Furnham

John Taylor

First published 2004 by
PALGRAVE MACMILLAN
Houndmills, Basingstoke, Hampshire RG21 6XS and
175 Fifth Avenue, New York, N.Y. 10010
Companies and representatives throughout the world

PALGRAVE MACMILLAN is the global academic imprint of the Palgrave
Macmillan division of St. Martin's Press, LLC and of Palgrave Macmillan Ltd.
Macmillan® is a registered trademark in the United States, United Kingdom
and other countries. Palgrave is a registered trademark in the European
Union and other countries.

ISBN 1–4039–3577–7

This book is printed on paper suitable for recycling and made from fully
managed and sustained forest sources.

A catalogue record for this book is available from the British Library.

A catalog record for this book is available from the Library of Congress.

10 9   8   7   6   5   4   3   2   1
13 12 11 10 09 08 07 06 05 04

Printed in China

For Benedict (AF)

For Abi and Rach (JT)

Contents

List of Figures

List of Tables

Preface

Betrayal is fascinating and many writers have used the theme as the centre-piece of their works. Romantic fiction, theatre and films rely heavily on people doing unpleasant things to each other. All too often, we find the reality close to us socially and in the workplace. In many ways the dark side of behaviour at work is more interesting than the light.

When planning the book we quickly became aware that while the issues were common and the subject of much chatter, serious analysis of what motivates people to do bad things is sparse, particularly amongst writers of management books. Specific subjects such as sabotage or fraud do have a number of books and studies to help the boss suffering those manifestations of employee perfidy.

There is a wealth of work on employee retention – how to recruit and retain the best staff being a frequent theme amongst writers of such works – but not much in-depth work on why people might want to resign in the first place. And yet so many people do leave their jobs – bosses included! Why is it so difficult to see in others what is, in effect, something already experienced by ourselves or those close to us?

Whistle-blowers these days almost have hero status. Their motive is clearly to expose a wrong, but few stop to think if there might be some other reason for their action. Fewer have tried to analyse their motivation. Could it be that to question the motive of a whistle-blower is not politically correct? When the press are chasing the whistle-blower (sometimes with tragic consequences) are we really not willing to examine whether he or she might have some ulterior motive that amounts to the rather less-attractive aim of revenge?

Whatever the reasons for the paucity of material on the subject of motivation of betrayers, we have tried to piece together such material as there is and to add our own thoughts based on observation and analysis. We have tackled these subjects in the hope that CEOs, bosses, managers and HR professionals will better understand why employees do bad things. It may be that managers themselves are in the dark with respect to the dark side of employee behaviour: one aim of this book is to turn the light on. In doing so, we hope that businesses and organizations will become more productive, profitable and efficient by the reduction of such counter-productive behaviours.

The authors met at various seminars and training events, many concerned with deception and employee dissatisfaction. The lack of material on these subjects provided their motivation to write this book. It is like many journeys of research, a beginning. They welcome comments – critical and supportive – on the book as well as stories of what might have caused employee commitment or rebellion in the workplace.

Please send any thoughts or contributions to feedback@artemis-uk.com.

ADRIAN FURNHAM AND JOHN TAYLOR
London

Acknowledgements

There are those who encouraged, those who cajoled, those who doubted and those who kept quiet and did not disturb. But all in their own way helped, both directly and indirectly. Sylva, Faye, Laura and Carole all put digit to keyboard and helped directly. Inspiration, support and motivation came from many: Alison, Aly, Ian, Anthony, Elizabeth, Pammie, Adrian, Jackie, Keith, Amanda, Cortland, Hilary, Mark, Jane, Christopher, Gerry, Brian, John, Peter, Nickie, Norah, Annie, Andrew, Simon, Roger, Nigel, Stephen, Penny, Debbie, Moira and the riff raff.

Stephen, who said yes to our proposal, and his team, who made its production as effortless as possible, deserve huge credit and our sincere thanks.

And of course, there are those who provided the substance. Most do not know they supplied the material, which is the basis of so much of the book. Some will speculate (in vain) about who inspired a particular story or conclusion. The sadness is that those who are the poor role models will probably never recognise themselves.

Amongst those who do not realise their positive contribution are The Angel Curry House and far too many vineyards from all over the world who sustained us through lunch times and evenings, when Alison tolerated our intellectual meandering – but only so much!

Thank you to you all.

The authors and publishers would like to thank the following for permission to use copyright material: United Feature Syndicate Inc. for permission to use the Dilbert cartoon on page xv; extracts from the *Guardian*; extracts taken from the *Financial Times*; material taken from the *Academy of Management Review*; material taken from The Centre for Retail Research, Nottingham; material taken from *The Economic Crime Survey 2003* is reproduced with permission from the Investigations and Forensic Services Department of PricewaterhouseCoopers; material taken from the *National Retail Security Report*, University of Florida; material taken from *Detecting Lies and Deceit*, A. Vrij (2000) with permission from John Wiley & Sons Limited; material taken from *Research on Negotiations in Organizations*, Vol. 6, Robinson et al., reproduced with permission from Elsevier; material taken from *Citizen Espionage*, Sarbin, with permission from Greenwood Publishing Group Inc.; material taken from *Telling Lies*, Ekman (2001), with permission from W.W. Norton; material taken from *International Journal of Selection and Assessment*, Kelloway et al. (2002) with permission from Blackwell Publishing Limited.

Every effort has been made to trace all the copyright holders but if any have been inadvertently overlooked the publishers will be pleased to make the necessary arrangements at the first opportunity.

Introduction

Source: Copyright © 1999. United Feature Syndicate, Inc. Reproduced by permission.

History is rich with examples of people cheating on their employers, leaders, work colleagues and friends. Some examples are notorious, some surprising and some, no doubt, contested. Even Ptolemy, Galileo, Newton and Mendel – who were all great men of science – are all believed by some to have misled the world on the research data that led to their great discoveries. They too might have been motivated by vanity or greed, like Herostratus or, more notoriously, Judas Iscariot.

More is known about the motives of employees in today's seemingly frantic and competitive world of work, but there are still surprises. Employers have to cope with the consequences of employees not just performing badly but behaving badly as well. The common managerial response is to remove the problem if it can be detected. This book endorses that approach, given that the 'crime' has been committed. But the authors believe the frequency and severity of the acts can be reduced, if not eliminated, by understanding why people do such things and therefore anticipating and removing the causes of the problem of dark-side or counterproductive behaviour at work.

On the night of 21 July 356 BC the Temple of Artemis, one of the Seven Wonders of the World, was burnt to the ground. The culprit was seized and he admitted just before his execution that he had done it in order to make his name immortal. His desire for fame, his act of unparalleled sabotage to satisfy his vanity, might have been frustrated because it was decreed that his name be removed from all records and that no one ever pronounce it. But we know his name was Herostratus.

Around AD 28 Judas Iscariot, one of the 12 apostles, betrayed Jesus to the chief priest for 30 pieces of silver. According to the Gospels of Matthew and Mark, he did it because of greed.

The normality of it all

It is, fortunately, rather rare to have employees who firebomb their boss's office; who sabotage computers; who poison food and blackmail companies. The deeply disgruntled, discontented employee who seeks to damage, defraud, even destroy their organization or the working lives of individuals is not necessarily a deranged demon.

It is, alas, not at all uncommon, for people at various points in their working lives to feel angry, resentful, hurt and vengeful. Just as everybody at some point can and does feel depressed at home or stressed at work, so it is extremely common for people to feel angry, defiant and vengeful at work. The crucial questions are the *cause* of the problem (boss, co-workers); the acute (how deep) and chronic (how long) *nature* of the problem(s) and most importantly how the individual *copes*, deals with or reacts to the issue. These negative feelings can occur for a host of different reasons:

▷ They are passed over for promotion.
▷ Their boss picks on them or is demanding and rude.
▷ Promises are reneged upon.
▷ Their workload is suddenly and inequitably increased.
▷ Various perks are removed.
▷ They get a poor, and in their view, unjust appraisal.
▷ Company policy over particular issues (for example maternity leave) changes.
▷ The CEO or some prominent leader takes an overtly political stand on some issue.

The most important characteristics of the above reasons for feeling discontent is that they are all subjective. In this sense they are peculiar and particular to the individual. Two people in the *same* job see things *differently*. The one feels a sleight; the other is amused. The one feels personally put upon; the other understands the necessity for the actions.

But one does not have to be a sensitive flower to feel unfairly dealt with. It is a very common reaction: in all organizations, at all times, on all levels people feel, from time to time, disgruntled. Indeed life is not fair. The slings and arrows of misfortune engulf us all.

The question, however, is how we react to these feelings. But first it may be important to ask some fundamental questions:

1 Are there cultural, economic and political forces that are more likely to lead to personal workplace malcontentedness?
2 Are some organizations likely to have more malcontents than others?
3 Do some management behaviours cause more malcontentedness than others?
4 To what extent does the nature of the job people do make them more prone to malcontentedness?

5   Are some people more prone to malcontentedness than others?
6   And finally, what leads people to express their malcontentedness in such different ways?

There are three sorts of forces and factors that relate to these issues. In the nineteenth century, the desperate, abused factory employee burnt down the factory in frustrated rage. In the twentieth century there was a huge growth in institutions and procedures that attempted to cope with grievances, inequalities and so on. Trade unions, workers' councils, arbitration services and human resource specialists – all attempted to resolve conflicts before they got out of hand. In the twenty-first century, the workplace is more complex and many workers more sophisticated. Some of the ways of dealing with grievances now seem inflexible, out-of-date and discredited. But the need for them has not reduced. Different countries respond to this quite differently and, therefore, in part account for variations at a national level.

Cultural, economic and political forces

Big international companies with subsidiaries in different companies know that rates of theft, disruption, absenteeism and strikes differ widely. There are cultural attitudes to, and beliefs about, theft: *what* and *when* and *how* and *why* certain things can be 'liberated' and what cannot. People often have a very elaborate, even sophisticated, set of ideas and rationalizations about these moral and ethical issues, which are deeply embedded in the culture. What one culture punishes another turns a blind eye to because of history, religion and so on.

There are also economic forces that inevitably relate to particular types of counterproductive behaviour at work. Where a country or company is in the economic cycle (boom, bust, growth, decline) could make a difference as can the differences between the remuncrations of the most well-paid. Economic conditions also determine the worth of different phenomena so that what is valuable in one country is nearly worthless in another.

Equally, political forces play their role. A politically unstable country is, no doubt, much more likely to see more counterproductive behaviour at work. The nature of a political system (democratic vs. autocratic) and the popularity of that system as well as its stability all make a difference.

Cultural, political and economic forces – nearly always complicatedly intertwined – in part determine different patterns in counterproductive behaviours at work.

Organizational factors

There is a long list of danger signals for organizations that make them more likely to be growth beds for the malcontent. Almost every one is sufficient but not necessarily a cause of the problem. But each is certainly a sign of a poorly managed company. This list is far from conclusive:

▷ An 'us vs. them' feel to management/employee differentiation.
▷ An assumption that loyalty and commitment is a one-way street: that employees should show unquestionable loyalty but that management need not reciprocate this.
▷ A culture of surveillance and suspicion where nobody trusts each other and there is excessive, probably growing, use of electronic surveillance methods.
▷ Having no, poor, outdated or rigged grievance procedures that people have not agreed to or had any personal say in shaping.
▷ Hypocritical messages where managers say one thing and do another.
▷ Where sticks are preferred to carrots to motivate and where only top managers get the 'carrot method'.
▷ Where there is no long-term view: management is reactive not proactive with a short-term view of everything, particularly profit.
▷ Where people are promoted (and rewarded) by nepotism, corruption and ingratiation rather than for their ability and effort.
▷ Where it is believed work is/has to be extrinsically satisfying only: there can be no joy in the work itself.
▷ Where communication channels are blocked, non-existent or noisy so that people do not realize what is going on until too late.
▷ Where most employees feel alienated from top management and no one identifies with the company or its products.
▷ And where, paradoxically, lots of people overtly or covertly break company rules and even legal requirements.

Similar organizations in similar sectors in the same region can therefore experience very varied rates of counterproductive behaviour as a function of the way the organization is managed. Indeed some have noted that 'shrinkage' and 'sabotage' are indeed excellent objective measures of how well an organization is run. They also represent a good index of how organizational change policies are working.

Individual factors

These are equally important and can be categorized in terms of ability, personality and values. Personality and values are most likely to influence counterproductive behaviours at work. Extreme extraverts may do things for the sheer thrill of the activity – practical jokes and so on. Neurotics may bear grudges longer and be more sensitive to negative comments. Less agreeable people may, through their lack of empathy, thoroughly 'piss off' their colleagues and customers.

However, values and personal morality may be the most important factor here. Some people seem utterly incorruptible, quite able to resist all temptations, while others act impulsively and immorally at any opportunity. Integrity is perhaps the value or trait that is most relevant here.

A personal ethical or moral system may be both rigid and flexible. It can change over time, but studies on the life history of cheats at work tend to show that signs of lack of integrity appear very early. The ethical/moral value systems are strongly influenced by primary (parental) and secondary (schooling) education. Most parents and schools are eager to teach moral values: about telling the truth, being honest, about loyalty, about trustworthiness, about justice and honour. Not all heed the lessons and there are quite obviously major differences between individuals. There are some individuals, though mercifully few in number, who cannot it seems differentiate between honesty and dishonesty; many names apply to them from moral imbeciles to psychopaths. They are dangerous but rare.

The workplace deviant is likely to engage in acts of theft, serious drug and alcohol abuse, lying and deceit, insubordination, vandalism, sabotage, chronic absenteeism and even assault. The files of workplace deviants are likely to contain numerous warning letters and threatened suspensions, grievance dispute records, worker compensation claims and accident reports. Some workplace deviants steal because of temporary life pressures – because of gambling losses, substance abuse or some other secret problem.

Consider two common and problematical issues: theft and lying. In some organizations, there is the possibly justified assumption that everyone is stealing. It becomes an opportunistic norm known by the technical term 'shrinkage'. It is a grey area with varying degrees of localized tolerance, even acceptance.

In most organizations, there is a balance of encouraging and inhibiting factors that determine levels and types of theft. Some organizations seek out personality types that may lie but are likely to be good at the job. Many have been 'arrested in their moral development' which can be tested by simple moral reasoning tasks. They also tend to have poor ego strength and can't resist easy temptation. They seem vulnerable to group norms and appear not to have that internal quiet voice of conscience. We know that the workplace deviant is likely to score very low on three related concepts of prudence, integrity and conscientiousness. These are not difficult to measure and there are various questionnaires which do just that. However, it should be admitted that they are fairly transparent and the lying workplace deviant may be able to spot the 'correct' desirable answers. So the best solution is to get the potential employee's nominated (or better still, not nominated) former employers and colleagues to complete these questionnaires for him or her. Many of them have probably been victims of the workplace deviant and their ratings of his/her imprudence, lack of integrity and conscientiousness should be highly predictive. The many hurt and angry people left in the wake of workplace deviants means there is likely to be no shortage of those willing to tell the truth about them.

Thieves, for that is what they are, may have a whole series of rationalization techniques for their clearly unacceptable behaviour:

▷ *Minimization:* 'it's only a pen; the company can afford it and won't miss it'.
▷ *Externalization:* 'the boss made me do it; I was framed'.
▷ *Normalization:* 'everyone does it; this is what we do round here'.
▷ *Superordination:* 'they owed me; it's only fair repayment'.

However, the theme of much of this book is that the dark side of behaviour at work is often simply the 'flip side' of the light or good side. Counterproductive behaviour at work is common though often its causes are not well understood. This book is about the many factors that lead people into committing a range of counterproductive behaviours – and what to do about it!

1 The Overview

Introduction

This book is about the cause, manifestations and consequences of individual infidelity to the employer. It is concerned with why employees become angry, disgruntled and spiteful towards their employer and how they attempt to seek to damage or take revenge for their feelings. But more importantly it seeks to help employers both prevent it occurring in the first place as well as 'recover' individuals who feel vengeful towards their company. It aims to help people identify and manage those who are likely to cause considerable damage to the organizations that they work for through theft, sabotage, fraud or a range of other counterproductive behaviours.

There is nothing new about institutional infidelity. Legends, myths and stories in all cultures celebrate and moralize about employees who have committed acts of vengeance against their employers. Judas Iscariot is one of the most notorious, but more recent ones have taken on similar infamy in their own fields – Nick Leeson (Barings Bank) and Jeffrey Wigand (Brown and Williamson, the American Tobacco company). Many of these stories deal not only with the shortcomings of the employee but also with those of the employer: infidelity *is a two-way street*. So is loyalty. Some organizations are more likely to produce betrayers than others: their values, management practices and hypocrisy turn the loyal and trusted employee into a potential saboteur, whistle-blower or thief.

In this book we consider what leads particular individuals to specific acts of infidelity and vengeance at a particular time. The questions are 'Why some individuals and not others?'; 'What is it about some people that they lie steal and cheat, while others with similar experiences do not?'; 'Why a particular act of vengeance and not others?'; 'Why do some individuals embezzle, others whistle-blow and still others simply leave?'; 'Why an act of betrayal occurs at one time and not another?'; 'What series of historical events occurred to provoke an act of betrayal or vengeance at a particular period of time?'

Managers and those employed in human resources seek to develop staff loyalty, even commitment. They want dedication born of mutual trust, respect and even affection. But loyalty acts both ways: both parties have to give and receive.

> *I don't want loyalty. I want* loyalty. *I want him to kiss my ass in Macy's window at high noon and tell me it smells like roses. I want his pecker in my pocket.*
> Lyndon B Johnson 1972,
> President, United States

If a marriage or partner relationship breaks down, each individual feels wounded and tends to blame the other. In this sense a job may be seen as a long-term (and very complex) relationship between employer and employee.

Many organizations and institutions can appear faceless, soulless and uncaring. To those running the institution, it is often hard to accept that they have a responsibility for specific employee problems. To them, it is the individual through his or her act of leaving, whistle-blowing or sabotage who is to blame. Little attention is paid to how the institution as a whole, and senior managers in particular, might have contributed to that individual's breaking away and severing the bonds of trust and loyalty.

In the introduction to her book *How Institutions Think*, Mary Douglas says:

> Writing about co-operation and solidarity means writing at the same time about rejection and mistrust. Solidarity involves individuals being ready to suffer on behalf of the larger group and their expecting other individual members to do as much for them. It is difficult to talk about these questions coolly. They touch on intimate feelings of loyalty and sacredness; anyone who has accepted trust and demanded sacrifice or willingly given either knows the power of the social bond. (Douglas 1986 p 1)

Psychologists talk of various attribution errors. This refers to explanations for the causes of success and failure. Perhaps the most noticeable attribution error is to explain away failure elsewhere. Thus the failed student blames the teacher, the text books and the exam format, but never themselves. Similarly, when asked to account for betrayal (senior) managers in organizations seek explanations exclusively in the pathology and immorality of employees. It is as if their management style and the organization culture are blameless or at least not involved in the causal explanation for the act of betrayal.

Part of the problem is that it is difficult to talk about organizational factors and processes as causal agents in the story of any individual. We are all psychologists in the sense that we choose to explain events at the level of the individual; not the group, not society as a whole but the individual. People are the origins of causes. Thus, confronted with different types or levels of explanation we often choose the most familiar. In this sense betrayal is explained in terms of the betrayer; not that which is betrayed. Betrayers are pathological not organizations – though individual managers can be.

Companies and organizations usually seek high retention rates, not just because it hurts to see former colleagues leave but for good economic reasons as well. Staff turnover is desirable in moderation in most organizations but when it becomes a haemorrhage the costs of recruitment and loss of skills and knowledge become intolerable and affect the efficiency of the business.

Most institutions suffer petty pilfering (and hardly any employee is innocent of misuse of the phone or using office stationery for personal reasons), but when Nick Leeson started breaking the rules at Barings Bank in the early 1990s he single handedly brought down one of the UK's most respected banks. One single 'rogue trader' destroyed a 300-year-old institution. We discuss Leeson's case in detail later, but commentators were generally agreed that Barings' management contributed significantly to its own demise (see Chapter 3).

Through the understanding of what influences employees to turn against an institution, managers and HR specialists should be able to avoid its worst excesses and manage disloyalty when it does occur, without it becoming a virus spreading through the rest of the organization and possibly destroying it. They could use that knowledge to build on institutional loyalty and even go further to create a workforce which is committed and willing to go that extra mile.

There are three factors of importance here: those unique factors that are relevant to betrayal; those unique factors that influence loyalty; and those that influence both. Just as psychologists argue that money affects job dissatisfaction rather than satisfaction, so certain organizational processes such as lack of appraisal may exclusively influence infidelity. But there are also processes that if not applied (or applied inappropriately) affect betrayal, but if applied correctly effect loyalty.

Much of this book is a study of *infidelity*, but its primary purpose is to use the understanding of *why* people betray in order *to build* on loyalty and commitment. Understanding why things go wrong can be most helpful in understanding why they function well. Illness tells us about health. We are interested in the anatomy and physiology of betrayal and the counterproductive acts that typify it – and its opposite, namely loyalty and commitment.

The concept of fit

It is now common practice for companies and organizations to devote considerable energy to working out what skills and qualities they want in their staff. The word 'competencies' is now commonplace. It is the right place to start, for if staff are employed who do not have the right skills or do not fit in the institution, something somewhere will soon go wrong.

Competencies identified by companies and public sector organizations tend to focus on skills such as literacy, numeric ability, accuracy or, at a higher level of management, influencing others, giving purpose and thinking strategically. They also seek to encourage qualities such as integrity, determination and responsibility. The competency list is an important tool and says something about the organization, but it says little about the priorities. It is interesting if an organization has integrity, honesty or fidelity as a desirable (indeed necessary) competency. It may say something about the organization as a whole. But what is perhaps more interesting is how recruiters and selectors go about evaluating integrity. What do they look for? How reliably do they detect it?

It is all too easy for staff to form their own perception of whether they are the right fit. The institution may form another view in terms of values, culture

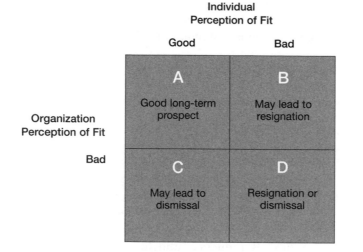

Figure 1.1 **The person–organization fit**

rewards, and so on. The interview, induction and probationary period are all about seeing if they fit together (employee as well as employer).

Box A: Both employer and employee agree and feel the fit is right. This is the condition to strive for, though it is often based more on perceptions and intuition than real data.

Box B: The employer feels the employee is good, but the employee is not content. This will lead ideally to the employee's resignation. Problems will develop if the employee stays on and the organization does not change.

Box C: Here the employee feels he/she is in the right job, but this view is not shared by the employer. This should lead to dismissal, but all too often this does not happen; the employee does not receive promotion or similar bonuses as his or her peers and begins to feel disappointment and then resentment. It often reflects the pusillanimity of senior managers to act early on once the misfit is apparent.

Box D: Again both employer and employee agree and there should be an easy resolution. It is probably best to let the employee resign and thus retain dignity. If engineered properly, the employee will leave feeling positively about the organization, which treated him or her well and fairly.

Those who fall into categories B and C present most problems, which may become noticeable over time rather than at the recruitment process. Figure 1.1 shows the most common consequences of getting it wrong. But if the fit is badly wrong or the individual feels badly treated, boxes B, C and D can result in much more dire penalties. Pilfering, fraud and sabotage can all precede the dismissal or resignation; whistle-blowing can feature both before and after the employee has left.

There are various problems with this simple model.

1 *Fit is multidimensional.* Potential employer and employee both see fit of various facets at various levels. Employees are interested in many job features both intrinsic and extrinsic: benefits and compensation, job security, training, maternity and crèche facilities and so on. The employer is after able, motivated, competent, honest, flexible staff. Thus there may be a perfect fit on one level/facet but not others. Hence both have to compromise in some cost–benefit analysis.
2 *Fit is dynamic.* Just as people find they change their interests, values and attitudes over time, so do organizations. The latter can change radically from their core business to their organizational structure. Many divorces occur because the partners change: once highly compatible they become incompatible when either party changes. If both individuals and organizations change, the more likely fit is to turn into misfit.
3 *Fit is hard to determine.* Neither interviewer nor interviewee is totally honest at interview. Errors of omission and commission mean that neither side presents a comprehensive picture. The tendency is to emphasize the positive. In this sense it can be difficult for both parties to determine their degree or level of fit.
4 *Fit may be impossible to articulate.* Neither employer nor employees always have a very good insight into their motives and needs. It is not that they are necessarily hiding something; rather they can not always accurately and sensitively report on those factors that drive them. In this sense fit or misfit only becomes clear over time, and even then it may be almost impossible for people at work to articulate precisely how this occurs.

Of course this is not the inevitable consequence of selecting the wrong people. People do not easily fit into such neat categories. Employees are often a near fit or near misfit to the ideal profile selectors are looking for. The issue then becomes one of performance. Where the recruiters have got it right, employee performance will (hopefully) be maximized. Where they do not quite make the right choices, performance is usually variable. This is recognized and accepted by organizations. But individuals often feel they are not appreciated and, especially when they are in a high performance business, often disagree with the labels given them. Figure 1.2 shows the relative performance of those who fit well – the high achievers; those who are a good but not quite perfect fit – the competent; and those who are not a good fit – the poor performers over the working life.

Loyalty over time

The working life is changing. Fewer and fewer people do the stint from 18 to their 60th or 65th birthday in the same company. More widespread education means that people start work later (in their mid 20s) and may take

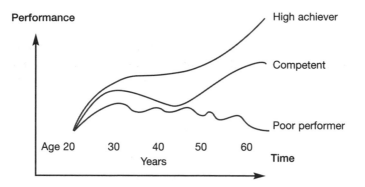

Figure 1.2 **Performance over time for three hypothetical types**

'early retirement' at 50 or 55. The impact of home working and the internet is still to be worked out.

Whether or not one works for the same company for a lifetime or simply
long periods of time, inevitably changes occur in one's attitudes to, and
beliefs about, the organization. People change in their needs and aspirations.
Managers change: they may have different preferences and styles, different
priorities and abilities, and they can powerfully impact on those working
with and for them.

Many social scientists have documented the different 'ages of man' – the
idea that people pass through various stages in their life. Labels such as the
'honeymoon period', the 'disengagement phase' or 'getting it together' to
'winding down' frequent their works. It is possible to plot time-lines for all
sorts of features of the job over the working life. Thus one could plot morale
over time or pay over time. Productivity, job satisfaction and commitment
could all be plotted, though the nature of the data upon which the time-lines
are based is variable. Generalizations and stereotypes abound and there will
be many exceptions, but it is possible to plot hypothetical time-lines such as
the one shown in Figure 1.2.

In this hypothetical situation, employees start work with a positive attitude and work to improve their performance. Where the fit is good and the
employee has talent (the top line), their performance takes off as they learn
and develop on the job. Most employees will go through a period between
their 30s and 50s when their performance does not match earlier promise.
This is not necessarily to do with their ability or motivation but opportunities in the organization.

What Figure 1.2 shows is the 'levelling off' phenomena in the late 30s,
40s and early 50s so often plotted in other studies. The idea is that in the
middle period of a working life, say 35 to 50 years, there is often a period of
disillusion and destructive emotions, where early hopes amid family commitments lead to a significant drop in many positive work-related attitudes and
behaviours. Studies have shown that those who actively betray their organizations are nearly all found in this age category.

The shape of the curve in middle age often predicts how the working life evolves. Some are enthusiastic, committed, hard working to the end. They refuse to retire; indeed nobody wants them to. The vast majority of people carry on steadily to the end of their working life. But it is the sour disengaged who are most problematic. These 'quit-but-stay' types do not resign or retire but carry on with minimal productivity and commitment. They appear to follow their own 'work to rule' agenda of minimizing their effort and commitment and hence productivity. They are perhaps the most prone to counterproductive behaviours.

The broken contract

Most of us have a work or employment contract. This is a quasi-legal document drawn up by the organization which specifies, in varying amounts of detail, issues around the work itself: hours worked, salary, holiday periods, even proposed retirement date. The contract is, by definition, a legally binding agreement between two parties. It is about terms and conditions and obligations. Contracts are used for hiring and firing. If one side breaks the contract, the other may sue or leave the relationship.

A legal, work contract is about economic and social exchange. The former is easy to specify, the latter more difficult. Psychological contracts, on the other hand, are about unspecified and even unspecifiable obligations, the major fulfillment of which is based on trust. They are about implicit or explicit expectations that people at work have of their boss and company policy.

Work contracts are explicit, specific agreements. But for over 20 years psychologists have talked about the psychological contract. By contrast these are implicit and more about expectations and values. Essentially the psychological contract is about the employees' perceptions of the reciprocal obligations between themselves and the organization. For instance, employees may expect job security for their entire working lives or promotion to senior positions in exchange for hard work and loyalty.

Herriot et al. (1999) believe contracts are broken when the organization or the individual offers more or less than they are obligated to. Further, they believe these contracts cover similar areas such as:

▷ *Work:* To do a good job in terms of quality and quantity measure.
▷ *Honesty:* To deal with clients and people in the organization honestly.
▷ *Loyalty:* To stay with the organization, guard its interests and reputation.
▷ *Property:* To be careful and frugal with property belonging to the organization.
▷ *Self-presentation:* To follow appropriate dress codes and social etiquette.
▷ *Flexibility:* To be willing to be adaptable, particularly in times of emergency.

There are a number of features about the psychological contract:

1 It is *inherently subjective*. It is not agreed by the employer, nor signed off
   by the CEO. It may be highly unrealistic, even fantastical in the correct
   sense of the word. Employers build up their contractual expectation from
   many sources including gossip, hearsay and media reports. Indeed it is
   the process of making explicit, and then managing those expectations
   that may be really very important.
2 It is a *promissory phenomenon* that consists of commitment to a future
   course of action. This can be actual verbal promises but is more likely to
   be perceived promises. The promises may be inferred from the past or
   present treatment of employees, be it actual or reputational. Promises are
   also about payment.
3 It implies actual as well as *tacit acceptance* by both parties. Acceptance
   implies that both parties are accountable for all the 'details' and terms in
   the psychological contract. Equally both are responsible for carrying it
   out and both, at any time, can chose to violate and break the agreement.

The psychological contract is essentially a way of representing the employment relationship in the mind of the employee. It is based on a very fundamental norm or reciprocity: reciprocal giving and receiving.

What is the function of the psychological contract?

It can fulfil many functions:

▶ *Sometimes, it occurs to* replace *an actual formalized contract. Not all
employers or unions provide clear contracts. Thus in the absence of a 'legal'
contract one formulates a psychological one.*

▶ *A psychological contract may* go beyond *the legal contract that is not
comprehensive enough. It fills in the cracks. It prevents uncertainty and
ambiguity by establishing fully the agreed-upon in appropriate detail.*

▶ *The contract can function to give employees an* increased sense of security. *Many people have a need for an 'understanding' with their employer.
And feeling they have a contract makes them feel safer.*

▶ *Contracts function to* direct employee behaviour *without managerial
control or surveillance. Employees act responsibly if they believe that this will
lead to rewards in the long or short term.*

▶ *They also serve to help people feel that they are personally able to* influence their destiny. *They can also choose to carry out their obligations or not.*

All employees want their working (and non-working) environment to be
stable, predictable and controllable. Psychological contracts reduce uncertainty and give the illusion of control that, in part, prevents stress.

Contracts can be seen as psychological schema that encapsulate how we
think about our jobs. They provide employees with a sense of order and
continuity in a subtle, important and complex relationship allowing for a

sense of both predictability and control. It is no wonder that when broken, threatened or violated people act so badly.

How do these psychological contracts get formed? What is the role of the individual and of the organization in the interview and acceptance process? Individuals, that is job applicants, have both complex motives and knowledge when applying for a job. They are motivated for many, often conflicting goals: good pay, job security, promotional opportunities, a sympathetic boss, helpful colleagues. The list of factors that may be relevant is long.

They can be categorical in many different ways: those which prevent dissatisfaction vs. those which encourage it; those that are about economic transactions vs. those that are really about social relations. The working student and mother may be particularly sensitive to flexible working hours while the ambitious post-graduate may be particularly interested in promotion projects, job titles and a good income.

Two things should be said about these job motives: first, they may be unrealistic, unconscious and contradictory. People have often very complex motives at work and may have little insight into their own motives. They may well project onto their boss and their organization their personal dynamics making them difficult to understand and even impossible to fulfill.

Second, these motives change over time so that those that drove the person to first seek employment may grow less important while others take their place. This implies that some features of the contract change over time.

Job seekers come to the job interview with motives but also knowledge, skills and values. They read about their prospective employer and may even search the web for details. The information they have may be comprehensive or sketchy; it may be accurate or inaccurate; it may be up-to-date or out-of-date. They also get information during the selection process. They observe various facets of the corporate culture and may, if wise, ask direct questions about issues that concern them. Whether they are given direct, honest and informative answers is another issue.

Further knowledge about the organization is likely to increase substantially after the person joins the organization. Their induction process and mentor – if they have one – may be very important in shaping the schema the new recruit has about the organization.

Thus the individual's contract is likely to be shaped by their motives and their knowledge of the organization and the world of work in general. This means that two individuals given the same information at interview may interpret it quite differently. This is of course a considerable problem for the organization and the interviewer.

What is the role of the organization in the establishment and maintenance of employees' psychological contracts? Organizations are inevitably made up of many different people. The first issue is the discrepancy between the story given by recruiters, who often 'sell the organization' to new recruits they want, and the version gien by the cynical 'old hands' who hold a different view.

However, recruiters are (quite rightly) not seen as very credible sources of information. The immediate boss or supervisor is seen as the most important, honest and reliable person and therefore the chief agent for establishing and maintaining the psychological contract. Many are not aware of this fact.

Co-workers inevitably play a role. They explain about roles and norms and more importantly, how fair a supervisor is and/or how trustworthy the senior management. They also provide comparative data showing how their new employee's contract is similar to or different from those in the organization. It is quite possible to have one's psychological contract violated very early in the employment relationship because of these factors.

It is possible to dimensionalize contracts from an organizational viewpoint:

▶ *Exhaustive (fully described) vs. fragmentary (incomplete, uncertain)*

▶ *Short term vs. long term*

▶ *Job focused vs. organizationally focused*

▶ *Flexible vs. fixed*

▶ *Individualized vs. standardized*

Some organizations need short-term, temporary employees; others long-term employees. One can make arguments about which is better for whom and when. The types of contract offered can have very significant consequences. Thus many people may favour individualized contracts tailored to their very specific needs but these may turn out to be inequitable when people compare their contracts.

Organizations change: hence trends for contract workers, temporary employment, early severance programmes. It is unwise and deceitful to try to cover this up when dealing with job applicants.

The violation of the psychological contract may be a major cause of personal disaffection or worse. Surprisingly it is quite common with as many as two-thirds of employees saying the employer patently violated their contract. There are some important issues in the violation process. Perhaps the most important are the attribution errors involved. That is, individuals discount their own poor performance, their disruptiveness or their incompetence in their reports of contract violation. Equally, organizations can be amnesic or in denial about corporate responsibility.

There are many features to the perceived contractual violation that are important: the size, type and frequency of the violation as well as, crucially, the perceived organizational (usually senior management) responsibility for the violation. Inevitably, how violations have been dealt with in the past is a relevant factor. Companies have procedures and policies for violation issues and these may powerfully determine whether people seek recompense for their grievances.

Violations can be about monetary or social issues. They can quite simply result from late or non-payment or from attempts to get people to work in a different way to those specified in their contracts. However it is more likely to be issues around trust, honesty and communication that lead to the most powerful reactions to violation. Anger, moral outrage and a desire for revenge are not uncommon reactions.

How people react to their contractual violations is quite simply a function of their attributions for it. Was the organization fully responsible or were there other issues involved (such as economic forces)? Did the organization do all it could to fulfil, even partly, the contract? Are the organization's appeal procedures fair?

Traditionally, people with real or perceived grievances do one of five things:

1 Attempt to voice their complaints to reinstate the original contract
2 Remain silent and do nothing
3 Retreat from their original position, possibly modifying their original contract
4 Carry out acts of destruction or revenge on the organization
5 Exit and resign.

Where the issue is about explicit economic issues, the most common reaction is the first. Where the issues are more social and about procedural justice, the characteristic reactions are more likely the other four. People may try more than one reaction – first sulking, then sabotage, then whistle-blowing, then resignation. Much is determined by the personality, motives and sense of justice/injustice of the individual worker with a broken contract.

In their analysis of betrayal in organizations, Pearce and Henderson (2000) put breaching the psychological contract as central. The betrayal of trust and experience of injustice in the organization inevitably leads to a breach in the contract. When the worker feels betrayed by the organization he or she becomes enraged by these threats to their identity, security and secrets.

The lessons of contracting are important. To prevent and repair broken contracts both parties need to acknowledge their expectations and review them periodically. The problem is that unless this occurs, one party may be unaware of the fact that the other feels the contract has been broken.

Loyalty and commitment

There are four critical stages in creating and fostering loyalty and development and, equally, where it can go wrong. Figure 1.3 shows the four phases: one and two are fairly close together and last about 2 to 8 months. Similarly the last phase is often short. The longest phase is that often extended period of up to 40 years between joining and leaving an organization.

Each plays a significant part in ensuring that employees in an organization become and stay loyal. If employees are handled well at each of these stages, not only will they be loyal but their productivity and their willingness to go that extra mile will be greater. Each of the above 4 stages will be examined in detail in the following chapters.

Figure 1.3 **Four opportunities to instill loyalty**

Recruitment and selection

Fostering loyalty and commitment begins at this phase even before the employee has been appointed. Companies now spend large sums on recruitment, recognizing that the key to success is the quality of their staff, and human resource (HR) departments now have a higher profile. *People Management,* the weekly magazine of the Chartered Institute of Personnel and Development (CIPD), regularly runs features encouraging boards to include the HR director amongst their number. But there are various myths surrounding recruitment, which are discussed in turn.

Recruitment as a discrete function can and should be outsourced

Those who adopt this practice believe that having identified the skills and qualities needed in the institution, it then becomes a semi-mechanical process of putting applicants through a series of tests and interviews. These will, it is argued, identify individuals who are the best and an offer can be made.

Organizations see the recruitment process as involved with attracting the best candidates. Recruitment drives seek to paint all aspects of the job in the most positive light. Photographs depict the most attractive scenes; attractive actors (rather than successful employees) pose as typical workers; the hoped for rather than the lived values of the company are stated; and many vague statements are made such as 'challenging environment'.

For many who work in the organization, the recruitment information simply 'does not square' with the organization they know. In this sense organizations may be deliberately or unintentionally misleading in the way they sell themselves. This in turn may lead to later problems which recruiters and selectors may blame on disenchanted or disillusioned individuals. Promises are not fulfilled; images are patently false. In effect, lies are told: told by the recruiters and selectors.

Recruiters naturally attempt to sell the organization. Potential employees sell themselves. Both are being economical with the truth. Both sides are aware of this phenomenon but it makes the whole business of selection and recruitment more difficult. If however in their recruitment literature organizations are particularly misleading it should come as no surprise that employees feel betrayed when they are confronted with the reality of the organization. In this sense organizations bring betrayal upon themselves.

Giving potential employees an honest and realistic description of specific jobs, the culture of the organization and their potential future in it is the first step in preventing individual infidelity and counterproductive behaviours. People join organizations for various reasons and with specific hopes and beliefs. They have expectations about money and promotion, about assessment and security, and about how they are to be managed. Some expectations may be inappropriate, even unfulfillable, and managers need to both explore *and* make appropriate every employee's expectations.

Assessment centres as a selection device are time absorbing and the senior managers will be eager to count the costs of staff needed to run them and declare that this function is not core to the business. And yet recruiting the right people is essential to the future of the organization, it is necessary to find candidates who have the necessary standards of intellect, the right mix of interpersonal skills and values. Many of these competencies can only be reliably and validly identified at an assessment centre.

Abilities, attitudes, beliefs, personality traits and values, particularly of top managers, play an important part in creating the culture of an organization. Too often the recruitment process does not take them into account.

There are two groups who can best judge these characteristics: the candidate and those involved in the core business. The candidates have to be able to see what people are like *in* the organization; they need to be able to meet them. And those that are suitable for the organization will be thinking 'when I'm 35 do I want to be like that person?'

Who does the organization choose? How does it mould and shape them? What do they turn out to be? The competent but timid person applying to a city firm because of peer pressure, lured by the money or that the advert for the job says the best mathematical brains are required and they have a first in mathematics, will only see that the pressures of the city trading floors are not for them, when they meet those testosterone filled men (and women) who inhabit the big banks and trading centres.

It might fly in the face of best practice, but those who are involved in the core business should also be able to use their abilities to judge candidates. This means not only the professional selectors but also, equally importantly, the middle and senior managers running the business. Potential employee and manager need to 'see' each other, that is have a real 'inter-view' of those likely to be working with each other. Managers can certainly be trained to be effective selectors, though some may resist the necessary training involved.

This is not to argue that there is no place for out-placement selection. Much of the initial sift and the early interviews can be done by outsiders or HR professionals. They can weed out those who do not meet the minimum requirements and present the institution with a short list.

The moral of the story is this. It is worth thinking about the integrity of candidates as a core competency *even before* the selection phase. Next the organization needs to be *honest* with the candidate. This sets the example to the candidate of what the organization is all about and also begins to manage expectations appropriately.

It seems particularly ironic for managers to complain about dishonest or counterproductive staff when they have made no attempt to select in or select out for these characteristics or, worse, when their whole recruitment and selection process is, in essence, a charade of half truths, hopes and spin.

Money is the overwhelming attraction for staff

Most people entering the job market look carefully at the salary offered. Often the subject is raised at the interviews and friends will talk about it when changing jobs. But rarely is it the most significant factor in deciding whether or not to take the job. There are many examples of staff leaving highly paid jobs in the city and joining the civil service. Money is a factor and people need to know that they are going to be able to earn enough to maintain a standard of living that suits them. They are conscious of market forces and the cost of money. Few are prepared to become simply wage slaves.

The vast majority are more interested in whether the company is going to provide a combination of challenge, security, interesting work and a pleasant working environment in a good location. Individuals have different priorities. The institution that has most sensitive recruitment methods will find the candidates whose individuality suits its culture best. Few people leave jobs exclusively because they are paid below the market rates. It can be the 'nail in the coffin' but only one among many.

The most highly qualified are the best for the job

Western industrial societies are becoming dominated by the need for qualifications and there is something of a culture of certification which is not synonymous with competence. Graduates are streaming out from institutions all over the world with university degrees, which on the face of it appear equally valuable. Employees are encouraged to obtain more and more education and if they come back with a qualification they will receive a supplement to their pay or be able to apply for promotion or a more highly paid job.

The encouragement to learn is a good thing, but only if managers and leaders realize that qualifications are worth nothing if the knowledge and skills acquired can not be applied in the workplace. Too often staff in HR departments have gone off to obtain the highest relevant qualification and returned to the workplace with no skill or understanding of how to handle employees or their managers.

A candidate for the civil service appeared before the British Civil Service Selection Board (CSSB) with a PhD in geography, having written a highly acclaimed thesis on the effects on sea levels if air temperature rises by various percentages. He was able to speak well on his subject and to explain the highly technical parts of his subject to a non-expert. The candidate was not however able to answer any questions on what society or governments should do to counter the resulting menace to coastlines and, worse, he seemed to have little interest. He was highly qualified in an area which is of interest to the civil service and with some good interpersonal skills, but he lacked the qualities of curiosity and intellectual flexibility to make a good civil servant.

A good deal is written about the selection process. But its role in the development of loyalty and commitment is often ignored or forgotten. It is the first impression that an employee gets and its effects can be long lasting.

Candidates are of course looking for different things when applying for a job. But there has been much research on what in general attracts staff and what continues to motivate them in their work. Herzberg (1992) identified the following top five factors which lead to extreme satisfaction:

1 Achievement
2 Recognition
3 Work itself
4 Responsibility
5 Advancement.

Salary itself was relatively low on the list, but it could become a source of dissatisfaction if it was inadequate (Herzberg 1992 p 72). Four of the five are easily recognized, but the 'work itself' is not entirely clear, despite much being made of it in the modern world. In essence it refers to how intrinsically interesting the actual job is to the individual.

Timothy Butler and James Waldroop (1999) found eight deeply embedded life interests for individuals drawn to a business career. Each one relates only to some people and not to everyone:

1 *Application of technology.* People in this group are curious about finding better ways of using technology. They do not need to be software or computer engineers.
2 *Quantitative analysis.* Some people are not just good with numbers they excel at them. They see mathematical work as fun.
3 *Theory development and conceptual thinking.* Abstract ideas and theoretical concepts attract this group.
4 *Creative productions.* These individuals are imaginative, can make something out of nothing.
5 *Counselling and mentoring.* For some nothing is more pleasurable than teaching and helping others.
6 *Managing people and relationships.* Counselling and mentoring people is one thing; managing them is something else. This group relishes the job of motivating, organizing and directing others.
7 *Enterprise control.* These people like to run projects and teams, they like to make decisions.
8 *Influence through language and ideas.* Communication and influence are what turns this group on. They are at their happiest speaking or writing and influencing others.

Understanding what the job essentially consists of not only helps the employer but also ensures the employee is more likely to fit the vacant position.

Induction

Few institutions take advantage of the opportunities afforded by the induction process. Most have them, but they attract little senior attention because they deal with junior staff who are learning basic skills. And yet this is when staff are at their most impressionable. New recruits enter the institution with hope and usually with positive thoughts about their employer who has after all just offered them a job and taken the burden of job hunting away from them.

This is the time when institutions should begin the process of *inoculation* against the possibility of disillusionment. Handled well, new entrants not only will obtain the necessary knowledge of the organization and the basic skills needed to operate, but they will be able to withstand the brickbats of the more cynical employees they will subsequently meet and work with.

Some induction is carried out in the training centre, some in the workplace. Some of the best induction programmes combine both. The process can be a few weeks or two to three years. If it is designed to give new entrants a sense of the purpose of the organization (vision, mission, strategy, products, processes), by showing how they contribute to the core business and reinforcing the values of the institution, their loyalty and commitment can be established.

The induction process is for both employer and employee the first real taste of each other. The new employee meets colleagues, supervisors and subordinates who were not involved in the recruitment or selection procedure. Many may speak to the individual and give quite different information from that they received from those doing the official induction.

Again induction should be factual and helpful. The aim is to make a person understand their job, their clients, and their place in the organization. It is designed to make the person as efficient as possible. It is about induction to the culture and values of the organization. For most, this is the start of the 'honeymoon period'.

It is a time of try-out for both parties; a probationary period where both sides are trying to make up their minds whether they have made the right decision. It provides an excellent (often wasted) opportunity for the organization to gain employee commitment, understanding and loyalty.

Production

This is where the real damage can happen. Considerable money has usually been spent on recruiting staff and giving them what skills they need to do their work. The employer is paying them and they can now qualify for the other benefits which are on offer. It is time for the employee to deliver.

If the recruiters have done their job properly and those running the induction have inoculated their candidates, the new employees should 'knuckle down' and start producing, even if their managers are somewhat

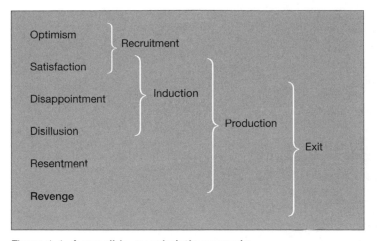

Figure 1.4 **A possible, pessimistic scenario**

inadequate. Toleration may however be tested if the employee's expectations are not being met. Other influences will also play their part in an individual's attitude to the institution.

An employee's emotional progress can be plotted, as shown in Figure 1.4. As they join a new organization, employees generally feel optimistic about the future and, assuming a reasonably competent recruitment and induction process, this will be followed by satisfaction. Disappointment and disillusion will set in if expectations are not met or dramatic changes occur in their private lives or the way the company is run. If the problem is exacerbated by other factors resentment begins to take over, a dangerous time. Resignation can still be the major consequence, but the departing colleague may bad-mouth the institution once gone and will think nothing of telling others about the poor management. He or she may go to the opposition and pass on confidences, knowledge or malicious stories designed to hurt.

Some will go that one step further and seek revenge. There are a number of options open to them, speaking ill of their former employer being the least damaging. Whistle-blowing, complaints to employment tribunals, sabotage, pilfering, poison pen letters and fraud are all manifestations of the revengeful. And even more damagingly they usually take place while the individual is still employed.

When staff leave or turn against an institution there is a danger that those still employed will demonize and outcast the 'perpetrators'. This is particularly true of the managers. The myths and phrases that build up about those who are no longer part of the 'club' vary considerably.

'He was too clever by half', 'She was never one of us', 'I always knew he had his fingers in the till', 'She was always a trouble maker', 'I never trusted him', 'She was always too friendly with (the competition, journalist ...)', 'He was a criminal', 'She had a personality disorder'.

It is common for people to blame others when something goes wrong. There may be truth in some of the above quotations. The perpetrator of a wrong has a responsibility. Wise employers will also look carefully at their own houses. Have managers contributed to this infidelity? Have the leaders failed to lead? Is there, at the core of business, deep hypocrisy?

There are three possible sources for betrayal: the individual, the institution and external societal forces. All of us have weaknesses and some times they lead to criminal acts or to infidelity. We have all been guilty of some, albeit minor, form of disloyalty. Most people have moved from one organization to another; most have spoken ill of their boss or others in senior positions in the organization; all have taken and kept small items from the office, which do not belong to us, all of us have used the office telephone for personal calls. The list could go on. It is surprising that when we see others fall significantly, we find it so hard to understand what might have motivated them.

Greed, borderline personality, vanity, need for excitement, personal life style and excessive ambition are all the responsibility of the individual. It is also necessary to have a recruitment process which weeds out those candidates who suffer these undesirable characteristics.

Rarely can the 'blame' for infidelity be exclusively the responsibility of one individual. Others have played their part; if only to give cause or excuse to the perpetrator. The institution plays a major part. Most of the problems stem from failed expectations.

The list is long. If employers fail to live up to these high expectations disillusion begins to set in and if the problems are compounded by other forces, the results can lead to a major betrayal. The question is threefold: what the (implicit/explicit) expectations on the part of the individuals are; how or why individuals have different expectations; and (most importantly) how the organization manages these expectations over time – shaping and fulfilling staff expectations needs clarification (and resources).

'Realistic' but often unfulfilled expectations

▶ *I will be recognized and thanked for good work*

▶ *People will be promoted and given new responsibilities using fair and open systems*

▶ *I will have some status in the company and be valued by peers and superiors*

▶ *The organization will train me and develop my potential*

▶ *I will be given work which is challenging and carries responsibility*

▶ *I will not always be bored or unduly stressed*

▶ *I will be paid sufficient and that the pay will be a fair reward for the effort I put in and the results I produce*

> ▶ *I will be working in a safe and comfortable place with interesting colleagues who share similar values to me*
>
> ▶ *The work will be worthwhile and interesting, the business will not present me with any ethical or moral worries*
>
> ▶ *There will be adequate welfare facilities for me and my family should I fall ill or need help*
>
> ▶ *There is sufficient security in the company to ensure work for the foreseeable future.*

External forces have their part to play. Competitors (headhunters, other companies) will always be on the look out either for good employees or for information about what else is happening in the market. If they can poach someone already trained by their competitors, they have achieved substantial savings as well as dealing a blow to the competition. Perhaps there are not many companies and organizations out there which are aggressively poaching staff or trying to persuade staff from their competition to provide information, but some are. Ideally headhunters enhance mobility in the labour market rather than encourage dissatisfaction in individuals.

Various *criminal* groups can seek to persuade people on the inside to give them information about where the valuables are or how to access the computer database to make the transactions.

Families are usually ambitious for their own. Parents can put a lot of pressure on their children to move to a 'better job' or to earn that bit more so putting the offspring under pressure to pilfer, be overambitious or to feel that they are not being appreciated enough. Friends can do the same.

Journalists looking for a good story will listen to those wanting to spill the beans. They will encourage and pay for indiscretions. Headhunters have card and data systems with the names of all the valuable staff in your company and will approach them directly to tempt them away.

These unsettling forces, whether they are explained as personality, failed expectations or external forces regularly combine. When they do there is a result and usually that means broken contracts or damage to the institution. Understanding the causes will help anticipate problems in the future.

The 'product' period may last from 1 to 40 years. The average may be 10 to 20 years. There are of course many ups and downs but long-term trends can be plotted (see Figure 1.2) and need to be dealt with.

Exit

In Figure 1.3 we identified four stages of an employee's life critical to ensuring commitment and loyalty. The fourth is 'exit'. To some it might seem curious that an institution needs to ensure the proper exit of its staff to ensure loyalty. But the manner of someone's departure affects how that person will react once they have left *and* how those left in the organization view management. Where there has been a clearly criminal act of fraud or serious pilfering, dismissal is appropriate and staff expect that. Employees are likely to be critical of management if people are seen to get away with criminal acts.

Where there is a grey area staff want to see the due process of law. They also want to see people leave with dignity. Many people in the organization will have been friendly with the person concerned and they will want to stay in touch. A wise company will ensure that staff who leave for all but criminal reasons, have their dignity and are still valued and are not made to feel pariahs.

> It is hard to think of someone in the United Kingdom who is more establishment than the head of the British security service, MI5. When Stella Rimington left MI5 on retirement she was held in high regard both by politicians and by colleagues. Some no doubt will have had their disagreements with her when she was in office, but none so serious that she should feel an outcast. And yet in her autobiography, which itself caused the establishment some problems, she wrote in her Preface:
>
> > The draft [of her autobiography] was sent to the Cabinet Office ... After enquiries on my part as to what was happening, I was summoned to Whitehall to see the Cabinet Secretary, Sir Richard Wilson. His brief was to deter me and he fulfilled it very well. By the end of an hour or so of being bullied, threatened and cajoled in the more-in-sorrow-than-in-anger way the establishment behaves to its recalcitrant sons and, as I now know, daughters, I was very shaken. My protests that I had done nothing except submit a draft manuscript for clearance seemed to fall on deaf ears. I felt that I had become an outsider, a threat to the established order ... When at the end of it all he walked me to the door of the building, patted me kindly on the shoulder and said, 'Never mind, Stella, go off and buy something,' I did not feel any better.
> >
> > At the end of it all, it is only a slight exaggeration to say that even I, a seasoned Whitehall insider, was starting to feel the sense of persecution and fear of the main character in a Kafka novel, in the grip of a bureaucracy whose ways and meaning could not be discerned. (Rimington 2001 pp xii–xiv)

The rights and wrongs of Stella Rimington's case are not the purpose of this book, but her feelings do serve to show that if someone in her position can feel so bruised (and there is no suggestion that she would take any action which might cause alarm other than the writing of her autobiography), how might others less senior feel who perhaps are not even given the chance to explain their behaviour to someone so senior as the Cabinet Secretary.

And it is the sentiment of caring that will do more for the creation of loyalty than any other. There will be a time when it is right that some staff move on. Employers need new blood and should welcome a controlled turnover of staff. An exit policy based on the principles of dignity, fairness, transparency, caring and respect for the law and organizational rules will contribute significantly to the loyalty and commitment of existing staff and reduce the potential damage of those who have left.

Critical incidents

Employees' attitudes to an institution inevitably change during their career. The influences will, as we have discussed, come from various sources. Some consequences will be transitory; others will be more permanent. The former are unlikely to affect the employer's long-term attitude to the employee. But when the effect is enduring, the employee's loyalty and commitment to work are likely to be reduced.

The incidents which cause this change can be either chronic, where the offending act is persistent, or they can be acute, the result of a single, though in the eyes of the employee large, event. Chronic incidents may, for example, be the continued pursuit of an employee by a headhunter. It could also be the lack of recognition by a manager of an employee's good work.

Acute incidents may be the individual's lack of promotion in an organization, when many of his/her peer group have been promoted. It could also be the single act of a bullying boss or a conversation with a journalist who makes the employee see things in a different light.

There can be a combination of critical incidents (CIs), so that there is a chronic incidence, in the form of lack of recognition over months or years of substantial effort, that combines one day with an acute incident which may be sight of a job advert or the approach of a headhunter or criminal. These all give the employee the opportunity to see the world in a different light consciously or unconsciously, and to question their continued loyalty to the organization.

In the early stages or where the CIs are of no great importance, disillusion will set in and this will lead to one or more of the following:

▷ Performance falling off
▷ Absenteeism
▷ Accidents at work
▷ Sick leave
▷ Propensity to strike
▷ Petty pilfering (including increased use of the phone, photocopying for personal reasons)
▷ Resignation.

Where the CIs are more serious or have become more persistent, resentment will set in, possibly leading to revenge. The form this takes may be:

▷ Whistle-blowing
▷ Fraud
▷ Persistent pilfering
▷ Sabotage
▷ Malevolent behaviour (bad-mouthing the company, poison pen letters)
▷ Malicious litigation.

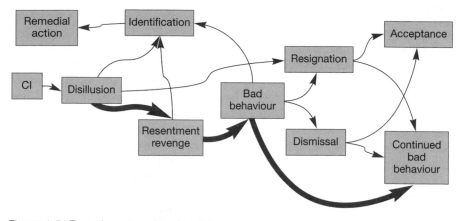

Figure 1.5 **Reactions to critical incidents**

The employer's job is to identify when this is beginning to happen and to avoid the damaging consequences. In Figure 1.5, the employer will aim to stay as close to the top as possible.

The challenges are many. The first is to identify problems early enough to do something about them. This book's aim is to help employers achieve that and to avoid the lower bold line in Figure 1.5.

At every stage of an employee's career, recruitment, induction, production and the exit employers need to manage fairly and with dignity. The seeds of disloyalty can easily be traced in the saboteur and whistle-blower.

Analoui and Kakabadse (2000) in an in-depth study of counterproductive behaviour in a service business describe six ways of 'getting even' or actions to express resentment in the workplace:

1   *Pilferage:* Also called stealing, fiddling, knock-offs, perks or shrinkage. In essence it is the unlawful and unauthorized acquisition, possession or disposal of workplace property, products or money. Money, raw materials and equipment are favourites. Sometimes goods (usually food and drink) are consumed on the property but most is removed.

    The pilferer needs two essentials: access and mobility. Managers and staff take part as well: often the former have better access and mobility. Pilferers often work in small groups but can do so alone. Dogsbodies and assistant general managers have different opportunities. Senior people can indeed invent (and pay) bogus employees such as foreign students or casual labourers.

    When caught, pilferers explain their behaviour in terms of being undervalued and underpaid: but some talk of necessity, frustration, challenging authority figures and the desire to exercise control. More senior people – often the biggest pilferers – do so for power, for control or simple vanity.

Pilfering can be surprisingly open and institutionalized. It is a way to restore balance/fairness. Equally, those caught are liable to be forgiven with a light warning or immediate dismissal.

2   *Rule breaking:* The workplace for most people is highly rule bound. Health and safety, HR, and senior managers are famous for their rules (sensible, logical, helpful – and those not so). There are rules about working conditions, especially time keeping; about production time and quality; about service; about raw materials and disposing of damaged goods.

Some simple rules simply get overruled by greed. 'First come, first served' can be broken because heavy tippers get preference. Managers break rules they see as unfair, stupid or simply additional work. Rules can be ignored, forgotten and disobeyed either overtly or covertly. Managers make and break rules certainly with more consequences.

3   *Destruction:* Ludditism is one of the oldest acts of defiance. Through acts of both omission and commission, vengeful employees can ensure equipment and goods are burnt, flooded, poisoned, broken and therefore wasted. Perhaps the newest form of this is to destroy valuable, perhaps irreplaceable, databases on computers. Not fixing something may have as negative consequences as breaking it in the first place.

In this instance, employees are more likely to carry out acts of destruction than managers because the latter are held responsible and tend to identify with the goals and objectives of the organization.

4   *Non-cooperation:* This is more subtle and passive than rule-breaking. It is usually the overt and covert refusal to meet objectives. It's about letting people down; refusing to go the extra mile; turning up late. Managers are less likely to choose this particular form of reaction than are employees.

5   *Disruptive practices:* There are lots of ways of causing chaos at big gatherings: letting a mouse go at a wedding, mixing up coat tickets, hiding or changing keys, swapping signs, having a bomb hoax. Disruptive practices are as much about entertainment as defiance. They relieve tedium and stop people thinking too much about the fact that they are in dead-end occupations.

6   *Misuse:* Managers have lots of opportunities to misuse 'facilities', cars, office equipment, computers.

Analoui and Kakabadse (2000) suggest there are four styles of reaction based on whether the expression of discontent is overt or covert and whether or not others are involved. Essentially this means whether people like working individually (on their own) vs. collectively (in groups) and whether or not they like to air their views.

The four categories are:

1   *The Lone Ranger:* An individual showing an overt response. By definition the lone ranger is a loner: independent, often believing they are misunderstood and mistreated. When they take action, they do so overtly and on their own so it is relatively easy to spot.

2 *The Sniper:* This individual has also lost faith in the system. Unlike the lone ranger, they often appear gregarious, socially skilled, conformist even respectful. But the overtly law-abiding citizen takes part in covert actions which could (and should) provoke serious repercussions. Snipers wait for their moment to inflict maximum damage.

3 *The Protester:* They work together joining or forming legitimate 'law abiding' groups that share similar values. While critical, they seek safety in numbers to protest their anger or hurt. They feel groups bear joint responsibility and face similar repercussions. Their actions are overt.

4 *The Rebel:* These are anti-establishment, often creative, deviants who may feel or portray themselves as victims. They enjoy recognition from other malcontents who they may or may not work with.

Activities of getting even are designed to solve a problem, make life difficult or simply show how angry people are. They may show tangible or intangible gains. Most have underlying meanings and motives.

Different sectors have different opportunities, cultures and products which affect how, when, where and why defiant vengeful behaviours occur. In their study of the hotel and catering industry, Analoui and Kakabadse (2000) offer advice on issues, many of which are salient to all occupations.

▷ *Adopt team management* to ensure total quality. They offer a TQM approach where a team designs tasks and jobs around individuals and customer needs and effectively runs itself. It is, in many ways, the opposite of top-down, command-and-control, rules-and-regulation controlling management.

▷ *Reduce work dissatisfaction.* Improve work conditions; install and maintain necessary equipment; provide a comfortable common room/association area; design work units according to task.

▷ *Better recruitment and training.* Understand seasonal peaks and troughs; provide training and a coach rather than a minder; link training to rewards; and ensure managers give feedback.

▷ With respect to pay and conditions, don't compensate poor pay with gratuities and fringe benefits; *relate pay to skill*, responsibility and length of service; install an equitable bonus system; make work units responsible for breakage, losses and wastage, and make sure pay is competitive.

▷ Try to ensure supervision involves *goal setting*, support and feedback rather than simply control. Supervisors need training, authority and responsibility appropriate to their role. Supervisors need to be responsible for morale as well as output. They need regular two-way meetings with staff and represent the staff to senior management. Supervisors also need clear goals and to know they are role models. All this becomes more important when introducing new ways of working which need to be carefully explained as well as genuinely useful.

An important question is how these problems are identified before they get out of hand. This might be by using questionnaires, meetings and quality circles. Also managers need ways of getting regular and reliable feedback on their and their staff's performance.

Finally organizations need to reduce legislations. Pilfering can be reduced by better surveillance and more controls but the best way is to get the staff to set up and monitor a security system themselves. Rule breaking can be reduced by having fewer, clearer, flexible sensitive and non-conflicting rules. Cooperative behaviour in the sense of (possibly) unexpectedly taking on extra work needs to be properly discussed and rewarded. Threats and punishments do not work. Destructive practices are last-resort, futile actions perpetrated by the outraged and powerless. Better management in combination with more secure access to sensitive areas usually works. Disturbances are also managed by ensuring that people have neither too much nor too little work to do. Ideally staff should be selected and trained for multiple roles and feel able to have some say in what they do.

> *It is necessary to the happiness of man that he be mentally faithful to himself. Infidelity does not consist in believing, or in disbelieving, it consists in professing to believe what one does not believe.*
>
> Thomas Paine, *The Age of Reason* Part 1 (1794)

Conclusion

The road from hopeful candidate to disenchanted employee is a long one. The ideal fit between employer and employee may not last and the psychological contract is easily broken. Organizational fidelity or loyalty is dynamic and even fragile. It has to be nurtured and tended and cannot be guaranteed to endure all situations.

Organizations try to deal with these problems by doing such things as public shaming of the culprits (for example newspapers naming people who have been tried and convicted for such offences as drunk driving), or having corporate hotlines (for whistle-blowers). Others try to target and assist those with temporary serious problems or to rotate group membership to break stealing norms; and, of course, most fundamentally, to select out those prone to lying, stealing or sabotage.

It is important, indeed necessary, to take an organizational, as well as an individual, perspective. Lying, deceit and subterfuge are characteristics of some organizations more than others because of the nature of jobs and organizations. Consider the following, quite reasonable, hypotheses:

▷ The more skilled the job holder, the less he/she will be likely to cheat.
▷ Flexibility in time keeping will be negatively associated with lying.
▷ Higher performance expectations on the part of the boss or the company will be associated with more lying.
▷ People having more than one formal role will be more likely to try to deceive.

▷ People with considerable demands (for example parental) outside the organization are likely to be more deceitful.
▷ People reporting to more than one boss are likely to be deceitful.

Each of these hypotheses has received empirical support. What they suggest is that certain job factors are implicated in the workplace deviants by bosses.

There are various stages in the working career when expectations need to be clarified and set. Recruitment and induction are essential. Most recognize the importance of the post-induction phase as the crucial time but many completely overlook the exit phase as crucial to the post-employment loyalty as well as an important indicator for those left in the organization about their own treatment when they leave.

As with many other aspects of business it is possible to have both virtuous and vicious cycles. This book is mainly concerned with the latter; with how disappointment can lead in turn to disillusionment, resentment and bitterness and finally to behavioural revenge in the form of serious counterproductive behaviours at work. But the overall message is that by understanding why people behave badly and the critical stages when loyalty can be either lost or gained, employers will be able to build a workforce which is both loyal and committed.

2 Theories of Dark-side Motivation

Introduction

This book is about what motivates people to leave, thieve and deceive at work. It assumes there are three sorts of factors that motivate individuals to take revenge on and betray their organization. First, there are individual difference factors unique to the individual: ability, personality, values and needs. These determine how people experience their world at work and how they react to specific experiences. They account for why individuals with much the *same experience* in jobs react *quite differently* when faced with setbacks, opportunities and temptations.

Second, there are social forces such as the work group, the manager's style and the organizational structure, culture and stability that act upon individuals to vary their commitment, productivity and satisfaction. These forces may be remarkably powerful yet unstable over time.

Third, there are societal factors such as the economic and political climate that may, at certain periods, be more conclusive to organizational betrayal. Thus in a prosperous, democratic, just and stable society that temptation (and opportunity) of betrayal is likely to be much less than in an unstable, autocratic and corrupt society where morality and the rule of law are not considered of much importance.

The question of motivation is central to all the social sciences as well as inevitable to the topic of this book. Great novels and plays explore the complex and subtle factors that motivate people to commit acts of crime and courage. In this chapter we will briefly overview salient psychological theories on motivation, trying to specify their relevance for the topic of this book.

Motivation is what activates and directs behaviour. It is what makes behaviour more vigorous and energetic. The word comes from the same Latin root as motion: it literally means to move people. Motives are about self-regulation, self-preservation and self-restoration. People are motivated to seek pleasure and avoid pain. They are motivated first by biological and social needs.

Older concepts of motivation fell into these categories. *Drive theory* saw motivation as a driver: an internal state of ill-ease, unrest or irritation that energizes actions. Drive-reduction theories do not consider that drivers come from the outside as well as the inside (for example a driver for food comes from hunger as well as from attractive food being available) nor do they take into account the differential desirability of individual goals.

Homeostasis theory saw people trying to maintain comfortable steady states. It too overlooks the power of environmental factors to arouse motivated behaviours (for example eating to be sociable rather than being hungry). *Incentive theory* stressed the attractiveness of incentives to behave in a particular way. More recent theories have picked up these ideas and developed them further.

Psychologists have naturally found it easier to describe and explain very specific (simple and physically based) motives such as the motive to eat. But even this has proved to be immensely complex because there are not only psychological factors (for example glucose levels) associated with hunger, but also personality, social and cultural factors. What motivates a Zulu tribe member to eat (and what to eat, where to eat and how much to eat) may be radically different from that of a New York banker even if they are the same age and size. We start and stop for different reasons. People differ in the way they metabolize food and in what foods they enjoy and find disgusting.

There are numerous, non-overlapping theories of motivation at work. They reflect in a way the complexity of the topic. They will be reviewed in brief and considered in the context of this book.

Need theories

There are many different theories of this type which all argue the same basic point. People have basic needs they strive to fulfil. But they also have rather different 'higher order' needs, which drive them to fulfil those needs. If a need is not gratified it generates tension and a drive to act. A satisfied need does not motivate any more than a satiated person wants to eat.

The most sophisticated theories attempt to describe *all* the needs. Murray (1938) came up with a list of 16 (see Table 2.1). The idea is that we all have a particular profile which predicts our behaviour. The stronger the need, the stronger the motive to reduce it.

Murray (1938) defined need as a force in the 'brain region', which energizes and organizes perceptions, thoughts and actions, thereby transforming an existing unsatisfying situation in the direction of a particular goal. However the 'hard' question is where these different and powerful needs come from. Are they biological, genetic and inherited or are they learnt? If they are learnt, when and why and how does that happen?

Ascertaining an individual's needs is not an easy task. Some needs are inhibited or repressed because of their unacceptable nature, rather than overt and readily observable. This may mean people *can not* rather than *will not* be able to say what they are. A need may focus upon one specific goal or it may be so diffuse as to permit satisfaction by many different objects in the environment; or an activity may provide its own pleasures, rather than being directed to a particular goal (see Table 2.1). Furthermore, *needs often operate in combina-*

Table 2.1 Murray's original taxonomy of needs

Need	Description	Accompanying emotion(s)
Abasement	To submit passively to external force; to accept blame, surrender, admit inferiority or error	Resignation, shame, guilt
Achievement	To accomplish something difficult; to master, manipulate, surpass others	Ambition, zest
Affiliation	To draw near and enjoyably cooperate or reciprocate with liked others; to win their affection, loyalty	Affection, love, trust
Aggression	To overcome opposition forcefully; to fight, revenge an injury, oppose or attack others	Anger, rage, jealousy, revenge
Autonomy	To get free of confinement or restraint; to resist coercion, be independent	Anger due to restraint; independence
Counteraction	To master or make up for a failure by restriving; to overcome weakness	Shame after failure, determination to overcome
Defendance	To defend oneself against assault, criticism, blame; to vindicate the ego	Guilt, inferiority
Deference	To admire and support a superior; to praise, be subordinate, conform	Respect, admiration
Dominance	To control one's human environment; to influence, persuade, command others	Confidence
Exhibition	To make an impression, be seen and heard; to excite, amaze, fascinate, shock others	Vanity, exuberance
Harm avoidance	To avoid pain, physical injury, illness, and death; to escape danger, take precautions	Anxiety
Infavoidance	To avoid humiliation; to quit or avoid embarrassing situations, refrain from acting because of the fear of failure	Inferiority, anxiety, shame
Nurturance	To give sympathy and gratify the needs of someone helpless; to console, support others	Pity, compassion, tenderness
Order	To put things in order, to achieve neatness, organization, cleanliness	Disgust at disorder
Play	To act funny without further purpose; to like to laugh, make jokes	Jolliness
Rejection	To separate oneself from disliked others; to exclude, expel, snub others	Scorn, disgust, indifference
Sentience	To seek and enjoy sensuous impressions	Sensuousness
Sex	To form and further an erotic relationship; to have sexual intercourse	Erotic excitement, lust, love
Succorance	To have one's needs gratified by someone sympathetic; to be nursed, supported, protected, consoled	Helplessness, insecurity
Understanding	To ask or answer general questions. An interest in theory, analysing events, logic, reason	A liking for thinking

Source: Adapted from Murray 1938.

tion: one may assist another, as when a person actively persuades a group to complete a challenging task (dominance need subsidiary to achievement need), agues passionately for freedom (dominance subsidiary to autonomy), or rules others through the use of force and punishment (aggression subsidiary to dominance). Alternatively they may *fuse* into a more equally weighted composite. Thus, an individual may humbly serve a domineering master (defence fused with abasement), or become a prizefighter (aggression fused with exhibition). Needs may also *conflict* with one another (for example affiliation with dominance) and needs can be triggered by external as well internal stimuli, so personality cannot be studied in isolation from environmental forces.

As well as needs, there are pressures which are environmental factors that facilitate or obstruct a person's efforts to satisfy their need by readily focusing on or avoiding a given goal. These pressures may be real or imagined but act in much the same way. Hence the idea of a good fit between a person and his work environment.

Thus, people seek out work that fulfils their needs, which may change and evolve over time. Hence, the frustration that may occur if people find themselves in the wrong job (due to selection or promotion) or more likely when organizations suddenly change meaning that previously satisfied needs are no longer (easily) satisfied or satisfiable.

It is possible to imagine potential betrayal having strong needs on each of the first five (abasement to autonomy) but much less so for others (nurturance, order, play). It is very much a descriptive theory because it does not tell us where these needs come from nor precisely what a person has to do to fulfil the need.

Some needs are easier to satisfy at work than others but strong needs for achievement, autonomy, exhibition or order can easily get individuals frustrated and into trouble. And they can explain, at least in part, why they begin to turn to counterproductive behaviours.

It is possible to screen individuals for their needs profile. One way of doing this is to get them to rank order or trade off (forced choice) various benefits at work. Thus one could trade off high salary for job security; job title for office space; up-grade technology for better canteen facilities. It may then be possible to get some idea of an individual hierarchy of needs: a person's needs for self-esteem, or power or achievement. Indeed it is often these three needs – sometimes called narcissism or vanity – that get them into trouble. But because people often can't or won't describe their profile these have to be inferred.

Essentially the problem is this, even if it is possible to understand perfectly the needs that predominantly drive an individual it still may not be possible to predict with any degree of accuracy when or where or how or why that person may take part in counterproductive behaviours at work (throughout the rest of the text we shall refer to these as CWBs – counterproductive work behaviours – which has become the accepted abbreviation at work (Ones 2002)). However, it should certainly increase the *probability* of making those predictions. Thus those driven by affiliate needs may be more likely to join others in CWBs to feel accepted by the group. Equally, those driven to get ahead (achievement and dominance) may 'cut corners' to ensure they come first.

The terrain of needs and desires is an interesting 'murky' world inhabited by crime writers and amateur Freudians. It may be easier to explain CWBs *after* the event by trying to understand an individual's crime profile rather than by using needs analysis to screen individuals for specific jobs.

Equity theory

This is entirely concerned with perceived fairness. The motivation is to be fairly treated. It is frequently associated with revenge. In the workplace this is all about performance-related pay, fair treatment and non-discrimination. It is perhaps the most fecund of the general theories that may usefully be applied to CWBs.

Equity theory, borrowed by psychologists from economics, views motivation from the perspective of the comparisons people make among themselves. It proposes that employees are motivated to maintain fair, or *equitable*, relationships among themselves and to change those relationships that are unfair or *inequitable*. Equity theory is concerned with people's motivation to escape the negative feelings that result from being, or feeling that they are unfairly treated in their jobs once they have engaged in the process of *social comparison*.

Equity theory suggest that people make social comparisons between themselves and others with respect to two variables – *outcomes* (benefits, rewards) and *inputs* (effort, ability). Outcomes refer to the things workers believe they and others get out of their jobs, including pay, fringe benefits and prestige. Inputs refer to the contribution employees believe they and others make to their jobs, including the amount of time at work, the amount of effort expended, the number of units produced, and the qualifications brought to the job. Equity theory is concerned with outcomes and inputs as they are *perceived* by the people involved, not necessarily as they actually are, although that in itself is often very difficult to measure. Not surprisingly, therefore, workers may disagree about what constitutes equity and inequity in the job. Equity is therefore a subjective, not objective, experience, which makes it most susceptible to being influenced by personality factors.

Employees compare themselves to others. Essentially they have four choices:

1 *Self-inside:* An employee's comparison to the experiences of others in a different position inside his or her current organization.
2 *Self-outside:* An employee's comparison to the experience of others in a situation or position outside his or her organization.
3 *Other-inside:* Compare another individual or group of individuals outside the employee's organization.
4 *Other-outside:* Compare another individual or group of individuals inside the employee's organization.

Equity theory states that people compare their outcomes and inputs to those of others in the form of a ratio. Specifically, they compare the ratio of their own outcomes and inputs, which can result in any of three states:

1   *Overpayment inequity* occurs when someone's outcome:input ratio is *greater than* the corresponding ratio of another person with whom that person compares himself or herself. People who are overpaid are supposed to feel *guilty*. There are relatively few people in this position.
2   *Underpayment inequity* occurs when someone's outcome:input ratio is *less than* the corresponding ratio of another person with whom that person compares himself or herself. People who are underpaid are supposed to feel *angry*. Many people feel underbenefited.
3   *Equitable payment* occurs when someone's outcome: input ratio is *equal to* the corresponding ratio of another person with whom that person compares himself or herself. People who are equitably paid are supposed to feel *satisfied*.

According to the equity theory, people are motivated to escape these negative emotional states of anger and guilt. Equity theory admits two major ways of resolving inequitable states. *Behavioural* reactions to equity represent things people can do to change their existing inputs and outcomes, such as working more or less hard (to increase or decrease inputs) or stealing time and goods (to increase outputs). In addition to behavioural reactions to underpayment inequity, there are also some likely *psychological* reactions. Given that many people feel uncomfortable stealing (goods or time) from their employers (to increase outputs) or would be unwilling to restrict their productivity or to ask for a salary increase (to increase inputs), they may resort to resolving the inequity by changing the way they think about the situation.

Because equity theory deals with perceptions of fairness and unfairness, it is reasonable to expect that inequity states may be redressed effectively by merely *thinking* about circumstances differently. For example, an underpaid person may attempt to *rationalize* that another's inputs are higher than his or her own, thereby convincing himself or herself that the other's higher outcomes are justified. There are various reactions to inequity: people can respond to overpayment (that is, being underbenefited) inequities in behavioural and/or psychological ways (that is being overbenefited), which help change the perceived *inequities* into a state of perceived *equity*.

Another way of seeing this is to point out that people have six possible reactions to perceived inequality:

1   change their inputs (for example exert less effort)
2   change their outcome (for example individuals paid on a piece-rate basis can increase their pay by producing more 'widgets' of lower quality)
3   distort perceptions of self (for example 'I used to think I worked at an average pace; now I realise that I work a lot harder than everyone else')
4   distort perceptions of others (for example 'Her job isn't as easy and desirable as I previously thought it was')

5 choose a referent (for example 'I may not make as much as my brother,
   but I'm doing a lot better than my next-door neighbour')
6 leave the field (for example quit the job; take early retirement).

An analogous set of behavioural and psychological reactions can be identified for overpayment inequity. Specifically, employees who lower their own
outcomes by not taking advantage of company-provided fringe benefits may
be seen as redressing an overpayment inequity.

If people believe they (their parents, group, ancestors) have been unfairly
treated (their land taken away; their mobility blocked; victimized generally),
they are motivated to correct the balance and restore justice. Justice restora-
tion can occur via propaganda or force or CWBs. It may involve punishing
the perpetrators, or their heirs, or simply changing the balance of things.
Thus if their land was 'stolen' the motive to get it back will drive people to
various acts until that is achieved. Inevitably people perceive the just or
unjust situation very differently. Furthermore, some restitution acts are
driven by guilt where people see their (privileged) position as being unfairly
acquired (say through inheritance).

Justice, fairness, honour, rights and reconciliation are the motives here.
The more these words occur in the speeches, writings of individuals or
groups the more the justice-motive should be considered important. As we
shall see people have used equity theory to explain theft as sabotage at work
Certainly the concept of justice and fairness which is at the heart of equity
theory is for all people a powerful motivator. Being thought of as unfairly
treated is a primary motivator to achieve revenge.

Rewards and fulfilments come in many forms: salary, title, job security. A
seemingly easy way to react to injustice is to move to another job. But when
various factors prevent this there is a temptation to assert personal justice
through theft, sabotage, whistle-blowing and fraud.

Of course people do not all have similar codes of justice. Furthermore,
people can differ in their sensitivity and reactivity to injustice. Nevertheless,
one of the most constant, powerful and persuasive reasons people give for
vengeful counterproductive behaviours at work is to re-establish distributive
justice. Certainly the concept of fairness is at the heart of much dark-side
behaviour at work. People can feel it is *fair* to steal to compensate themselves for their inequitable pay; sabotage 'pays back' others for what they did.

Justice at work

There is abundant evidence that justice at work has powerful consequences
on such things as job satisfaction/dissatisfaction, intent to leave and well-
being, (Dailey and Kirk 1992; Schmitt and Dorfell 1999).

Academically it has been common to differentiate three types of justice:

1 *Organizational justice.* This justice is people's (manager and employee)
   perceptions of fairness in an organization's policies, pay systems and practices. The concept of justice and how justice is meted out in any organ-

ization must be fundamental to that organization's corporate culture. The psychological literature tends to be *descriptive* (focusing on perceptions and reactions); whereas the moral philosophy writings are more *prescriptive* (specifying what should be done).

Questions of justice and fairness occur whenever decisions have to be made about the allocation of resources, whatever they are in a particular business. Concern about the outcomes of justice decisions is called *distributive* justice. However, there are also questions about how fair decisions are made and about the procedures each organization has in place to make those decisions. Concern about fairness policies is called *procedural* justice.

2   *Distributive justice.* Research in distributive justice goes back to ideas of 'rules of social exchange'. It is argued that rewards should be proportionate to costs, and the net rewards should be proportionate to investments. Most of the current research focuses on employees' perceptions of the fairness of the outcomes (both rewards and punishments) they receive. Results show clearly that fairness perceptions are based on relative judgements. That is, how happy one is with fairness decisions, such as decisions about pay, is dependent on the perceptions or knowledge of others' pay. It is not the absolute amount of reward people focus on but their relative rewards compared with salient others.

The question is who one compares oneself to, on what criterion of one's job, and for how long. It seems that most employees are able to distinguish between unfavourable outcomes (not as good as one hoped) and unfair outcomes. Clearly, employees react much more strongly and angrily to unfair, compared with unfavourable, outcomes. There may be various cultural factors that relate to distributive justice; that is, in collective cultures equality may be seen as more fair than equity decisions; whereas the reverse is true of individualistic cultures.

3   *Procedural justice.* Procedural justice concerns the *means* rather than the *ends* of social justice decisions. Employees are more likely to accept organizational decisions on such things as smoking bans, parental leave policies, pay, and even disciplinary actions, if they believe the decisions are based on fair procedures.

The evaluation of procedural justice issues depends on both the environmental context within which the interaction occurs and the treatment of individuals. There are all sorts of factors built into a justice procedure which seem to be crucial – consistency, non-partiality, accuracy, correctability, representative and openness. They include:

▷ Adequate notice for all interested parties to prepare
▷ A fair hearing in terms of giving all parties a fair chance to make their case
▷ A perception of all judgements made upon good evidence rather than on intuition
▷ Evidence of two-way (bilateral) communication
▷ The ability and opportunity to refute supposed evidence
▷ Consistency of judgement over multiple cases.

Although there are, or should be, general context-independent criteria of fairness, there are always special cases. All employees are very concerned with interactional justice, which is the quality of interpersonal treatment they receive at the hands of decision-makers. Two features seem important here: social sensitivity, or the extent to which people believe that they have been treated with dignity and respect, and informational justification, or the extent to which people believe they have adequate information about the procedures affecting them (Cropanzano and Greenberg, 1997).

Quite simply, procedures matter because a good system can lead people to take a long-term view, becoming tolerant of short-term economic losses for long-term advantage. Research has demonstrated many practical applications or consequences of organizational justice. Using fair procedures enhances employees' acceptance of institutional authorities. Further, staffing procedures (perceptions of fairness of selection devices) can have pernicious consequences.

People at work often talk of particular types of injustice: unjustified accusation/blaming; unfair grading/rating and/or lack of recognition for both effort and performance; and violations of promises and agreements. Miller (2001) argues that the perception that one has been treated disrespectfully leads to anger.

A number of factors relate to people's reactions to injustice. These include the perception of the motives/state of mind of the wrongdoer (did they do it intentionally and with foresight of the consequences). Next, the offender's justification and apologies play a role along with how others reacted to the unjust act. The relationship between the harm-doer and the victim is also important as is the public nature of the injustice. Victims of injustice want to restore their self-esteem and 'educate' the offender. Usually they retaliate by either withdrawal or attack. What is clear however, is that people's perception of fairness and justice at work is a powerful motivator and demotivator and often a major cause of negative retaliation behaviours.

Most organizations assert fair treatment of all employees and try to provide some way of dealing with complaints because they believe it directly affects employee commitment, productivity and loyalty. Typical procedural justice systems include:

▷ Grievance procedures, by which an employee can seek a formal, impartial review of a decision that directly affects him or her.
▷ Ombudspersons, who may investigate claims of unfair treatment or act as intermediaries between an employee and senior management and recommend possible courses of actions to the parties.
▷ Open-door policies by which employees can approach senior managers with problems that they may not be willing to take to their immediate supervisor. A related mechanism is a 'skip-level' policy, whereby an employee may proceed directly to the next higher level of management above his or her supervisor.

▷ Participative management systems that encourage employee involvement in all aspects of organizational strategy and decision making.
▷ Committees or meetings that poll employee input on key problems and decisions.
▷ Senior management visits, where employees can meet with senior company officials and openly ask questions about company strategy, policies and practices or raise concerns about unfair treatment.
▷ Question/answer newsletters, in which employee questions and concerns submitted to a newsletter editor and investigated by that office are answered and openly reported to the organizational community.
▷ Toll-free telephone numbers that employees can use anonymously to report waste, fraud and abuse.

The key characteristics of making these systems work are:

1 Simplicity – easy to use by everybody.
2 Accessible – open and comprehensive.
3 Well administered – work with follow-ups and corrections.
4 Response – to needs and on time.
5 Non-retributive – non-punitive.

There have been some very interesting studies that have examined employee 'revenge' as a consequence of what they see to be unjust behaviour. Lind et al. (2000) were interested in what predicted workers to complain that they had been 'wrongfully' terminated after being laid off. They hypothesized that how fairly workers felt they had been treated during the course of their employment and in the termination predicted the type of claim they made. In addition they tested such claims because claiming is related to the perception that termination of employment is the employer's fault. And further, that the relationship between claiming and blaming is stronger in those fired rather than merely laid off.

Their study showed that three factors were directly relevant to whether people considered they would claim: fair treatment at termination, their expectation of winning the case, and their perception of fairness/justice while at work. They agreed that the results of this study, which involved interviewing 996 employed adults, have clear practical implications for all organizations which include:

▷ Treat employees fairly throughout their employment and foster the impression that the organization is interested in justice (procedural and distributive)
▷ When terminating people be honest and treat them with dignity and respect
▷ Being honest about the causes of unemployment results in a legal saving of around £10,000 per person
▷ The dignity and self-respect of those terminated can be enhanced by such

things as providing transitional alumni status, symbols/gifts of positive regard and offers of counselling
▷ Attempts at litigation control through lobbying and particular settlement practices have only limited success.

Values

It is argued that value systems are organized summaries of experience that act as general motives. One researcher (Rokeach 1973) differentiated between terminal values (or end-states to be achieved) and instrumental values (ways of achieving them).

Value systems are systematically linked to culture of origin, religion, chosen university discipline, political persuasion, and generations within a family, age, sex, personality and educational background. It is possible to measure an individual's values system which may cover important issues such as morality, ethics and injustice. Personal values relate to which CWBs seem acceptable and which not.

Note that some of these values can be contradictory. Freedom and equality are good examples. Values in part determine where people choose to work: that is, if the avowed values of an organization (expressed in its

Table 2.2 Terminal and instrumental values from the Rokeach value survey

Terminal values	Instrumental values
A comfortable life (a prosperous life)	Ambitious (hardworking, aspiring)
An exciting life (stimulating, active life)	Broad-minded (open-minded)
A sense of accomplishment (lasting contribution)	Capable (competent, effective)
A world at peace (free of war and conflict)	Cheerful (light-hearted, joyful)
A world of beauty (beauty of nature and the arts)	Clean (neat, tidy)
Equality (brotherhood, equal opportunity for all)	Courageous (standing up for your beliefs)
Family security (taking care of loved ones)	Forgiving (willing to pardon others)
Freedom (independence, free choice)	Helpful (working for the welfare of others)
Happiness (contentedness)	Honest (sincere, truthful)
Inner harmony (freedom from inner conflict)	Imaginative (daring, creative)
Mature love (sexual and spiritual intimacy)	Independent (self-reliant, self-sufficient)
National security (protection from attack)	Intellectual (intelligent, reflective)
Pleasure (an enjoyable, leisurely life)	Logical (consistent, rational)
Salvation (saved, eternal life)	Loving (affectionate, tender)
Self-respect (self-esteem)	Obedient (dutiful, respectful)
Social recognition (respect, admiration)	Polite (courteous, well-mannered)
True friendship (close companionship)	Responsible (dependable, reliable)
Wisdom (a mature understanding of life)	Self-controlled (restrained, self-disciplined)

Source: Rokeach 1973.

product, procedure, production methods) are contrary to those of the individual so he or she may choose not to work there. But companies change and furthermore, the values that people and organizations say they endure and the things they *do* may not be far from compatible. Once individuals realize there is a value gap or clash they may be motivated to punish those with a different value set from their own. This may occur after an M&A (merger and acquisition) where the values of one company are clearly different from that of others.

Further, the values that people and groups publicly expose may be quite different from those that they actually hold. However trying to map the values of leaders and followers may give one a partial clue to their motivation.

Values theory, a bit like needs theory, is interesting but of limited use in understanding CWBs except perhaps after the event. Not everyone can talk about their values; some are reluctant to and others simply say what they believe their listeners want to hear. For some individuals, values are extremely important. They are for many whistle-blowers and for some individuals who resign from an organization once they realize their values and those of the organization are deeply antithetical.

Reinforcement theories

This theoretical approach is the most simple and emphasizes the *consequences* of a person's activity. If the outcome is positive they will continue the activity; whereas if it is negative they will stop it. All behaviour, it is argued, is shaped and sustained by contingencies. For every action there are essentially four outcomes: positive reinforcement (praise, money, fame); negative reinforcement (threats to do better, try harder); punishment (physical, verbal); ignore the behaviour. The former two increase the behaviour, the latter decrease it. But punishment can also lead to anger, humiliation and the desire for revenge.

It makes no difference what the person needs, expects, values or wants, although these factors impact on the differential power or effect of each reward (and punishment). It is sufficient merely to establish the reinforcement contingency or relationship in order to effect a behavioural change. Reward any form of behaviour regularly and valuably and you get more of it.

Individual differences of various sorts dictate what is a reinforcement and what is not. The argument is that people perform certain work-related acts that are subject to reinforcement (or punishment and extinction) contingencies. People work with a certain degree of effectiveness, and when a particular behaviour results in a reward (there is a reinforcement contingency between, say, payment and work efficiency), performance improves.

A second type of reinforcement theory is the *social learning theory*. The individual (who has unique traits, cognitions, perceptions, attitudes, emotions) and the environment (which provides reinforcement) combine to perfect performance. It is not enough to say merely that a person works because he or she is reinforced; one needs to take the person's cognitions, attitudes or emotions into account as well.

Some managers self-evidently use social learning theory in the workplace. Some of the strategies have been directed at changing the environmental stimuli that set the occasion for rewarded behaviour, whereas others have manipulated the consequences of behaviour in such things as performance appraisal schemes.

There are some fairly general rules of reinforcement that are applied by all managers:

▷ *Do not reward all people the same.* Pay, praise, responsibility and other reinforcements should be distributed *fairly* to all employees, according to relevant sensitive and measured performance criteria (not sex or marital status, for instance). Reward must be linked to personal input.

▷ *Appreciate that failure to respond can have reinforcing consequences.* Withdrawing reinforcement (ignoring performance) causes a behaviour to cease; so does the act of not applying reinforcement in the first place.

▷ *Tell people what they must do to receive reinforcement.* Workers should know whether to concentrate on quality, quantity or something else.

▷ *Tell a person what he or she is doing wrong and find out why it is happening.* Organizations should institute performance evaluation systems that include regular and comprehensive feedback to help change behaviour.

▷ *Do not punish in front of others.* In using punishment, individuals should attempt to reduce dysfunctional secondary consequences associated with it. By keeping punishment private, the need for workers to 'save face' with their co-workers or subordinates, which may cause them to act in ways detrimental to the organization's goals, is reduced.

▷ *Make the consequences appropriate for the behaviour.* Reinforcements, such as praise, bonuses, promotions or demotions, should fit the type of behaviour reinforced.

There has been a debate concerning the usefulness or otherwise of punishment as a strategy. Problems such as resentment and sabotage may accompany a manager's use of punishment. It is always wise to remember that:

▷ *Although behaviour may be suppressed as a result of punishment, it may not be permanently abolished.* For example, an employee may be reprimanded for taking unauthorized breaks. The behaviour may stop, but only when the supervisor is visible. As soon as the threat of punishment is removed from the situation (when the manager is no longer present), the employee may continue to take or even increase breaks.

▷ *The person who administers punishment may end up being viewed negatively by others.* A manager who frequently punishes subordinates may find out that he or she has an unpleasant affect on the work unit, even when not administering punishment, because the manager has become so associated with punishment.

▷ *Punishment may be offset by positive reinforcement received from another source.* A worker may be reinforced by peers at the same time that punishment is being received from the manager. Sometimes, the positive value of such peer support may be strong enough to cause the individual to put up with punishment, and the undesirable behaviour continues.

Reinforcement theories are at the heart of teaching. But they do not seem particularly useful to explain counterproductive behaviour. The theory recognizes that any complex behaviour leads to many outcomes. Some of which may be positive, others negative. Further, it recognizes that not all outcomes are anticipated or expected.

To understand why an individual starts, but more importantly continues to take part in a CWB activity one needs to look at the balance sheet of outcomes for the individual. Over time one can get a better picture of what 'really turns somebody on' by the way they attempt to maximize certain activities.

Expectancy theory

This theory focuses on the *rational* side of motivation – specifically people's expectations of the outcomes of their activity. People start jobs usually with clear expectations. They have expectations about promotion, training and security. The theory suggests that people will only take part in an activity if first, they believe their efforts will result in the desirable outcome. Next, they must believe that particular outcome will be rewarded. Third, it is essential that the rewards are valuable to them personally.

If any of these three beliefs are not held the motivation will stop. These beliefs are multiplicative. Multiply anything by zero and you have zero. To motivate others, the theory suggests that leaders need to clarify expectations, link rewards very clearly to performance, and give rewards that are most positively valued.

An employee may believe that a great deal of effort will result in getting much accomplished, whereas others believe hard work will have little effect on how much gets done. For example, an employee operating a faulty piece of equipment may have a very low *expectancy* that his or her efforts will lead to high levels of performance, and hence probably would not continue to exert much effort.

It is also possible that even if an employee works hard and performs at a high level, motivation may falter if that performance is not suitably rewarded by the organization – that is, if the performance was not perceived as *instrumental* in bringing about the rewards. So, for example, a worker who is extremely productive may be poorly motivated to perform if he or she has already reached the top level of pay given by the company. If behaviour is not explicitly or implicitly rewarded, people are unlikely to repeat it.

Even if employees receive rewards based on their performance, they may be poorly motivated if those so-called 'rewards' have a low *valence* (worth) to them. Someone who doesn't care about the rewards offered by the organization would not be motivated to attempt to attain them. It thus behoves an organization to determine what rewards its employees value, because rewards of low valence will not affect motivation. To a large extent personality factors determine what rewards valence – the value of rewards.

According to this model, job performance is a multiple combination of abilities and skills, effort and role perceptions. If individuals have clear role perceptions, if they possess the necessary skills and abilities, and if they are motivated to exert sufficient efforts, the model suggests that they will perform well.

One important recommendation is to *clarify people's expectancies that their effort will lead to performance*. Motivation may be enhanced by training employees to do their jobs more efficiently, thereby achieving higher levels of achievement for their efforts. Where possible, therefore, a manager should make the desired performance level *attainable*. It is important to make it clear to people what is expected of them *and* to make it possible for them to attain that particular level.

A second practical suggestion from expectancy theory is to *link valued rewards to performance clearly*. Managers should therefore attempt to enhance their subordinates' beliefs about instrumentality – that is, make it clear to them exactly what job behaviours will lead to what rewards. Further, the introduction of sensitive and fair performance-related pay systems enhances this. Expectancy theory specifies that it would be effective. Performance increases can result from carefully implemented merit systems (management–performance systems).

One most obvious practical suggestion from expectancy theory is to *administer rewards that have positive valence to employees*. The reward must be valued by employees for it to have potential as a motivator. It is a mistake to assume that all employees are about having the same rewards made available to them by their companies. Values are in part personality dependent. Some might recognize the incentive value of a pay rise, and others might prefer additional vacation days, improved insurance benefits or day-care facilities for children, free health insurance, a motor car, or an impressive job title. With this in mind, more and more companies are instituting cafeteria-style benefit plans: incentive systems through which the employee selects their fringe benefits from a menu of available alternatives. The success of these plans suggests that making highly salient rewards available to employees may be an effective motivational technique.

Expectancy theory is better at explaining poor work behaviour than counterproductive behaviour at work, but it certainly has clear implications for the manager. Certainly at selection and induction a person's expectations need to be established (see Chapter 1): the need to believe that hard work not luck is important at work; that CWBs are unacceptable; that effort will be rewarded in terms of things that are valuable for them. Equally expectations need to be realistic. It is too tempting as a recruiter and selector to promise more than one can deliver. Soured, unfulfilled promises and expectations are frequently the first step on the road to revenge.

Conclusion

Motivation is a fascinating but difficult topic to understand. A number of (difficult and salient) questions arise.

▷ *Where do drivers/needs/motives come from?*
The answer is three sources: biology, shared experience, personal experience. People do inherit abilities and temperaments. These predispose them to certain routes in life. Abilities affect education; temperaments how one gets on with other people.

> *While behaviour is almost always motivated, it is also almost always biologically, culturally and situationally determined as well.*
>
> A H Maslow, *A Theory of Motivation*

Individuals grow up in a particular culture which shapes their values, expectations and the way they see the world. Religious, historical and economic factors shape culture which impacts everyone living in that culture. Thus growing up in a Pakistan village will have a very different imprint on an individual compared, say, with a Canadian town.

Third, we all have unique experiences that shape us. Our parents, family and individual history, which may involve trauma or not, also have an important impact on later life. The more extreme any of the above three factors, the more likely they are to influence the motives on an individual.

▷ *Do people have mixed (even contradictory) motives/drivers?*
Most complex behaviour has a rich mix of benefits and drawbacks. Every day, people do things they know are bad for them (such as smoking). Behaviour is multidetermined by push and pull factors (approach/avoidance). It is extremely likely that all people at work who take part in counterproductive behaviours have conflicting motives. Some will find this difficult and frustrating and expand their efforts in trying to reduce the dissonance that this causes. Some cultures (for example Asian) seem more comfortable with holding mutually contradictory views than others.

▷ *Do drivers (motives) change (much) over time?*
Some people argue that once needs are satisfied they have less motivational force and therefore motives do change dramatically over time. Others argue that motives do change but less dramatically and that some are never really fulfilled. Thus the drive to accumulate wealth is never fully satisfied because the amount is never really enough. The same is true of excitement; even possibly of fame. Autobiographical studies of individuals do seem to imply that motivational patterns established early in life never really change very dramatically.

▷ *Are motives/drivers conscious or unconscious?*
Some psychologists believe that the (real) motivations underlying our behaviour may not be obvious, even to ourselves. For instance, patients

with psychosomatic illnesses are often unaware that the cause is mental not physical. They may explain how people react to them in terms of the other person's beliefs and behaviours rather than their own.

If motives are unconscious or preconscious it means people can not (as opposed to will not) tell you about their real motives. They have limited insight into what drives them. Further, the Freudians argue that people characteristically adopt what they call *defence mechanisms* to 'protect themselves' from anxiety. These mechanisms, in part, explain a person's motives. Seven of these mechanisms are well known:

1 In *repression*, a threatening idea, memory or emotion is blocked from becoming conscious. It refers to the mind's effort to keep a lid on unacceptable feelings and thoughts in the unconscious, so that one is not even aware of them. Repression is only partly successful and can cause havoc with memory. Killers repress the awfulness of their deeds.

2 In *projection*, one's own unacceptable feelings are attributed to someone else. A person who has uncomfortable sexual feelings about members of a different ethnic group may project this discomfort on to them, saying, 'those people are dirty-minded and oversexed'. Some cultures institutionalize the whole process of projection. That which you hate in yourself is projected on to your enemy and eradicated.

3 In *reaction formation*, the feeling that produces unconscious anxiety is transformed into its opposite in consciousness. Usually, a reaction formation gives itself away by being excessive: the person asserts the feeling too much and is too extravagant and compulsive about demonstrating it. Thus the hater expresses love; the intolerant totalitarian a form of participant democracy.

4 *Regression*. Freud believed that personality develops in a series of stages, from birth to maturity; each new step, however, produces a certain amount of frustration and anxiety. If these become too great, normal development may be briefly or permanently halted and the child may remain fixated at the current stage; for instance, he or she may not outgrow clinging dependence. People may 'regress' to an earlier stage if they suffer a traumatic experience in a later one. Adults occasionally reveal 'partial fixations' that they never outgrew (such as biting nails, sucking the thumb) and often regress to immature behaviour when they are stressed. The temper-tantrums of some adults may be very similar to how they behaved as children. People can regress to the sulkiness of adolescence or the clingingness of childhood; hence many delinquent acts at work expressed as CWBs.

5 In *denial*, people simply refuse to admit that something unpleasant is happening or that they are experiencing a taboo emotion. Just as a person who is dying can be in a state of denial, these people deny their evil thoughts and behaviours and refuse to accept what they really are and stand for. They may deny their support for others who commit CWBs.

6 *Intellectualization* and *rationalization* are higher-level defences that depend on complex cognitive processes. Intellectualization is the unconscious control of emotions and impulses by excessive dependence on 'rational' interpretations of situations. In rationalization, the person finds excuses to justify actions that were caused by repressed and unacceptable feelings. Some people find that a university education trains them to be highly sophisticated at rationalization. Clever, articulate people can have impressive, but bogus, theories for why they have or should do certain things.

7 In *displacement*, people release their 'pent-up' emotions (usually anger) on things, animals or other people that are not the real object of their feelings. People use displacement when they perceive the real target as being too threatening to confront directly. Thus loathing can be displaced on to innocent others. If motives are unconscious to those who do things it means we are not helped by talking about them. Breaking machinery may be displacement for trying to break the organization.

▷ *Can people (ever) tell you about their motives/drivers?*
The answer to this question is to a large extent based on the answer to the previous one. If motives are unconscious, almost by definition, people cannot tell you about them. Even if conscious, there are two further factors which inhibit a full, frank account of motivation: vocabulary and shame. Many individuals do not have the (psychological) language through which to describe why they behave as they do. This may be partly also a function of their education and ability. Secondly, many individuals may, quite simply, be ashamed of their motives and hence unwilling to disclose them fully.

▷ *What is the difference between intrinsic and extrinsic motivations?*
Intrinsic motivation is to do something for its own sake: because of the sheer joy of the activity. *Extrinsic* motivation is based on the rewards and punishments that the act may bring. Most activities have a combination of the two: artists paint out of creative joy and instinct (intrinsic) but also for profit (extrinsic).

Money is nearly always an extrinsic factor. Paradoxically perhaps, people paid to do interesting, even absorbing tasks, become less interested in the activity. For some, sabotage may be intrinsically satisfying because of the way it fulfills the need for excitement or identity. However, even something like religious motivation can be both intrinsic and extrinsic. Extrinsically religion can provide comfort for sorrow, security, opportunities for social interaction, status and a means of self-justification. Intrinsically religion can be used to bring the whole of life into harmony with faith. There are many different, but not contradictory theories of general and work motivation. None has been developed specifically to understand CWB, though each is relevant to it.

3 Betrayal: The Unsettling Forces

The advantage of emotions is that they lead us astray. (Oscar Wilde *The Picture of Dorian Gray*)

Introduction

Few people experience a trouble-free and perfectly stable work career. Everyone at some stage feels a career move is due and would be beneficial. Most people, who want to, still succeed in finding a new and 'better' job. Their motives for moving and staying will probably be a mixture of personal and organizational factors, together with influence from significant others. People's circumstances change, though their ability, personalities and values do so very little. Any organization will change as a function of market forces, technology and management style and philosophy. The ideal fit can quite easily become a misfit.

It is not too difficult for managers to recognize the motives of staff who resign. The surprising and perhaps less palatable realization is that people who pilfer, deceive or leak information have often similar motives to those who leave seeking greener pastures. They may be more extreme and the individuals willing to go much further than the majority of their colleagues, but essentially their reasons for acting in this extreme manner are the same as those who choose the less dramatic path and resign.

For this reason much of the language used in this chapter will be familiar. The following pages describe in detail the motivations that influence employees as they feel the need to move on or take other counterproductive action while remaining at work.

A study of people who leave or break the rules has to feel its way through the mists of perceptions, deceptions and half-truths rather than hard fact. Many parties get involved in rationalizing, defending or even mystifying the behaviour of themselves and others to explain their motives. While most make an attempt to explain some of their reasons for going, few do or perhaps even can tell the whole truth. People's perceptions of why they leave, for example, are often complex and not always easily defined, even by the person concerned.

Consider for a moment why you left your last job? If you are still in your first job then think of someone who has moved recently.

Table 3.1 The reasons for changing jobs

a.	The new job is better paid
b.	I read a very attractive ad in the paper/internet
c.	I was not fully appreciated in the old job
d.	I was sacked/made redundant
e.	I was not being developed (that is trained, stretched) enough in my old job
f.	The old job was not sufficiently challenging; essentially tedious, boring
g.	I had to move for personal reasons (that is family, schooling, climate)
h.	My old boss did not like me or treat me fairly
i.	I was approached by someone outside the company
j.	I did not get promotion when I should have
k.	I did not like the office building/surroundings
l.	I feel more comfortable with the ethics and values in this organization
m.	Others in the old company were getting promotion because they were friends of the boss/management
n.	I felt under too much pressure and continually stressed
o.	I was being bullied/harassed

Which of the statements in Table 3.1 applied to you? You probably identified more than one factor which influenced you or your recently departed colleague. Some will be more important than others.

Reasons for leaving can be categorized into three groups. There are those which originate primarily with the individual concerned; there are those which are stimulated by the employer and finally there are external forces which can influence and persuade someone to take action (Lock and Wells, 1996 p 258).

Two (b and i) of the factors in Table 3.1 relate to *external persuaders*. Those at c, h, j, l, m and o might be the *responsibility of the organization*. The rest are largely the responsibility of the *individual*.

Some work has been done to analyse the motivations of scientific researchers, though the frustrations of those investigating are apparent.

> What we do not know far outweighs what we do know. Most of the wrongdoers have been bright, accomplished scientists who have engaged sometimes in honest and, other times dishonest research … No obvious link seems to exist between a predilection for unethical behaviour and any particular type of training or institutional employer.' (Lock and Wells 1996 p 9)

Iain Gillespie (1996), 'From the Head of Department's Point of View', in his contribution to Lock and Wells's book identifies five principal reasons for deceit in medical research:

▷ *Personal ambition.* There is a natural desire to please the boss who might be unreasonable. The personal ambition is also sharpened by looking sideways at the rate of progress at of one's contemporaries. It is only natural to feel resentful at a colleague's apparently much more rapid progress, and short cuts may be tempting.

▷ *Need to publish.* There are pressures to publish quantities of material as well as quality. There are also pressures of the deadline and of holding on to grants which might be reliant on the published material.

▷ *Financial pressures.* When a payment is offered for each subject introduced into a trial, the inducement to ensure that a complete set of values is entered and to use imagination to fill any occasional blanks is one which some people will find hard to resist.

▷ *Health problems.* Gillespie separates this into two parts:
  – The first act of fraud may be the symptom of a personality disorder
  – The temptation to fake a figure just for the sake of doing it – for the excitement.

Broad and Wade focus more on the self-deception argument. 'The desire to win credit, to gain the respect of one's peers, is a powerful incentive for almost all scientists … The thirst for recognition has brought with it the temptation to "improve" a little on the truth' (Broad and Wade 1985 p 24). Self-deception they believe is a problem of 'pervasive importance in science. The most rigorous training in objective observation is often a feeble defence against the desire to obtain a particular result' (Broad and Wade 1985 p 109).

Work provides both rewards and punishment; sources of frustration and stress as well as satisfaction. It is possible to distinguish between good and bad jobs and good and bad unemployment as shown by Warr (1987) (see Table 3.2). Of course some people are trapped in bad jobs due to their lack of skills or geographic mobility.

A salary is necessary to lead a comfortable life; many enjoy the challenges and social interaction employment provides; some believe in their work and want to improve the lot of fellow man. But others would rather be doing something else, or at least claim that is what they want.

Table 3.2 Good and bad jobs and unemployment

	'Good' jobs have:	'Bad' jobs have:
Money	More	Less
Variety	More	Less
Goals, traction	More	Less
Decision, latitude	More	Less
Skill use/development	More	Less
Psychological threat	Less	More
Security	More	Less
Interpersonal, contact	More	Less
Valued social position	More	Less

Source: Adapted from Warr 1987.

Good work provides tangible and intangible benefits. Sigmund Freud argued that love and work (*lieben und arbeit*) were fundamental to our mental health and well-being. Indeed that is why we have occupational therapists who see work as therapeutic. It is often difficult to see the benefits of work – and how not having these benefits leads to frustration.

Based on her work on the unemployed dating from the 1930s, Jahoda (1982) has developed a theory based on the idea that what produces psychological distress in the unemployed is the deprivation of the latent or implicit, as opposed to explicit, functions of work. These include:

▷ *Work structures time.* Work structures the day, the week and even longer periods. The loss of a time structure can be very disorientating. A predictable pattern of work, with well-planned 'rhythms', is what most people seek.

▷ *Work provides regularly shared experiences.* Regular contact with non-nuclear family members provides an important source of social interaction. Social isolation is related to disturbed mental states. Social support from family and friends buffers the major causes of stress and increases coping ability, so reducing illness. If one's primary source of friends and contacts is work colleagues, then the benefits of social support are denied precisely when they are most needed. One of the most frequently cited sources of job satisfaction is contact with other people. We are, in short, social animals. Restrict our social interaction: increase our frustration.

▷ *Work provides experience of creativity, mastery, and a sense of purpose.* Both the organization and the product of work imply the interdependence of human beings. Take away some sense of relying on others, and them on you, and the unemployed are left with a sense of uselessness. Work, even not particularly satisfying work, gives some sense of mastery or achievement. Creative activities stimulate people and provide a sense of satisfaction. A person's contribution to producing goods or providing services forges a link between the individual and the society of which he or she is a part.

▷ *Work is a source of personal status and identity.* A person's job is an important indicator of personal status in society – hence the often amusing debates over job titles, such as 'sanitary engineer' for street cleaner. Furthermore, jobs give a certain status that also extends to families. Never underestimate the importance of job titles. You are what you do. You take on the reputation of the organization you work for. And your job title speaks to your success at your job.

▷ *Work is a source of activity.* All work involves some expenditure of physical or mental effort. Whereas too much activity may induce fatigue and stress, too little activity results in boredom and restlessness, particularly among extraverts. People seek to maximize the amount of activity that suits them by choosing particular jobs or tasks that fulfil their needs.

Workers' balance between contentment or passive acceptance of their lot and hostility to their boss or employer is fragile. Negative feelings are easily magnified if employers fail to satisfy expectations. Yet so many managers find it hard to recognize what is happening when their subordinates feel both dissatisfied and unsatisfied.

Employers and colleagues often feel that a good person who has left, has somehow betrayed the organization. Their departure is often explained by problems experienced by the individual concerned or their particular and peculiar personality. Of course some employers are delighted to 'see the back of' particular individuals. Further, in some industries (insurance, sales, fast food delivery, telesales) there is considerable, expected and understood turnover. However, the problem for many is the opposite: their talented, enthusiastic, productive people leave. It costs considerable time and money to recruit, select and then train people 'up to standard'. It is then a major setback if they resign (in large numbers) after all this money and effort has been spent. The question for the manager is why did they do it?

The individual job leaver will often tend to put the blame on his or her employers, especially when speaking to friends, contacts outside the office and especially in interviews with the new employer.

But the statements identified in Table 3.1 do not just apply to those who leave. They apply to anyone who does something which might be much more damaging to the organization: passing on unauthorized information, sabotage, fraud, pilfering or deceit.

The development of disappointment, dissatisfaction and defection

Rarely does a single motive or experience or issue bring individuals at work to react negatively. Many dynamic factors motivate individuals who may or may not be able to articulate their feelings. These complex motives can also rapidly change over time. The final, extreme act of leaving, thieving or deceiving is the culmination of a number of factors and influences, often over a considerable period. And the motivation changes as new influences play their part.

Some bad event may trigger an overwhelming feeling of revenge and the inevitability of further action is set. People are likely to go through a number of stages before they are ready, emotionally and intellectually, to take action. There are often as many as four identifiable stages.

There are drivers or susceptibilities in an individual that predispose him or her to CWBs. There are the needs that come from poverty, despair and greed. There are needs stimulated by hatred, resentment and anger. And there are ideological needs to root out corruption or to remove those who do not share your beliefs. Many people have a desire to develop skills, knowledge and experience, and the need for thrills, excitement and of moving out of their comfort zone.

These individual qualities and factors interact with the culture, management style and work of the organization. In the early days of a job the individual is usually optimistic, sometimes a little apprehensive: Am I up to the job? Will I like the people there? As the job continues, then the individual can measure their expectations with reality. And of course the organization is doing the same thing, often called the 'probation' period.

People's expectations can be disappointed for a host of reasons. Many should be made explicit before entry, if the individual asks the right questions and if the organization is honest about its business, the nature of the work and the rewards on offer. Mistakes and bad judgements are easily made at this stage, but this takes time to discover or people will continue because they do not want to go through another job search with all the uncertainty that involves. They may well opt to stay with the 'devil they know'.

A more difficult issue arises when there is change. The two issues that affect an individual's satisfaction rating in a company are how well the company matches up to the expectations of the employee and how well it manages change. If the organization fails on either of these counts, the individual's loyalty will be weakened resulting in some form of negative reaction.

Most people are subject to some form of outside influence; for some it is subtle, for others it is overt. Job advertisements are ubiquitous. How many people when feeling unhappy at work turn to the job vacancy pages? Others may be approached by headhunters, journalists or others seeking to prey on an employee's discontent.

Finally, after provocation, the employee takes some action. Initially it may be a loss of enthusiasm, an unwillingness to put in the extra effort to complete a task or find new jobs which could be done. It can also lead to more counterproductive activities.

There is no clear moment when someone moves from stage to stage and for some it is possible to leap a stage. Some will be ready to take on action without going through all stages. Motives develop; they rarely remain static. And for every individual there is a unique set of motivations.

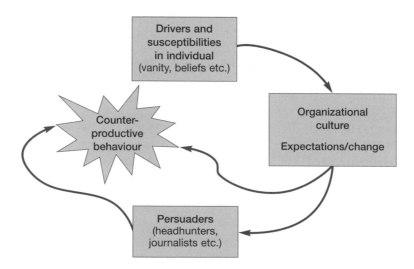

Figure 3.1 **The unsettling forces**

Individuals' attitudes and motives can change as they absorb new experiences and come into contact with new people. The power of the group or of an inspirational leader or friend cannot be overestimated. Similarly being bullied or seeing someone else being badly treated as, for example, they leave an organization can have a lasting impact on the individual. Being humiliated by your boss deeply affects your commitment to the cause.

'When dealing with people, remember we are not dealing with creatures of logic; we are dealing with creatures of emotion, creatures bristling with prejudices and motivated by pride and vanity' (Carnegie 1936). These words are applicable to those who are behaving badly in the workplace, just as much as those identified in the title of Dale Carnegie's book *How to Win Friends and Influence People*.

Drivers and susceptibilities to retaliate against the organization

What factors in an individual are likely to make them prone or susceptible to take anticorporate counterproductive behaviour? Employers expect their new recruits will bring specific, desirable skills and qualities which will add value to the work of the organization, be it more profits, greater efficiency, more security or better research. Some will have less welcome qualities that can undermine, negate their advantages or even work against the company. Some of these may be recognized at recruitment. No one is perfect and some weaknesses are acceptable.

Beliefs/values

The nature of the organization, its methods, products and customers are important to many people. This could be about whether the company is pursuing a good environmental policy or uses animals to test its products. Some feel unhappy about arms manufacture even if what they do is make products only some of which are used in the manufacture of arms. Some feel more comfortable in the public sector, others in an overtly capitalist venture. Most of these factors are clearly visible to candidates as they join, but some may be hidden or there may be change. The issue here is the gap or misfit between the beliefs and values of the individual and those of the organization which may be more about what it does, than what it 'says' through mission statements, press releases and advertisements.

The following changes or hidden factors commonly cause staff to change their minds about the company:

▷ Discovery of corruption or fraud in the company at a senior level or which is condoned by top management.

▷ New CEO or management who brings in different policies. Wigand was deeply distressed by the appointment of Thomas Sandefur at Brown and Williamson. The policies he introduced reduced the work on the health risk factors at the expense of profits.

> Paul van Buitenen, an accountant with the EU, blew the whistle on the Commission and eventually brought down the Commission (Buitenen 2000). He worked in the Financial Control Directorate of the European Commission in Brussels and exposed misappropriation of funds, corrupt dealing with contractors and jobs for friends or family. He subsequently lost his job as a result of his whistle-blowing. Buitenen was motivated purely by his beliefs and desire to root out corruption.

See also Whistle-blowing in Chapter 4.

Social needs

There are those whose employment is a way of creating relationships. Maslow identified the need for 'belongingness and love' in his hierarchy of needs. He suggested that people will

> strive with great intensity to achieve this goal. Attaining such a place will matter more than anything else in the world and he or she may even forget that once, when hunger was foremost, love seemed unreal, unnecessary, and unimportant. Now the pangs of loneliness, ostracism, rejection, friendlessness, and rootlessness are pre-eminent. (Maslow 1970 p 20)

The language is strong but the ideas are recognizable. Some people do go to work because it provides a social environment in which they can flourish. If they cannot satisfy this need or it is threatened, their bitterness will grow. People even try to punish individuals by isolating them. Solitary confinement is after all a form of torture. People have strong needs to be part of a group, though they can have conflicting motives to both 'get along with' others as well as 'get ahead of peers'.

Vanity

Vanity is, according to the dictionary, the 'excessive pride in or admiration of one's own appearance or achievements'. The people concerned do not have to have their accomplishment in the public eye. Often they will be content to look at

> *Desire for approval and recognition is a healthy motive but the desire to be acknowledged as better, stronger, or more intelligent than a fellow being or fellow scholar easily leads to an excessively egoistic psychological adjustment.*
>
> Albert Einstein (1879–1955)
> *Ideas and Opinions* 1954

themselves in the mirror in the morning or as a saboteur might read the newspaper headlines next morning and say to him- or herself 'I did that'.

Vanity takes two forms:

▷ *Reputation.* Fame and notoriety are highly stimulating and become a major force in pushing individuals into extreme action.
▷ *Identity.* Where their action provides an individual with an identity and when their actions become known their status in and outside the community increases. Their place in the community becomes more secure.

See also section on narcissism in Chapter 5.

Money

All of us in the modern world need money. Our system demands it, but for some accruing enormous sums goes beyond any perceived need we might envisage. At its best it is a symbol of our worth and the contribution we make. But some will be tempted down the criminal path in order to make money and most of us would like more money. It is therefore worth spending a little more time exploring the fascination and desire for material wealth. Most people have their price: that is, what they are prepared to do for money.

Money has a deep symbolic value. People are not rational about money though they are prepared to do a great deal to acquire it. For psychoanalysts, money has psychological meanings: the most common and powerful of which are security, power, love and freedom (Goldberg and Lewis 1978).

Security

For the poorest it is their means to survival, not just for them but also for their families. In many communities young men are brought up to believe it is their responsibility to look after the family. For those who are more fortunate and who have sufficient to survive, money can still provide an emotional security blanket, a method of staving off anxiety. Yet turning to money for security can alienate people because significant others are seen as a less powerful source of security. Building an emotional wall around themselves can lead to fear and paranoia about being hurt, rejected or deprived by others. A fear of financial loss becomes paramount because the security collector supposedly depends more and more on money for ego-satisfaction: money bolsters feelings of safety and self-esteem.

Power

Because money can be used to buy goods, services and loyalty it can be used to acquire importance, domination and control. Money can be used to buy out or compromise enemies and clear the path for oneself. Three money types who are essentially power grabbers are:

1 *The manipulator.* These people use money to exploit others' vanity and greed. Manipulating others makes this type feel less helpless and frustrated, and they feel no qualms about taking advantage of others. Many lead exciting lives but their relationships present problems as they fail or fade due to insult, repeated indignities or neglect. Their greatest long-term loss is integrity.
2 *The empire builder.* They have (or appear to have) an overriding sense of independence and self-reliance. Repressing or denying their own dependency needs, they may try to make others dependent on them. Many are likely to become isolated and alienated, particularly in their declining years.
3 *The godfather.* They have more money to bribe and control so as to feel dominant. They often hide an anger and a great oversensitivity to being humiliated – hence the importance of public respect. But because they buy loyalty and devotion they tend to attract the weak and insecure. They destroy initiative and independence in others and are left surrounded by second-rate sycophants.

Love

For some, money is given as a substitute for emotion and affection. Money is used to buy affection, loyalty and self-worth. Further, because of the reciprocity principle inherent in gift giving, many assume that reciprocated gifts are a token of love and caring.

Freedom

This is a more acceptable, and hence more freely admitted, meaning attached to money. It buys time to pursue one's whims and interests, and frees one from the daily grind and restrictions of a paid job. For these people money buys escape from orders, commands and even suggestions that appear to restrict autonomy and limit independence.

Money can become the focus of fantasies, fears and wishes, and is closely related to denials, distortions, impulses and defence against impulses.

Money is associated with:

amour, ardour, admiration, freedom, power and authority, excitement and elation, insulation survival and security, sexual potency, victory and reward. Thus, money may be seen as a weapon or shield, a sedative or a stimulant, a talisman or an aphrodisiac, a satisfying morsel of food or a warm fuzzy blanket … so having money in our pockets to save or to spend, may provide us with feelings of fullness, warmth, pride, sexual attractiveness, invulnerability, perhaps even immortality. Similarly, experiencing a dearth of money may bring on feelings of emptiness, abandonment, diminishment, vulnerability, inferiority, impotency, anxiety, anger and envy. (Furnham and Argyle 1998)

Michael G. Kessler & Associates, Ltd interviewed employees in the US in 1999 who admitted stealing from their employer. They asked 'What made an otherwise loyal and honest individual feel the need to steal when placed in a work environment?' The answers showed that:

▶ *49% steal due to greed*

▶ *43% steal due to vindictiveness or need to get even for poor treatment*

▶ *8% steal due to need.*

Most people can be bought at a price though they are loath to admit it. They fantasize about what money can do for them, believing it to be a crucial component in their ultimate happiness. They will therefore be tempted to CWBs in return for money.

Envy

Much is made in the Bible and in the Book of Common Prayer about the sinfulness of envy. But why is it so reviled? The dictionary definition provides a clue 'Discontented or resentful longing aroused by another's possessions, qualities or luck'. And yet it is a fairly normal

If I esteemed you less, envy would kill pleasure.
Shelley to Byron

emotion. We look longingly at another's kitchen fittings, their clothes, their car, their spouse, their happiness or their success.

The issue is closely associated with perceived fairness; that is, how others are treated. Individuals will look at those in their peer group, but also to their seniors. The boss who is known to earn a whacking great salary or who has a large and flashy car that takes him to work can still produce feelings of envy.

Comparison with others is said to be invidious. In the civil service there is a fairly transparent and easily perceived promotion ladder. Personnel officers have to explain the decisions of promotion boards to those who had not succeeded that year. Some are more or less content with the explanations of their own shortcomings. But many compare themselves to others and feel they deserve promotion at the same time. They were certainly disappointed and they feel justified in their complaint. They would not admit to feelings of envy, but unfair it certainly does seem.

It is not just the big issues that can eat away at an individual's contentment. The size of another's office or their benefit package can be an issue. These are containable by management but not, we suggest, entirely. Only the manager or the personnel officer truly knows the relative value of each individual's contribution. They usually cannot share that with the discontented. The latter have to take their word for it and this is often not enough.

We are all prone to comparisons with others, particularly our peer group.

When the competition gets keen and there are many fighting for advancement the decisions of management are that much more closely scrutinized. It is a thin or at any rate a blurred line between fairness and envy, but managers have to tread it and get it right. Where criteria and procedures are obscure, suspicion and then envy creep in, leading to feelings of disillusion and resentment.

Ambition

> *All ambitions are lawful except those which climb upward on the miseries or credulities of mankind.*
>
> Joseph Conrad, personal record

Ambition, as the dictionary defines it, is good: 'a strong desire to do or achieve something; desire for success, wealth or fame'. If only we had more desires like that. But the ambition that Conrad describes in the above quote is not usually beneficial. The clever ambitious person will go to some lengths to hide the miseries which they have caused to others, but all too often they are found out – though few will tell them so. They continue until the boss finds the disruption amongst the rest of the workforce too great and has to ask the culprit to leave or move him or her on elsewhere.

The considerable psychological work on need for achievement or achievement motivation can be traced back to the personality theorist Murray (1938), who included achievement as one of his 20 basic needs. It was defined thus:

The desire to accomplish something difficult. To master, manipulate, or organize physical objects, human beings, or ideas. To do this as rapidly and independently as possible. To overcome obstacles and attain a high standard. To excel one's self. To rival and surpass others. (p 164)

> *Men do not desire to be rich but to be richer than other men.*
>
> John Stewart Mill, *Essay on Social Freedom* 1907

The following are said to be the characteristics of persons high in need for achievement:

1 Exercise some control over the means of production and produce more than they consume
2 Set moderately difficult goals
3 Maximize likelihood of achievement satisfaction
4 Want concrete feedback on how well they are doing
5 Like assuming personal responsibility for problems
6 Show high initiative and exploratory behaviour

7 Continually research the environment
8 Regard growth and expansion as the most direct signs of success
9 Continually strive to improve.

There is perhaps a thin line between 'healthy' need for achievement and 'unhealthy' greedy ambition. The real danger is those whose ambitions far exceed both their talent and taste for hard work.

Excitement

Many, but not all individuals feel both frustrated and let down when the company has no chance of providing what the individual wants. They will display signs of boredom, but there will also be something else they need. It is hard to weed out those whose sensation-seeking needs are so high that they become a problem. Adventurers are attractive people by and large. They also are often associated with risk taking and companies and organizations often look for an element of this in their candidates. Usually they look for those who know how to calculate the risk, but this is difficult to define let alone identify in a candidate.

The dangerous-sports addict is an adrenalin seeker. Like hyperactive children, they are calmed down by excitement and risk. They need excitement to feel human. And they are prepared to break the law just for the sheer thrill of it.

The foolhardy will risk not just their own prosperity (or physical safety) but that of the company's. The thrill of the chase is all. It can be seen in the money markets where managers have to leave the decisions to young and relatively inexperienced people who have to calculate profit and loss at a phenomenal speed. They clearly love it; but if it is combined with an unsympathetic management structure that will not tolerate mistakes, the bad deal will be hidden. Then risks to the company's profits will be great.

But it is not just the banking world that attracts the risk taker. The armed forces admire the physically strong and the courageous. There is a fine line between that and the dangerous, not just to the soldier himself but to the men he is leading as well.

Journalists can also take risks and become hooked on it. The obvious are the war correspondents. But there are also those who pursue their investigative journalism to the limits and who begin to pursue because of the chase and lose the perspective of the story. Courage and bravery are admirable in an individual – foolhardiness is not.

Finally in this section there are those who suffer from some psychological disorder, sometimes described as personality disorders or psychopaths. More often people in the workplace describe them in less technical and more graphic terms. They are unsettled and unsetting people to have as employees. There are probably very few of them, but they do represent a real threat to the company. Chapter 5 therefore discusses them in detail.

Aldrich Ames

Betrayer of his employer, the CIA and his country, the United States of America

Aldrich Ames, an employee of the CIA, became an agent of the Russian Intelligence Service, the KGB, in 1985. He betrayed not only his employer, but also his country, perhaps the ultimate form of treachery.

He received millions of dollars from the KGB for his work and greed is certainly a major part of his motivation. For many commentators, including most of the press at the time, this was the the only reason. But were there other factors influencing him?

On the face of it Ames is an unlikely betrayer. He came from a middle-class family and his father was himself a member of the CIA. At no stage did he demonstrate that his political beliefs rejected democracy and capitalism or favoured communism and a command economy. Beliefs or as some would describe it 'ideology' played no significant part in his decision to spy.

Nor was he persuaded by a Russian intelligence officer to work for the KGB. He knew very well that they would be delighted to accept him as an agent, but there were no direct external influences pulling him towards espionage.

Personal relationships

Ames appeared to care about people and wanted good relationships. Both his mother and father while demanding were important to him. His sister's death was a major sadness. All died before he started working with the Russians.

He enjoyed a close relationship with his first wife and while later it lacked passion, they were still able to conduct a civilized relationship without tension. When his wife took up politics in 1972 he joined in, probably against the rules of his employer. But their lives did drift apart and Ames went on a posting to Mexico in 1981 alone. In Mexico Ames had a number of affairs, before meeting and falling in love with a Colombian diplomat. This relationship enjoyed much passion and survived until Ames' arrest in 1985.

Ames flirted with the theatre and magic. He enjoyed creating illusions and seemed comfortable with role-playing in the CIA, training and operational activities.

> I recognize that I am often unable to open myself up fully or allow any true familiarity to show in many situations. I am not the sort of man who can talk easily about his feelings or gush with strangers. (Earley 1997 pp 42, 43)

Of his alcohol use he said:

> I guess I should mention that an enduring pattern to my drinking has been its social aspect. I have always felt inhibited, uncommunicative, unable to make small talk and to enjoy intimacy with others, even friends and colleagues. Social drinking, together with the effects of alcohol itself, made me feel more able to relate to and deal with others. (Earley 1997 p 54)

There are friends from school and college who vouch for him as a good friend; there are others who found him less easy:

> He was an awkward boy. I remember he used to try and run after me and try to

kiss me! He wore a sarong for a few days, but he didn't know how to sit prop-erly. (Earley 1997 p 257)

Attitude to employers

Ames joined the CIA having failed at university and with the help of his father. His career in the CIA seems chequered. He did receive good reports, but he received some poor ones. He had, by the time he started working for the KGB, become an expert in the KGB and been involved in running some major cases in New York.

There were some indications that Ames resented his treatment. He was passed over for promotion in 1985 and developed a reputation for 'being argumentative, resentful' (Earley 1997 p 257).

He said after his arrest:

It's interesting to think how different not only my career but my own feelings and thoughts, too, might have been had I not encountered such a rogues' gallery of incompetent and sometimes vicious [in the sense of behaviour and habit] superiors in my field assignments. In Turkey, New York City, Mexico City, and to a lesser extent Rome, I worked for a collection of men who were almost universally despised, pitied, or condemned ...

I am not exaggerating about the nearly dozen men I say were incompetent and generally contemptible, mostly professional but often personal as well. (Earley 1997 p 205)

Beliefs

Ames claims that by the time he decided to turn to the KGB his respect and belief in the US and its political and intelligence institutions had evaporated:

A lot of barriers which should have stopped me betraying my country were gone. The first barrier was that political intelligence matters. It doesn't ...

I had also become to believe the CIA was morally corrupt ... It was a danger-ous institution.

By 1985 I also felt that I knew more than anyone else about the real Soviet threat, the real Soviet tiger, and I did not believe that what I was about to do would harm this country.

And finally, I personally felt totally alienated from my own culture ... I did not feel part of our society.

The truth is there was only one barrier left, and that was one of personal loyalty to the people I knew and, unfortunately it was not a very strong one. (Earley 1997 pp 145, 146)

Money

Ames admits freely he needed money. He was in debt at the time, he thought to the tune of $45,000. His first request to the KGB was for $50,000. However having received this payment he continued to work for the KGB and eventually earned some millions of dollars.

Why did he need this money? Was it to buy security, power, freedom or to buy the love of his new wife, Rosario? Most commentators point to the last and there is no doubting her expensive tastes and love of the high life.

> It [continued work for and payment from the KGB] seemed to be the only way for me to guarantee that the us I desired so desperately would survive. It would make us possible and, therefore, make our love a lasting one. I wanted a future. I wanted what I saw we could have together. Taking the money was essential to the recreation of myself and the continuance of us as a couple. (Earley 1997 p 147)

Money was the prime motivator: he needed freedom from his debts and he needed to ensure his future through the love of Rosario.

External influences

There is no evidence that another party directly persuaded Ames to become a spy. The decisions were his own. But that is not to say others did not influence him, both in his decision to betray and in the subsequent and sustained acts of betrayal.

Rosario resented having to renounce her Colombian citizenship and lost few opportunities to remind Ames that she was a Colombian. She complained she could barely afford to buy groceries. She longed for the big city life with all its cultural trappings. Suburban life in Washington did not appeal. Rosario further undermined Ames' loyalty to the CIA and put considerable pressure on him to provide her with a comfortable and culturally rich life.

The KGB did not identify him and develop him as a potential agent, but they did look after him and sustained him as a source.

> I had walked away from the protection that the agency gave me and I was in the cold and I didn't like it so I moved to the other camp and said 'Okay, guys, now you protect me.'

> I do feel a sense of continuing obligation and gratitude to the KGB, and I think the men who became my handlers developed a genuine warmth and friendship for me. (Earley 1997 p 147)

Conclusion

Ames needed money to pay off debt and to give Rosario the lifestyle he thought she needed to stay with him. That was the immediate and dominant motivation.

But money on its own would probably not have brought him to betrayal. The need for the love of others, his use of alcohol, the erosion of belief in the US political direction and resentment of CIA management all played their part.

Dysfunctional organizations

If failed expectations and poor management of change cause employee shocks, what are the elements that produce these? Most researchers on employee motivation concentrate on the positive: what makes employees work harder, better, more effectively, go the extra mile. There are fewer that have researched the negative motivators: why people become disillusioned, slow down, resign or worse start pilfering, embezzling and committing sabotage.

Herzberg most famously categorized motivators in the workplace, based on research he conducted in the late 1950s. According to this research the following factors caused greatest dissatisfaction in the workplace: company policy and administration; supervision; recognition – lack of; salary; inter-personal relations – supervision; the work itself; working conditions (Herzberg 1993 p 72).

The point he made was this. If all of the above are good (good working conditions, good salary) the individual will not be dissatisfied. They prevent dissatisfaction, but in and of themselves they do not lead to satisfaction.

In 2001 the Hay Group published a report entitled *The Retention Dilemma* in which they analysed the motivations of staff staying and leaving. They measured the satisfaction levels of those staff who were committed and those who were planning to leave in the next two years. They identified some significant gaps in expectations between the two groups. Those leaving felt significantly less satisfied than did those staying in the following areas:

▷ Use of their abilities and skills
▷ Ability of top management
▷ The company's sense of direction
▷ Advancement opportunities
▷ Opportunity to learn new skills
▷ Coaching and counselling from own supervisor
▷ Pay
▷ Training.

Senior management courses, leadership seminars and similar develop-ment courses often include sessions when delegates identify what motivates and demotivates them in the workplace. Analysis of the 256 replies by senior civil servants and senior managers in the private sector shows strikingly similar concerns in the UK in 2003. Phrases such as 'excessive interference', 'lack of planning', 'false priorities', 'thankless ministers/CEOs', 'tolerance of poor standards', 'change of emphasis', 'lack of reward/appreciation' appear with considerable regularity.

The methods of collection in this kind of exercise are not sufficiently rigorous to make it a reliable source for research. It does however confirm that workers today have similar concerns and provides language that is more modern.

A group of workers of particular interest in the last ten years is the IT sector. The Hay Group report identified the top five reasons why IT staff resign. They were:

1 No opportunity for advancement
2 Lack of confidence in top management
3 Unappreciated for work well done
4 Skills and abilities underutilized and unchallenged
5 IT pay is not up to par (that is, comparable) to that in the marketplace.

From these studies and data it is possible to draw up a list of common factors, the responsibility of employers, which cause workers distress. Each will be considered separately.

▷ Top management/organizational policy and administration
▷ Day-to-day management including interpersonal skills
▷ Recognition, advancement, proper use of employee skills
▷ Salary
▷ Work itself
▷ Environment, work conditions and colleagues
▷ Development opportunities.

Top management/organizational policy and administration

Today's media ensure that information, some would say too much information, is available to everyone including employees about company executives, senior civil servants and ministers. Inconsistencies and mistakes are highlighted and often publicized. The internet makes such information available to all, but more significant for organizations is the proliferation of the intranet, some including provision of chat rooms for staff to air their views.

The *British Medical Journal (BMJ)* carried out a number of studies on job satisfaction amongst doctors working in the National Health Service in the UK. In January, 2003 it published a report which concluded that 'job satisfaction is an important factor underlying the intention to quit.' More specifically the survey revealed that the principal causes of general practitioner discontent lie within the wider environment. The organization and governance of general practice have greatly changed in recent years, and doctors may be experiencing difficulties in adapting to these changes (Sibbald et al. 2003 p 26).

Whether the information that people have about their organization is accurate or not it is often a source of immense dissatisfaction. Often policies such as chief executive pay, closing down plants or even something as simple as de-layering or going open plan can be a source of major discontent.

Day-to-day management including managerial interpersonal skills

This refers to a manager's skills and styles: IQ (intelligence quotient) and EQ (emotional intelligence quotient). They include all variants of communication skills, favouritism and the general as well as the more serious issues of bullying and harassment. The last two are particularly crucial for companies who harbour or protect such people, as they become vulnerable to legal sanctions.

The following account, written by a 25-year-old graduate, illustrates what happens when a manager is incompetent in her dealings with staff.

The company I worked for was going through some obvious troubles. We (the employees) were not stupid and knew what was going on. However, we were kept in the dark and treated like idiots. The CEO of the parent company appointed a new MD for our company. We all knew from the start that she was inept at her job and didn't know how to lead a team.

Slowly the new MD started marginalizing two of the account directors who had served the company loyally for over 7 years each. They were humiliated by her and treated with no respect. It was clear that the MD was dealing directly with the CEO of the parent company now and that our CEO was also being pushed out. The two account directors were made redundant in a very unprofessional way and they left on very bad terms. The rest of us began to hate the MD.

She was a terrible leader. When briefing people for projects, she was vague and unsure of what she wanted, leaving those around her to scrabble around to hold things together. She was blatantly having an affair and would come in late every day. Meanwhile the main CEO thought she was doing a fantastic job.

Suddenly we were told that the CEO of our company had been asked to leave. He had been told not to tell us and just not turn up on the Monday morning. We were all devastated and felt as if we were being left to deal with this awful woman on our own.

The two Directors who had been ousted were not saying the nicest things about the MD and the company while they were talking to friends in the industry and to other companies. I stopped putting effort into my work because I didn't want her to look good due to my efforts. Most of us were looking for jobs and when I went to interviews the first question people asked was why I was leaving; I didn't hold back. I know others were doing the same. Our industry is a very small world and most people now know that the company is in trouble and that there is a witch at the helm. About 5 people have jumped ship in the last 5 months and when I meet up with old colleagues, I am told that things are getting worse and that the majority of them are looking for other jobs.

When I told her I was leaving she was childishly bitter and called me into her office and said 'you know, you just missed a trip to New York'. I didn't rise to her bait but I thought 'how old are you?' I was given no exit interview and I will continue to bad-mouth her.

Recognition, advancement, proper use of employee skills

It is part of most societies' culture to train young people to say thank you and show gratitude for things done or given. Failing to show gratitude to those who deserve it offends against the norms of society.

The unrecognized person in the workplace soon becomes dispirited. It

There are two things people want more than sex and money – recognition and praise.

Mary Kay Ash (1915–2001) US entrepreneur, business executive and founder of Mary Kay cosmetics is all the more extraordinary in this materialistic world because it costs nothing to ring up or go to the office and say thank you. Recognition and praise are cheap and done effectively and judiciously can be particularly motivating.

Most staff-opinion surveys report that staff feel unappreciated and that they do not feel valued. It is not a question of money; it is in most cases a lack of courtesy. Recognition and appreciation come in other forms – job titles, certificates, pictures and interviews in the in-house magazine. For some, status is important because they want others to know they hold a senior position or have a particular expertise. Labels mean something to them.

In some organizations status is deliberately underplayed. 'Flat structures' mean fewer ranks and people become one of only a few homogeneous groups. For those at the bottom of the pile this is good news, but for how long? Some more senior people may feel their contribution and experience count for nothing.

Another method of recognition is salary. Many senior executives receive proportionately huge salaries and benefits. Prolonged negotiations take place over the size of their package. The cash involved is largely immaterial; what matters is that this is a measure of how they are valued. During the heady days of the stock market boom, the bonus received each month was a symbol of success as much as a means of acquiring even more material goodies.

Just as staff enjoy recognition, gratitude and an appropriate salary, they also desire advancement and to feel that their skills are being properly exploited. In some organizations, particularly the public services and military, promotion issues dominate the thoughts of many employees as they come into the zone. While some only become aware of them as they see others, often their peers, being promoted and they themselves feel passed over.

Not everyone can be promoted and this is recognized. But the systems by which people are promoted are often opaque, clouded in mystery and the rules and procedures obscure. The more this is so, the more individuals not promoted will feel the 'system' is against them and will feel resentful.

There is currently another trap for the employer, which is becoming more frequent: overqualification. Universities are proliferating and producing well-trained and skilled graduates, but the number of demanding jobs has not increased by the same proportion. Many employees now find themselves in jobs for which they are grossly overqualified. Graduates can be found in most civil service departments standing for hours by the photocopier or putting basic data into a computer. Most recognize this should only be a temporary phase and they will advance. But if the delay is too long their motivation will fall. Their most likely course is to walk, but where the labour market is against a move, their minds might turn to more mischievous ends.

Salary

It comes as a surprise to many managers that money is not a major factor in people's motivation. A senior British political figure in the 1980s would frequently anger his civil servants by telling them that the principal motivation for everyone was money and that by introducing a performance pay scheme, productivity would increase. In fact within the civil service it created more resentment than almost any other management scheme introduced in the second half of the twentieth century.

It features as a dissatisfier when the employees' perception is that they are not receiving a fair day's pay for their work. And the definition of fair is influenced by many things. In the first place, workers need to satisfy their standard of living – this has little to do with sufficient to live, but more to do with the repayments on a large mortgage, a new car, a larger family or an annual skiing holiday.

> *A fair day's wages for a fair day's work: it is as just a demand as governed men ever made of governing.*
>
> Thomas Carlyle (1795–1881)
> *Past and Present* 1843

The salaries of friends or colleagues at work might also play their part in influencing someone to believe they are not being paid enough. The salary of the fat cat CEO compared with the paltry sums paid to the workers can have negative effects.

> Almost all of my working career I have stolen from my employers in a number of different ways – whether it was stealing their time by adding on extra hours worked, or stealing materials that I could then use for my own work, or stealing money directly.
>
> I started my employment with a medium-sized construction company and was paid very little but worked extremely hard. They had big contracts and our wages didn't reflect the profit they made and the work we did. Because of this I thought that the company owed me. I was angry about the way they used me. This justified my stealing rather than gave me the reason. My reason was because I thought that they are a big company and they can afford it and I needed it more. I took materials from the company's stock and charged it to my own customers. (Australian plumber 2003)

Work itself

Where the work is boring or repetitive, the climate bullying, the management callous, staff will quickly feel disenchanted and leave. Where the nature of the work is not what they expected or offends their sensibilities, employees might feel the need to take more drastic action. Graduates of the 1980s were less concerned about the ethics of work. In the twenty-first century they are beginning to care more about the nature of work.

Hollyforde and Whiddett (2002 p 159) conclude that the following elements should be part of a satisfying job:

▷ Jobs should be interesting, significant, autonomous, and a 'whole job'.
▷ Somewhere job standards should be made clear and challenging (perhaps

in the employee's listed objectives rather than in the employee's job description).

▷ People should be able to get regular feedback on their performance. Feedback should be designed to be informational rather than controlling in order to ensure that intrinsic motivation is not adversely affected.

▷ The things most people accept as 'given' should already be in place (policies, salary, good working conditions, and so on).

▷ Those affected (or their representatives) should ideally be involved in job design from the start.

▷ People are most likely to respond to well-designed jobs if they are looking to grow and develop. However, even those that are not are unlikely to respond negatively.

▷ People who are seeking to meet the most basic of human needs (food, shelter, and so on) are likely to be extrinsically motivated more by the rewards a job brings than by the content of the job itself. However, by designing jobs that cater only for such needs, organizations are in danger of alienating those who have 'higher' needs and not allowing for personal development and growth.

Environment, work conditions and colleagues

The work can be intrinsically satisfying, staff are developing well, the money is good and management comes straight out of Harvard business school. But still people are unhappy. Most people spend more conscious hours at work or going to work than doing anything else. It is an important part of our social life. We need to feel comfortable there. Companies increasingly spend money on their buildings and the facilities; for good reason – they want their staff to be happy at work.

> *The job for big companies, the challenge that we all face as bureaucrats, is to create an environment where people can reach their dreams – and they don't have to do it in a garage.*
> Jack Welch *Fortune* May 1995

It is more than just a great canteen however. It is the atmosphere, morale, camaraderie. Some of the happiest memories are associated with some poorly maintained buildings, with few facilities. But the friendships and fun are more than enough compensation. Modern clean buildings can not, on their own, lead to satisfaction.

Where staff find their colleagues less than conducive, where the surroundings do not offer good shopping or restaurants, where staff feel physically threatened as they leave the building, they will leave the company.

Development, growth and challenge opportunities

On its own insufficient challenge or development will probably lead to nothing more than a speedy departure of the individuals concerned. It is however one of the most potent forces in keeping staff and that is why it features again later in this book (see Chapter 10).

Challenge comes in various forms. For some it is a need to continue to learn new skills, more knowledge, a better understanding of the world or the issues facing the company. In short and modern jargon it is the need for development. For others it is the need for something new, excitement, the thrill of the unknown, the adventure. Harnessed this can be a very effective force for the company. If it is unrequited it can start to work against the company.

Others will need a different kind of challenge. The perfectionist will find it hard to work in an ambiguous environment where quality of work is not so important as quantity, for example. Some will want to apply their knowledge and skills to known problems. The analyst and the investigator will want to tackle new problems but they may well be content without the unknown.

> *Companies ... have a hard time distinguishing between the cost of paying people and the value of investing in them.*
>
> Thomas Stewart US journalist
> *Intellectual Capital*

Graduates are looking increasingly for challenge. The need for security is now less important. Even when the economic climate is looking stormy, people today have less reason to think that this is no more than a temporary condition and that prosperity is not far away.

The organization hopefully should provide the right kind of challenge and at the right moment to the individual. Where this involves new skills or knowledge then it has to provide that as well. If employers advertise jobs as being challenging or demanding, they have the responsibility to provide that. Frequently however these words are used as synonyms for stress.

Without the right kind of challenge (and development or learning is challenging in its own right) staff become bored. If they can leave that is fine and, if the company cannot provide the challenge, the sooner they go the better. If however they are tied, because of a volatile and threatening job market or because the company has tied them in through some financial package, this boredom becomes destructive.

Bored members of staff will find something to distract them. This might be reading a book or the newspaper. It might become more damaging and lead to longer telephone calls to family or friends. In the modern era it will mean long hours spent on the internet, emailing friends or, much worse, surfing the net and exposing company computer systems to viruses or just clogging up the system with unnecessary files. The bored worker might well turn to whistle-blowing or collecting names of clients to pass on to the next company. In many incidents of sabotage, particularly by those working on conveyor-belt-type activities, it is reported that they did it simply to relieve the unutterable tedium of their repetitive work.

The corollary to boredom is stress brought on as a result of too much challenge. Badly managed change or providing staff with too challenging work or objectives is often the cause. Again on its own this will do little more than produce a resignation. However, the individual is unlikely to admit the reason, because they will feel it is their failure. It is often the manager's failure to recognize that he or she was asking too much.

In some cultures there is pressure to produce, to achieve. Without results people cannot progress. This can breed deceit. It might manifest itself in presenting data in an academic environment which is not original. It might encourage individuals to commit fraud in the company, by falsifying the accounts to present them in a more favourable light. If managers set unattainable targets and provide only little support to achieve them and, worse, threats of punishment for not achieving them, deceit and fraud are very likely to occur.

Nick Leeson

Broke the rules and caused the collapse of the UK's oldest bank, Barings

Nick Leeson rose through the ranks of Barings Bank and in 1994 was the floor manager of its trading operation on the Singapore SIMEX. He used a bogus account (the 88888 account) initially to cover a loss created by a junior work colleague. He subsequently used this account to cover other unsanctioned business. As the markets in 1994 fell the debts increased and Leeson fled Singapore to escape the auditors.

The obvious conclusion is that he was trying to make money for himself – he was, in short, greedy. But money was not his motive. He at no stage stood to gain financially from his wrongdoing. The Serious Fraud Squad investigated the case and found insufficient evidence to make a case against him in the UK.

Leeson's mother pushed him to achieve from a young age. He had ambition and planned his moves into the city and up the ladder to financial success. But there was nothing extraordinary in his behaviour in these early years. He was unusually successful but not a rebel.

By the time he joined Barings in 1989 he was seen as a hard working, competent employee. Later he would comment on those early months:

> Although I wasn't that interested in who or what Barings was – it was just the next job for me – I did find out some of its history. It was hard not to when it was drummed into you every time you walked along any corridor to the gents. (Leeson 1996 p 32)

Whatever the induction process was, it clearly had little impact on Leeson. History and tradition permeated the company, but it did nothing in this case to swell Leeson's pride in Barings. Of his colleagues Leeson commented at that time:

> I got my head down and stuck to it, and I wasn't afraid of asking the most stupid questions. People at the London end of Barings were all so know-all that nobody dared ask a stupid question in case they all looked silly in front of everyone else. (Leeson 1996 p 38)

Leeson moved to Singapore in 1992 to activate Barings' trading seat on the floor of the Singapore International Monetary Exchange (SIMEX). Leeson was doing well at this stage and the bank thought highly of him.

A few months after setting up the new operation, one of his staff made a mistake on the floor which cost £20,000, a lot of money for Leeson at that stage. Leeson chose not to report it or to take action against the staff member, largely because, he claims, of the attitude of his immediate boss at that time. Instead he hid the mistake and took on responsibility for the loss himself, by using a bogus account known as 88888.

This was a critical time for Leeson. Whatever his subsequent motives, Leeson's explanations for his decision at this time were:

> It had been a madhouse. Nobody could have known what they were doing. It was all Simon Jones's fault, I swore, and Mike Killian's in Tokyo: the mean tight fisted bastards wouldn't let me employ anyone. They wanted to keep the costs down to the bone; Simon Jones hired this girl on a salary of £4000 a year. It was disgusting, and all so he could look good on the bottom line. Everyone else I'd wanted to employ had all been turned down, either because they cost too much or because the sales people didn't think the surge in volume would continue. (Leeson 1996 p 55)

His feelings for Barings were apparent. It is worth recalling that Leeson himself did nothing here for his own personal financial gain.

Throughout the saga, Leeson's feelings about management in Barings were never far away. He recalls a minute of a meeting between Peter Baring and Brian Quinn, a director of the Bank of England on 13 September 1993, in which Peter Baring is recorded as saying: 'The recovery of profitability has been amazing following the reorganization, leaving Barings to conclude that it was not actually very difficult to make money in the securities business.'

Leeson goes on to comment:

> As I stood in the box and grabbed phones, signalled to George or Fat Boy, bought and sold, watched the market lurch about, gobbled sweets and even chewed the trading cards themselves, I imagined Peter Baring's quiet voice in some splendid lofty office in the Bank of England as he sat back on a leather sofa and stirred his Earl Grey tea and admired his brightly polished toe caps.
>
> ... not actually terribly difficult.
>
> They should have known better. Certainly Peter Baring should have known better. Making money is never easy. (Leeson 1996 p 98)

Insights into Leeson's personal motivation are also revealing. While he still felt that he had some control over the 88888 account, he wrote:

> I could see the whole picture. I was probably the only person in the world to be able to operate on both sides of the balance sheet. It became an addiction. (Leeson 1996 p 87)

However, the markets continued to fall and Leeson became desperate. As he and his wife were fleeing Singapore in February 1995, he recalls:

> 'It was for you', I almost said, 'I did it to make you happy, because I could win that way.' But then I knew it was also for me: I'd had to win that way so that I

> *could run my own team, be my own boss, tower over the trading floor, earn my bonus. The pity of it was that now I realized Lisa would have loved me if I'd just joined my dad as a plasterer. (Leeson 1996 p 10)*

Vanity, excitement and ambition all played a part. His wife Lisa is also an important player, but not directly. She remained unaware of his illegal activities and when she was given glimpses reacted strongly against and told him not to do it again. There could therefore be an element of fear of being caught by Lisa, as well as by the authorities that played a part.

The dominant factors behind Leeson's actions were his feelings about the management of Barings. He was not alone. In July 1996 the *Daily Telegraph* commented in an editorial:

> *The report reflects badly on the Bank of England, badly on Mr Leeson, but worst of all on the senior management of Barings ... it is the Board of Barings who emerge from this story as almost sublime incompetents, blithely counting their own booty on the promenade deck, oblivious of the torrent cascading into their ship from below the water line.*

Footnote

He gave himself up and the courts in Singapore sentenced him for 6½ years for deceiving the auditors of Barings in a way 'likely to cause harm to their reputation' and for cheating SIMEX.

In October 2003 Leeson gave an interview to the *Financial Times*. Nearly ten years after the event, when asked if he was still driven by the same destructive influences that drove him to lose more and more money at Barings he replied: 'I certainly push boundaries and overstep them if they are not strong enough to stop me,' he admits, remarkably frankly. 'I'll go to the gym and come back completely exhausted. I just like to push hard.'

Would he say he was honest now? 'Erm ... I'd like to think so,' he replies after a long pause. 'I don't hide anything from Leona, maybe I'm too honest sometimes. But you know, I suppose I'm not really in a situation where I could do something dishonest.' He takes another sip of tea and, for the first and last time during our chat, he cracks a mischievous smile. 'But if I could fudge some expenses, I probably would.'

(Financial Times 18 October 2003)

The persuaders

If internal bad management pushes people away from the organization external forces can also *pull* the individual away. If the individual has some personal factors that make him or her vulnerable, the chances of the external force having the power to influence are that much greater. They can be enormously powerful if played by someone with a very strong personality. If they are perceptive and can see some nascent weakness perhaps produced by resentment or an overriding personal quality, an outsider can bring havoc to the organization, significantly weaken it or in some cases bring it down.

Thus the perceptive headhunter be they professional or not may easily seduce a talented and valuable person away from his or her work.

Competition

Competition threatens companies in two ways: Other companies can poach staff and they can seek information about specific products. Both can, and often do, involve persuading staff to betray their employer.

The weekend newspapers groan with job offers and now the internet has ever-easier ways of tempting us away from our jobs and into the arms of another company. Direct competitors may not necessarily be poaching staff from our company through the media but a good many employees will be aware of what is being paid or offered elsewhere.

Where there is a group of companies whose employees know each other well (for example in journalism), competitors may well target individuals and contact them directly. In Britain, the move of Desmond Lynam from the BBC to ITV to do a very similar job demonstrates how it can be done.

Many companies are now setting up intelligence units. They scour the press and the internet for intelligence on what the competition is doing. They may be more unscrupulous and use tactics that border on, or go beyond, the illegal. It is also possible to employ private investigators.

If they can find someone who is vulnerable, offer more money, but also flatter and offer the thrill of a change, betrayal, or at least resignation is not far off.

Criminal

Criminals can use their guile to work their way into any organization, which can provide them with useful information or access to cash or goods. The bank teller, a security guard or a bonds trader, all have information very useful to the criminal. If a member of staff is vulnerable when he or she has some resentment or a personal weakness, which the criminal can identify, the latter will take advantage.

Philip Martin Ashley was a property entrepreneur and was a client of the London branch of United Mizrahi Bank ('UMB'), an Israeli bank with a head office in Tel Aviv. All his dealings were with senior bank employees John Doherty and Rafael Kellner.

Between May 1994 and December 1995 Ashley conspired with Doherty and Kellner to circumvent the bank's lending rules. For their part in the conspiracy, Doherty and Kellner received money from Ashley. For example, in one loan transaction of £1.1 million, a sum of £65,000 was paid into an account held at Credit Suisse in Zurich for their benefit.

SFO press release 22 January 2003

Family

Parents and others in the family are often deeply ambitious for their offspring. This happens in western and particularly eastern society and at all levels. But it can be particularly strong in other cultures. Asian society is noted for the strength of the family but it should not be surprising to find it elsewhere.

Whether or not families are ambitious for their children, they frequently offer advice and encouragement. When there is a problem at work it is often to the close family that people turn. What the husband or wife says can influence employees considerably.

Parents may not approve of, or understand, the jobs their children are doing. Many prefer older and established professions like lawyer or doctor to some modern, seemingly less secure and important job, like IT. Parents can maintain a powerful emotional source of pressure on their children for years; indeed even after death. Adults can be seeking parental approbation for job success well into middle age. Wives can be enormously ambitious for their husbands and vice-versa. The success (and failure) at work of one's spouse or relatives reflects on the individual; hence their pressure on him or her to succeed conspicuously – often at any cost. Expensive spouses can often be the start on the slippery slope to deception, fraud and theft.

Friends and minority group pressure

This group can play the same role as the family but they can go further and tempt people into excessive social activity, drinking, clubbing and so on, and thereby undermine the work culture of the organization. Peer pressure particularly among the young is substantial and certainly the major factor accounting for delinquency.

There is a slightly different phenomenon when an employee belongs to a minority group. We like to belong and if we are in an alien culture or where we feel outnumbered for whatever reason, we look for people who are like us. At its most benign and innocent it can be Scots living in London, Brits living overseas (the 'expats') or it could be Catholics in an otherwise Protestant community. These groupings are unlikely to cause problems, indeed they may well help the employee adjust to the society outside the office and thus make people feel more comfortable and relaxed.

Some communities are more intrusive, which can lead to a conflict of loyalties. There is much suspicion about the masons, although the worries come about because of their secrecy, rather than their actions. When we do not know what is happening it is a natural reaction to worst case the situation and prepare for any eventuality. Pressure can be brought to bear on people because of their religion, colour or nationality. We know that much undesirable behaviour in young people from binge drinking to delinquency is sustained by their peer group norms and pressures. Groups pre and proscribe good and bad behaviours. They can endorse CWBs or cause them to occur very rarely in an organization.

Headhunter/recruitment agencies

These people are employed to find staff and they nearly always find people who are already employed: by definition most of the successful indeed crucial 'knowledge workers'. The employee may come into the recruitment agency or contact the headhunter. But they are on the look out as well. Any indication that someone is not happy or is looking for a change and their name will quickly be in the carding system. Young ambitious people soon know what they are worth and are happy to tear up both their legal and psychological contract. Headhunters lure and can destabilize. They can sow seeds of greed and discontent as part of their otherwise quite legitimate process. At best they can help occupational mobility and act as a sort of vocational guidance. At worst they sow seeds of discontent to further their own aims.

Journalists and the press

Journalists have always looked for good stories (and scoops) and found them usually amongst the discontented. They have money to pay people (often quite large sums), but they have something else they can play on most effectively: vanity. The journalist can offer public retribution for wrongs done. He or she can ensure that the worker gets either maximum publicity or, if they wish, anonymity. The exposure of a company or individuals in that company, when satisfaction was not possible from within, can feel enormously rewarding. If combined with flattery (it is vital for the common good), the sense of importance felt by the perpetrator increases. They feel they have made a change and that it is only they who have brought this about.

Rarely does an employee leave, thieve or deceive for one of the above reasons alone. People take advice from others: friends, family and professionals. In any big decision they will usually talk with others, who may be highly skilled counsellors, who will lead us down the best path for us, but mostly they are friends with no counselling skills and they offer advice. It is true therefore to say that however the betrayal is manifested and however serious it is, an external force will play a part. It may be the criminal tempting someone away or the influence of a friend or family member.

The contrary is not, however, true. An external force will rarely succeed unless there is something deficient either in the workplace or in the individual's character that predisposes him or her to betray.

Motivations are complex, but the elements, which go to make them up, are not. Everyone has experienced something similar. And because we can empathize with people who are leaving, thieving or whistle-blowing, we might as well start by asking ourselves that question we asked at the beginning: how might I have contributed to this act of betrayal?

Jeffrey Wigand

Revealed the illegal activities of his employers, Brown and Williamson, the US Tobacco giant in the press and courts

Jeffrey Wigand was sacked by his employer, Brown and Williamson, one of the seven largest tobacco companies in the world, in 1993. In 1994 Wigand embarked on a course which would lead to his appearing on nationwide TV in the US and in the US courts testifying against the tobacco industry and Brown and Williamson (B&W) in particular.

Wigand has become a role model for whistle-blowers and has had a major film, *The Insider* starring Al Pacino and Russell Crowe, made on his story. But the cost to him personally and financially has been significant. Was he motivated purely by ethical principles? Or were there other factors which influenced him?

Beliefs

There is no doubt that Wigand believed the tobacco industry was causing great harm to many people, including young teenagers. He also believed B&W management was cynically ignoring the health risks. A major part of his motivation was to expose these wrongs.

> He was disturbed by a report that on average children begin to smoke at 15 ... 'I used to come home tied in a knot. My kids would say "Hey, Daddy do you kill people?" I didn't like some of the things I saw. I felt uncomfortable. I felt dirty.' (Vanity Fare *May 1996*)

And later after he had left B&W:

> He was in his den with Lucretia [his wife] when he watched Andrew Tisch, the chairman of Lorillard, testify, 'I believe nicotine is not addictive.' Then he heard Thomas Sandefur [CEO B&W] say the same thing. Wigand was furious. 'They lied with a straight face. Sandefur was arrogant! And that really irked me.' (Vanity Fare *May 1996*)

The management

Wigand was a good scientist. He had worked his way up the hierarchies of other firms, been successful and much appreciated. But his position changed soon after the appointment of Thomas Sandefur as CEO.

> Sandefur used to beat up on me for using big words. I never found anybody as stupid as Sandefur in terms of his ability to read or communicate ... In terms of his understanding something and his intellectual capacity, Sandefur was like a farm boy.

Wigand felt that Sandefur, when presented with data that showed cigarettes contained cancer-causing ingredients, would do nothing to change the product fearing it would impact sales. On 24 March 1993, 2 months after Sandefur's appointment as CEO, B&W sacked Wigand.

B&W suspected he was talking about his previous employment and the company threatened to remove elements of his severance package, unless he signed a new and stricter confidentiality agreement. His reaction was:

> If Brown and Williamson had just left me alone, I probably would have gone away. I would have gotten a new job. (Vanity Fare *May 1996*)

B&W's tough tactics and threats continued for a number of years. They served only to strengthen Wigand's resolve. He became deeply resentful of B&W.

Wigand's personality

Wigand is proud of his scientific achievements and skills. He had worked in the healthcare industry, including companies such as Boehringer Meinheim Corporation, Pfizer and Johnson and Johnson. He was brought up in a strict Catholic home in the Bronx and became a talented biology and chemistry student.

His stubborn, rebellious nature comes out often. His brother James recalled in his interview with Marie Bremner:

> He suddenly announced to his parents that he was dropping out of college and joining the air force. 'It was a rebellion to get away,' James said. 'My mother just about freaked out ... but if you make someone so suppressed, the anger kind of builds up.' (Vanity Fare May 1996)

And Wigand to Marie Bremner herself:

> I have a very bad problem – saying what's on my mind ... I don't take too much crap from anybody. (Vanity Fare May 1996)

This determination combines with anger bordering on rage. During interviews with Marie Bremner she frequently recalls such incidents:

> Wigand splutters with rage.

> I am accustomed to his outbursts. A form of moral outrage ... he is often irascible and sometimes, on personal matters, relentlessly negative.

> His need to control his emotions [at the office] caused him frequently to lose his temper at home, Lucretia remembered. (Vanity Fare May 1996)

Alcohol also played its role:

> Wigand himself had at one time been a drinker, but he stopped when he felt out of control. After he was fired he told me, it was not surprising he began to drink again. (Vanity Fare May 1996)

Persuaders

More by accident than design Lowell Bergman, producer on the CBS programme 60 minutes, met Wigand. Bergman needed help on an issue concerning another tobacco company, Philip Morris. Wigand could provide just the kind of technical advice Bergman wanted. Wigand was not, however, prepared to talk about his work at B&W – at least initially.

> It was the beginning of an extraordinary relationship. Bergman's presence in Wigand's life would eventually inspire him to come forward as a whistle-blower. (Vanity Fare May 1996)

Bergman was perceptive and recognised the problems:

> The bottom line is that this was a man with significant information, but it wasn't just that he had to worry about the obvious, which is Brown & Williamson crushing him, but he had to worry about what would happen in his personal life. (Vanity Fare May 1996)

Wigand's relationships with the FDA and others from the government and judiciary were also important as they persuaded and coached him towards giving testimony, but none was as influential as Bergman.

Conclusion

Wigand's action can be partly explained by personal belief. B&W's management style contributed significantly to the situation. But Bergman's intervention was crucial and provides the third of the big three factors in this case.

The route to revenge

People at work are remarkably resilient; they have to be. People do not move on just because of a failure. Most employees stick at the job for a long time – years if not decades, despite repeated upsets concerning or affecting work. They stay remarkably loyal and deliberate sabotage, deception or revenge never enters their minds.

Staff joining a company usually feel optimistic and anticipate working with the company with some pleasure. The recruiters will have presented a picture, hopefully accurate, of the organization as having the kind of qualities that the individual aspires to or admires. There are of course the discontents or criminally minded who from day one will take the company for all that they can get away with. (Chapter 9 addresses how organizations can protect themselves against disloyalty of all kinds.) Once the excitement of the new job has died down and we have not found anything radically different from what the recruiters told us, we become satisfied.

Soon the gilt becomes tarnished; tolerance begins to thin. At some stage, and it can happen on day one, staff become disappointed, or angry and then vengeful. The office has no daylight; the people in the office are not congenial; a best friend has also started work and she is getting more money. These are not enough to upset us and we soon forget them or put them aside because the benefits outweigh the deficits. They are temporary concerns or at least manageable.

If these negatives persist because they are part of the company's culture and no one is going to change them or it is not possible to do the job properly, those feelings of disappointment become disillusion with the company or ourselves. Those early positive feelings about the company dissipate. Staff no longer feel so committed and they put themselves first and are less willing to give that extra effort or lunch hour. They start to make excuses. They begin to think the office owes them something and they start taking from the organization. They slip from commitment to alienation.

The 'breaking point' for each individual is different. Some of us can accept more 'unhappiness' than others for a longer period. How many competency frameworks have inscribed 'resilience' into their appraisals. 'Copes with failure or disappointment' are also written in to the qualities which employers like in their staff. Recruiters look for these qualities as they select candidates. Organizational cultures often belittle those who give up on a task let alone the company. But we each do have a breaking point, however much the culture may resist it. Indeed the culture itself may be part of the problem.

> *Vote for the man who promises least; he'll be the least disappointing.*
>
> Bernard Baruch 1870–1968,
> US Presidential adviser

Disappointment leads easily to disillusion. The cause of disappointment either is too great or has happened too frequently. The cause may not be the organization itself. Staff can be disappointed in themselves, their own performance. They have committed to working for the organization, but are failing or they made a bad judgement and thought the organization would provide them with more than it did. The job could have been too challenging or more prosaically the commute to work may have become intolerable.

Similarly family or friends could undermine confidence in the organization. Others may be on a much higher salary or have better benefits. The adverts on TV or in the appointments pages of newspapers can cause employees to question whether they are working in the right place.

> *Blessed is he who expects nothing, for he shall never be disappointed.*
>
> 18th-century proverb

Whatever the cause, their beliefs or ideals as they joined the company have been eroded (or simply changed) and they are left with the feeling that there may be something better out there. The reaction to disillusion is more likely to be resignation than anything more dramatic, but in the mean time the disillusioned will tend to give less and the more unscrupulous will 'take more liberties'.

They will be less willing to put in the extra hours; they will spend more time on the phone; some may start to 'liberate' stationery. They can justify it to themselves because they feel they have 'given' a lot to the company and this is only due to them. Most companies can accept this level of dishonesty.

When staff perceive that these things have happened because of some deliberate act by individuals in that company and who are still thriving in that company, stronger feelings emerge: those of resentment. Reactions to this emotion vary. Some will harbour their feelings; some will talk about them to colleagues in the company, unsettling other staff; some will express their feelings to outsiders which can damage the company's reputation or worse give competitors useful insights; some will resign. Few will leave without expressing some of their disappointment to others – and there is retaliation in that act alone. They no longer feel loyal to the company and they are seeking some kind of revenge.

The target varies. It can be the office itself. It may be individuals, the CEO, department head, the supervisor or possibly, though least likely, colleagues. Where the hurt is particularly deep the individual may turn to more damaging forms of revenge: theft, fraud, deceit, sabotage or whistle-blowing (see Figure 3.2).

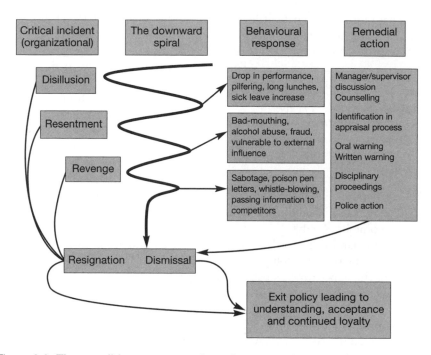

Figure 3.2 **The possible responses of employees as they experience poor management**

There may of course be justification for such action. Employment law is a major growth industry. Our language is full of litigious references and words. One personnel officer reports that when he started work in 1986 he never once had to consult the legal advisers. In 2001 barely a week went past without a fairly major discussion with lawyers about some potential case. Employers have to respect the workers and the latter have many more remedies available to them. The most obvious is to vote with their feet and resign. Others may not choose to leave but they can blow the whistle. Some will start taking from the company or deliberately damaging its interests.

The response to each of those emotions will vary for the individual and many have been mentioned already. Most typically they will consist of those listed in Table 3.3. So that for some individuals, they will never reach the theft or whistle-blowing stage in the normal course of organizational life. For others, the slightest excuse and they become disloyal.

Employees, like people everywhere, are moved by emotions. Managers and HR professionals seek to rationalize human behaviour. Economists call employees a factor of production, although the phrase is less fashionable now. Even using the common 'human resources' suggests that they are a commodity which can be moved around a shop floor and by applying hard learnt business principles they will respond in a foreseeable manner. People are not so predictable; but their motivations to take unusual even aberrant actions are understandable.

Table 3.3 Emotional states and responses

Employee state of well-being	Emotional and practical response
Optimism	Expectation of salary, good work, security, enthusiasm
Satisfaction	Desire to work well, to please, a feeling of commitment to the company's fortune
Disappointment	Sadness, temporary falling in performance, withdrawal of enthusiasm, but things can get better
Disillusion	Poor time keeping, petty pilfering (telephone, stationery), discussion of disappointment/disillusion in and out of the office, start to look or think about alternative jobs
Resentment	Bitterness, feeling of being wronged; theft, including taking clients, rubbishing company to current clients or customers, fraud, whistle-blowing, legal actions perhaps based on the individual's own mendacity
Revenge	Sabotage and other more serious counterproductive behaviours designed to cause deliberate damage

An employee establishes relationships, with colleagues, customers and competitors. One of the most significant is with their boss. These people are rarely chosen, they are supplied. It is not surprising that tensions between people in the workplace develop. Everyone can recognise that and everyone who has worked for any length of time has observed and experienced negative feelings.

These feelings and tensions will move people. They are the same feelings that are commonly experienced by employers and employees alike. Analysts can categorize them, as this chapter has in an attempt to make them more understandable.

Conclusion

The motives for disruptive behaviour in the workplace can originate for a variety of reasons and there is unlikely to be only one cause. They can be summarized as follows.

Individual drivers or susceptibilities

▷ *Beliefs and values.* People are increasingly conscious of and care about the nature of the business they are associated with. They can be motivated by positive (a belief in developing life-saving drugs or working in the social services) or negative feelings (fighting against corruption). Where the original feeling is a positive one their motive to rebel will be because of a change in the perceived business, reducing or reversing the positive nature of the business.

▷ *Social needs.* Many enjoy the social nature of work. People spend as much as 30% of their time there and strong social relationships are created. A threat to this interaction will have consequences for those for whom this is a crucial factor.

▷ *Vanity*. There are those who seek fame in their work to achieve a strong reputation and others who seek some identity amongst their peer group.

▷ *Money/greed*. Money can satisfy four basic needs: security, power, love and greater freedom.

▷ *Envy*. The promotion of others, when an individual perceives he or she is equally if not more deserving, causes considerable resentment. The issue may not just be about promotion.

▷ *Ambition*. A desire to advance is normal but when it becomes obsessive and at the expense of others it becomes destructive.

▷ *Excitement*. Thrill seekers can be risk averse and if the organization does not satisfy their needs, they may turn their attention to breaking company rules.

▷ *Personality disorders*. These are often hard to detect and because they are essentially a medical condition they are discussed in more detail in Chapter 5.

Dysfunctional organizations

▷ *Top management and organizational policies and administration*. Employees expect to be led and to be led wisely. They resent unnecessary administration or bureaucracy or 'absentee managers'.

▷ *Day-to-day management including interpersonal skills*. Few people leave an organization – they leave because of the boss.

▷ *Recognition, advancement, proper use of employee skills*. Some of the simplest day-to-day courtesies are all that are needed to make employees feel their skills and achievements are appreciated.

▷ *Salary*. This is more important for blue collar workers than white collar workers, but both need to feel their pay is sufficient. For some it is also a symbol showing how much the individual is appreciated.

▷ *The work itself*. People want their time at work to be interesting as well as worthwhile. Different people have different interests.

▷ *Environment, work conditions and colleagues*. Having a modern office (or an old fashioned 'comfy' office) matters to many. The ability to commute or shop easily is an important factor.

▷ *Development opportunities*. Employees want not only to feel that they are allowed to continue their learning but also to develop in the job. Responsibility and authority are an essential ingredient for the budding employee.

The persuaders

▷ *Advertisements and the media*. People are exposed to many different forms of inducements to move job.

▷ *Competitors*. Rival companies will be interested in poaching your best staff and some will go to illegal lengths to acquire your secrets. Staff are often the weak link.

▷ *Journalists.* Staff will often find a journalist provides just the vehicle to vent their feelings. Publicity is a good way of revenge, particularly when anonymity is guaranteed.

▷ *Friends and family.* Employees are often influenced by the friend and family who may be pushing them to greater deeds (and wealth).

▷ *Criminals.* Sadly staff can all too easily be seduced by the temptations of greater wealth. A professional criminal will always be on the look out for an insider to help achieve the misdemeanour.

▷ *Headhunters and recruitment agencies.* Employers and their competitors are always looking for the best talent; poaching is common. Their professionalism varies but the headhunter will target individuals and make an offer before the current employer knows about it.

The unsettling forces, strengths and weaknesses in individuals are recognizable; that staff should become occasionally resentful or disillusioned should not come as a surprise; some minor infringements are inevitable. And the consequences are usually met with resilience by the employees, who also recognize the world is not perfect. But when employers and their managers persist in negative behaviour or fail to notice and react to an individual's problems, the reaction escalates.

That may be enough. The ambitious individuals who seek thrills and excitement in their work will not tolerate a company where advancement and new challenges are absent. They will resign and, depending on the severity of their poor management experiences, will bad-mouth the company, seek to take with them information or clients or seek some other form of revenge. If during the process of disillusion an external 'persuader' discovers what is happening the consequences could be accelerated and turned into a more damaging act of sabotage.

The solutions for employers are not hard to grasp. It may be that the fault lies entirely with the individual and some external malevolent force. But before seeking refuge in this rather comfortable explanation, employers might pause and ask themselves if their own management skills and styles might have contributed to the process.

At the beginning of this chapter readers were invited to look at some responses to questions about why they left their last job (Table 3.1). Employers who have recently suffered a particularly hurtful resignation, fraud, theft, deception or other act of sabotage might consider the following taken from that set of questions. Could the perpetrators of the act have answered 'yes' to any of them:

▷ I was not appreciated in the old job
▷ I was not being developed (that is trained, stretched) enough in my old job
▷ The old job was not sufficiently challenging
▷ My old boss did not like me or treat me fairly
▷ I did not get promotion when I should have

▷ I did not like the office building/surroundings
▷ Others in the old company were getting promotion because they were friends of the boss/management
▷ I felt under too much pressure
▷ I was being bullied/harassed.

If employers really do want to prevent any repetitions, those sorts of issues have to be addressed. If the act was the result of an individual's problem or the influence of an outsider, the act will not be repeated. If, however, the problem lies within, then repetitions can be expected.

4 Counterproductive Behaviours at Work

Introduction

The list of antisocial, deviant and destructive behaviours at work is long: absenteeism, accidents, bullying, corruption, disciplinary problems, drug and alcohol abuse, sabotage, sexual harassment, tardiness, theft, whistle-blowing, white collar crime and violence are typical examples of what one could list as counterproductive behaviours or CWBs.

The term CWB is often used synonymously with antisocial, deviant, dysfunctional, retaliative and unethical behaviour at work (Marcus 2000). It costs organizations billions every year and many of them invest in ways to prevent, reduce or catch those most likely to offend. There are many different words to describe CWBs, such as: organizational delinquency, production and property deviance, workplace deviance. All agree it is a multifaceted behavioural syndrome that is characterized by hostility to authority, impulsivity, social insensitivity, alienation and lack of moral integrity. People feel frustrated or powerless or unfairly dealt with and act accordingly.

CWB is intentional and contrary to the interests of the organization. CWB may not in the shortfall be reflected in counterproductivity which is the cost of CWBs. The essence of a CWB is wrongdoing: not counternormativeness or hurting the organization. Thus taking sick leave when not sick may be a common occurrence, indeed the norm, yet still a CWB.

So what are we talking about? Sackett (2002) listed 11 groups of CWB:

1   Theft and related behaviour (theft of cash or property; giving away of goods or services, misuse of employee discount).
2   Destruction of property (deface, damage, or destroy property; sabotage production).
3   Misuse of information (reveal confidential information; falsify records).
4   Misuse of time and resources (waste time, alter time card, conduct personal business during work time).
5   Unsafe behaviour (failure to follow safety procedures; failure to learn safety procedures).
6   Poor attendance (unexcused absence or tardiness; misuse sick leave).
7   Poor quality work (intentionally slow or sloppy work).

8 Alcohol use (alcohol use on the job; coming to work under the influence of alcohol).

9 Drug use (possess, use, or sell drugs at work).

10 Inappropriate verbal actions (argue with customers; verbally harass co-workers).

11 Inappropriate physical actions (physically attack co-workers; physical sexual advances toward co-worker). (pp 5–6)

A central question for both the scientist and the manager is whether these eleven types of CWB are discrete or related. In other words, does each CWB have its own unique characteristics or are they are all related and the product of a mix of different personality types and organization situations?

At the heart of the matter is whether people who engage in one type of CWB (for example sabotage) are also likely to engage in others (for example theft). It should of course be recognized that work contexts limit and provide opportunities for specific types of CWB. However, various studies using different groups have revealed a fairly strong correlation between self-reported CWBs (Sackett 2002). In other words, people seem likely to (or not) take part in any/all or no counterproductive behaviours. Thus it seems that people could be put on a continuum in terms of how likely they are to engage in CWBs from very unlikely to very likely.

No doubt the choice of CWB to the individual is limited. Some thieve, others destroy, some go absent a lot, others do shoddy work. Perhaps their personality, opportunity, level of courage or anger determines how they act but the essential point is that people seek their vengeance where they can. Put another way, the essential causes of theft, sabotage, whistle-blowing or lying and cheating are probably the same.

Classification of bad behaviours

There are few more distressing experiences in the workplace for managers than having to cope with an employee who has deliberately done wrong. The implications of not taking action are often even greater and if situations are handled badly managers compound the errors.

The sooner problems can be identified the easier they are to handle and, if managed well, the potential costs of counterproductive behaviour are reduced. Staff are often described as a company's most valuable resource. It is often said and quoted by CEOs. The published material on managing employees prefers to emphasize the positive: how to maximize potential, retaining great employees, motivating for success, win–win. The list is long and extensive.

In an earlier study that tried to classify deviant behaviours, Robinson and Bennett (1995) came up with the impressive list on the page opposite.

▷ Employee stealing customer's possessions.
▷ Boss verbally abusing employee.
▷ Employee sabotaging equipment.
▷ Employee coming to work late or leaving early.
▷ Employee lying about hours worked.
▷ Employee gossiping about manager.
▷ Employee starting negative rumours about company.
▷ Boss sexually harassing employee.
▷ Employee physically abusing customer.
▷ Employee taking excessive breaks.
▷ Employee sabotaging merchandise.
▷ Employee overcharging on services to profit him or herself.
▷ Employee intentionally making errors.
▷ Employee covering up mistakes.
▷ Employee leaving job in progress with no directions so the job is done wrong.
▷ Boss following rules to the letter of the law.
▷ Employee gossiping about co-worker.
▷ Employee intentionally working slowly.
▷ Boss unjustifiably firing employee.
▷ Employee sexually harassing co-worker.
▷ Employee accepting kickbacks.
▷ Employee endangering him or herself by not following safety procedures.
▷ Boss leaving early and leaving his/her work for employees to do.

▷ Employee hiding in back room to read the newspaper.
▷ Employee stealing company equipment/merchandise.
▷ Employee acting foolishly in front of customers.
▷ Employee verbally abusing customers.
▷ Employee working unnecessary overtime.
▷ Employee calling in sick when not.
▷ Boss showing favouritism to certain employees.
▷ Boss gossiping about employees.
▷ Employee talking with co-worker instead of working.
▷ Employee stealing money from cash drawer.
▷ Employee misusing discount privilege.
▷ Employee wasting company resources by turning up the heat and opening the windows.
▷ Employee blaming co-worker for mistakes.
▷ Employee misusing expense account.
▷ Employee going against boss's decision.
▷ Employees competing with co-workers in a non-beneficial way.
▷ Boss blaming employees for his/her mistakes.
▷ Boss refusing to give employee his/her earned benefits or pay.
▷ Employee making personal long-distance calls or mailing personal packages from work.
▷ Employee endangering co-workers by reckless behaviour.
▷ Employee stealing co-worker's possessions.
▷ Boss asking employee to work beyond job description.

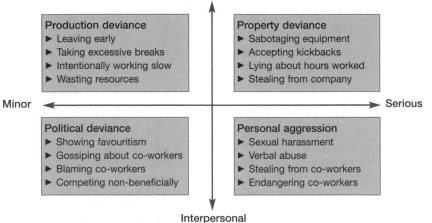

Figure 4.1 **Typology of deviant workplace behaviour**
Source: Robinson and Bennett 1997a.

Robinson and Bennett (1997a) describe CWBs as 'voluntary behaviour of organizational members that violates significant organizational norms and, in so doing, threatens the well-being of the organization and/or its members' (p 7). They also offer two-by-two categorization of CWBs (see Figure 4.1).

They offer both a simple model of the path to deviance (see Figure 4.2) and also a more detailed model that tries to predict which type of deviance will occur (Robinson and Bennett 1997b p 15).

They have five propositions based on this model:

P1: If the provocation produces an expressive motivation, an employee will be more likely to direct his or her actions at the perceived source of the provocation (individual or organization), with one of the most legitimate/least deviant action that is available, satisfying and unconstrained.

P2: If the provocation produces an expressive motivation, an employee will be more likely to engage in a more serious deviant act to the extent that more minor deviant acts are unavailable, unsatisfying, and/or constrained.

P3: If the provocation produces an expressive motivation, an employee will be more likely to direct his or her actions at a target other than the perceived source of the provocation to the extent that minor and serious forms of deviance directed at the perceived source are unavailable, unsatisfying, and/or contained. (p 22)

P4: If the provocation produces an instrumental motivation, an employee will be more likely to direct his or her actions at the target (individual or organization) that is most pertinent to resolving the disparity, with the most legitimate/least deviant action that is available, effective, and unconstrained.

P5: If the provocation produces an instrumental motivation, an employee will be more likely to engage in more serious deviant acts to the extent that more minor deviant acts are unavailable, ineffective, and/or constrained. (p 23)

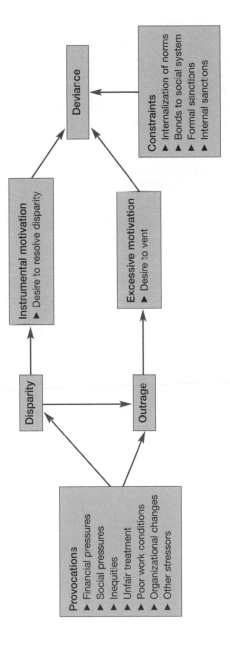

Figure 4.2 **A model of workplace deviance**
Source: Robinson and Bennett 1997b p 15.

Various researchers have placed emphasis on slightly different features. Thus Grover (1993) believes role conflict at work is a major cause of CWB. Triggers (felt injustice, stressors) provoke a deviant reaction; because of lack of constraints there are opportunities to perform CWBs in individuals with poor self-control.

There are not many theories specifically of CWBs but one exception is that of Martinko et al. (2002) who developed what they called a Causal Reasoning Perspective. Their aim was to demonstrate the relationships and similarities between and among various forms of CWBs. They define CWBs as those 'characterized by a disregard for societal and organizational rules and values; actions that threaten the well being of an organization and its members and break implicit and explicit rules about appropriate, civil and respectful behaviour'.

Martinko et al. (2002) reviewed over 20 relevant studies that looked at individual difference variables and situational variables that seemed related to CWB; individual differences included personality (for example neuroticism, Machiavellianism), demography (age, sex), morality (integrity), organizational experience (tenure, commitment) and self-perceptions (self-esteem, self-concept). The situational or organizational variables included organizational policies, practices, norms, rules, resource scarcity, job autonomy and appraisals.

Note that the attribution must be about stable causes, meaning stable over time. Unstable causes by definition come and go and lead to quite different attributions. Thus lack of ability is a stable attribution, but being in a bad mood or having a cold is an unstable attribution.

The theory shown diagrammatically (Figure 4.3) goes like this. An individual in a particular work situation, say a person with low self-esteem and low integrity in a difficult competitive work environment with adverse work conditions feels that things are not fair. The model talks of perceived disequilibria, or feelings of injustice or inequity. Associated with this feeling of unfairness is the cause or attribution that the person makes for this state of affairs. If they believe *they personally* are the cause (internal stable attribution) they are likely to take part in self-destructive behaviours, but if they feel the cause is *external* (that is, their boss, unfair company rules) they are likely to take part in retaliation behaviour.

What is attractive about this model is essentially three things. First, it attempts to differentiate between different types of CWB, here called self-destructive and retaliatory behaviour. Second, it offers a process whereby CWBs are likely to occur. Third, it describes some of the more important individual difference factors that are associated with CWBs.

Martinko et al. (2002) describe in detail six individual difference factors they believe to be heavily implicated in CWBs:

1 *Gender:* Overwhelmingly CWBs are more likely to be the province of males because they make more aggressive attributions and tend to be more self-serving by blaming others for their failure.

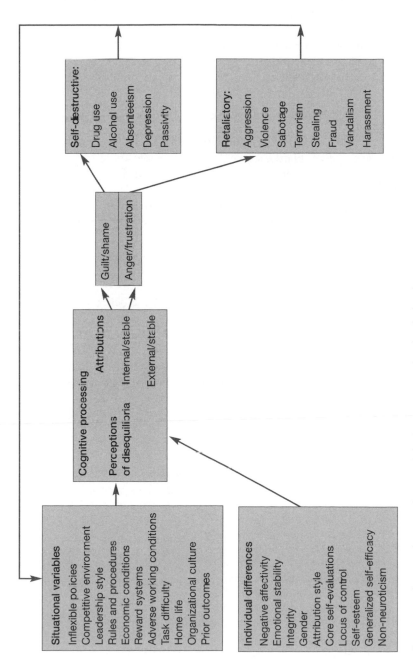

Figure 4.3 **A causal reasoning model of counterproductive behaviour**
Source: Adapted from Martinko et al. 2002.

2 *Locus of control:* Those who are fatalistic, believing their lives are determined by chance or powerful others, compared with instrumentalists who believe they control their own life outcomes, are more likely to commit CWBs.
3 *Attribution/explanation style:* Those with hostile and pessimistic attribution styles, in other words, those who attribute person failure either to external, stable and intentional causes (that is, a nasty boss) or internal, stable and global causes (that is, I have no ability) tend to cause more CWBs. In other words, how people characteristically describe their own success and failure is a good predictor of their likelihood to become involved in CWBs.
4 *Core self-evaluations:* These are fundamental beliefs about self and are similar to self-esteem. Hardy, stable, 'can do' people are less likely to feel victims or experience organizational paranoia and less likely to be involved in CWBs.
5 *Integrity:* People with integrity tend to be agreeable, conscientious, emotionally stable and reliable. They are clearly less likely to get involved in CWBs.
6 *Neuroticism* (negative affectivity): This refers to the extent to which individuals experience anger, anxiety, fear and hostility. Stable individuals tend to be more satisfied with their lives and focus on the positive. Neurotics often feel people in their environment are demanding, distant and threatening. Neurotics are more prone to CWBs.

Certainly this model is a promising start. The authors are wary of limitations but make a good cause for specifying a reasonable process which explains how, why and when individuals in certain work situations do, and do not, get involved in CWBs.

Theft

> *Companies around the world will spend an estimated US$75 billion this year on security-related products and services. That sum will include mountains of high-tech equipment, investigators' fees, and salaries for thousands of security officers. With losses from corporate fraud put at between US$250 billion and US$400 billion annually, the obvious question is: Is this money well spent?*
>
> The Enemy Within – report by Stephen Payne February 2000 http://www.cfoasia.com/ archives/200002-20.htm

Organizations often label theft as 'inventory shrinkage' and it may be 2–3% of retail sales. Up to half of this can be employee theft. These figures differ from country to country, sector to sector and year to year but are serious enough for many organizations to call for expensive countermeasures. Electronic security tags, cameras and observation mirrors, locks and chains and armed security guards are commonplace in many shops. They may or may not act as deterrents. They can make matters worse (see Chapters 9 and 10).

It is impossible to get accurate and reliable statistics on employee theft. Estimates vary as a function of the research and the business domains. It is also difficult to define theft or to suggest that 'taking home' a few envelopes is equivalent to stealing large sums of money or valuable goods. 'Ball-park' figures vary considerably that from a quarter to two-thirds of all employees are involved in some sort of theft at work.

There are all sorts of definitional issues. Employers and employees have different definitions particularly when the words thief and victim are used. Also there is trivial theft (a few paper clips), semi-trivial (pens and paper) and non-trivial theft (computers). It is possible to distinguish between *production theft* (poor output) and *material theft* (property/money). Production theft includes work slow-downs while material theft is quite clearly property theft. There is also theft of time (absenteeism) and theft of goods produced by the company.

Some have distinguished between *altruistic theft* (giving stolen goods to others) and *selfish theft*. This is often a post-rationalization of the thief who claims that he/she is more like Robin Hood than a common criminal. There is also *preventable* vs. *non-preventable theft*. This may be a more fuzzy distinction than can be made here. There is scarcely any crime that is totally non-preventable, although the risks can be significantly reduced.

Essentially theft is the unlawful taking, transfer or control of another's (the employer) property with the aim of benefiting the thief (and others) who are not entitled to that property.

In every company or organization there are staff who thieve. It may be mostly petty theft, but the extent is often surprising. The evidence is growing that employees regularly steal from their employers. Estimates vary considerably from researcher to researcher, from business sector to business sector and from country to country. But the overall picture is compelling: employee theft is hurting companies and organizations.

There is no single database that details the extent of the problem. The retail industry has always recognized that 'shrinkage' of its stocks is a problem. Until recently the blame was put on the customer and described as shoplifting. Now employers recognize that employees are also responsible. The 2002 National Retail Security Survey produced by the University of Florida reported that 'retailers attributed 48% of their inventory shrinkage to employee theft'. Shoplifting, often thought to be retailer's biggest problem, is only 32% (see Figure 4.4).

The report goes on:

> Assuming a total shrinkage dollar total of approximately $31.3 billion, this trans-lates into an annual employee theft price tag of slightly over $15 billion ... There is no other form of larceny that annually costs American citizens more money than employee theft.

According to this report convenience stores and supermarkets suffer the greatest losses (Hollinger 2002).

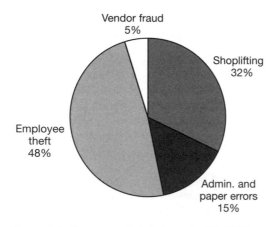

Figure 4.4 **Sources of shrinkage in US 2002**
Source: University of Florida, National Retail Security Survey 2002.

In Europe the situation is a little different. The third report of the European Retail Theft Barometer collected data from 16 European countries. The report estimates the costs of shrinkage in Europe to be €27,258 million in the year 2002/03 or 1.37% of turnover. Customers who shoplift represent 48% and internal error is 17%. Another 7% is the responsibility of the suppliers (Figure 4.5).

Taking each country separately the shrinkage problem is most acute in the UK, where staff theft accounts for 36% of shrinkage, with Denmark, Norway and The Netherlands 32%. Portugal and Germany have less staff theft at 22% and 23%, but, by the same analysis, a higher shoplifting rate (Table 4.1).

Retailers have responded by increasing the amount invested in security. They now spend €6364 million on security, an increase of 22% over the previous year (2001/02), but this figure includes measures to combat theft by customers and suppliers.

The opportunity for thieving is perhaps greater in a shop than, say, an employment agency, but opportunities exist in all businesses.

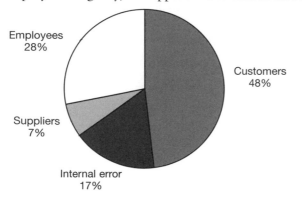

Figure 4.5 **Sources of shrinkage in Europe 2002/03**
Source: The European Retail Theft Barometer, Centre for Retail Research February–May 2003.

Table 4.1 2002/03 sources of shrinkage by country

	Customers %	Staff %	Suppliers %	Internal error %
Austria	53.0	23.5	6.0	17.5
Belgium/Luxemburg	46.5	29.5	6.0	18.0
Denmark	45.5	32.5	7.0	15.0
Finland	47.0	31.0	9.0	13.0
France	48.0	28.3	6.5	17.2
Germany	50.7	23.0	8.3	10.0
Greece	55.0	20.0	7.0	18.0
Ireland	46.2	29.2	7.2	17.4
Italy	52.3	22.9	10.8	14.0
The Netherlands	45.9	32.0	7.1	15.0
Norway	46.0	32.0	6.0	16.0
Portugal	53.0	22.3	9.7	15.0
Spain	52.0	26.5	5.5	16.0
Sweden	45.0	27.0	9.2	18.8
Switzerland	52.5	23.5	8.5	15.5
United Kingdom	42.4	36.1	4.0	17.5
Averages	47.8	28.5	6.8	16.9

Source: The European Retail Theft Barometer, Centre for Retail Research, February–May 2003.

In 2002 a dental practice in London discovered that their much loved receptionist had stolen over £5000 from the till over the previous three years. The receptionist had simply creamed off £20 or £30 every time she was on duty. Any one who has access to company cash has the potential to steal.

The hotel and catering industries suffer as much as any:

I started to get bored, so I began stealing small things like food and beer from the kitchen. But when I start stealing from a job it's like a snowball effect, an addiction, I can't stop it … I stole TV sets, lamps, chairs and furniture. (Martin Sprouse 1992 p 45, quoting a security guard in a hotel in the US)

Members of all the housekeeping groups band together when it comes time for stealing … For more major thefts it's back to the rooftop. Workers with pick-up trucks drive to the back of the hotel. Others throw boxes of linen, shower curtains, towels just anything, into the waiting trucks. (Martin Sprouse 1992 p 43, quoting a chambermaid)

In 1999 Michael G. Kessler & Associates, Ltd, the leading international investigative and forensic accounting firm specializing in corporate issues affecting today's workplace, completed an exhaustive study surveying over 500 employees in the US on the issue of employee theft in the workplace. Their report showed that employee theft is the cause for one out of every three business failures in the US today. Their study 'disclosed that employees readily admitted to stealing office supplies, falsifying expense reports and taking inventory, and almost 87% of those surveyed admitted to falsifying time sheets because they regularly stole time from their employers and were paid for hours they did not work. Those surveyed also indicated that these practices were increasing at an alarming rate. Previous studies revealed that the price tag on employee theft in the US was over $120 billion a year' (www.investigation. com/articles/library/1999articles/articles22). Their research also discovered that: 21% will never steal from an employer; 13% will steal from an employer and 66% will steal if they see others do so without consequence.

A UK-wide survey, for Bank of Scotland Business Banking by the Opinion Research Business, revealed that 24% of small and medium-sized businesses – almost 900,000 across the UK – reported having suffered staff fraud. Whilst losses of more than £5000 are very rare, the figures show small firms are more susceptible to cases of petty fraud and theft. Some 11% have lost up to £1000 through theft or fraud and 4% have lost between £1000 and £5000.

Whilst 19% of firms with fewer than 15 employees have experienced staff fraud, this figure more than doubles to 48% for businesses with over 36 staff. For some reason, firms headed by men are more likely to experience staff fraud than those headed by women (25% compared with 18%). Nearly one in ten respondents said that they have sacked or disciplined a member of staff as a result of fraud or theft over the last three years (www.smallbusiness-centre.net – 24 July 2003).

Singer (1996) noted 12 danger signs that possible indicate employees are embezzling a company:

1 Rewriting records for the sake of 'neatness'.
2 Refusing to take vacations; never taking personal or sick days.
3 Working overtime voluntarily and excessively and refusing to release custody of records during the day.
4 Unusually high standard of living, considering salary.
5 Gambling in any form beyond ability to withstand losses.
6 Refusal of promotion.
7 Replying to questions with unreasonable explanations.
8 Getting annoyed at reasonable questions.
9 Inclination toward covering up inefficiencies and mistakes.
10 Pronounced criticisms of others (to divert suspicion).
11 Frequent association with, and entertainment by, a member of supplier's staff.
12 Excessive drinking or associating with questionable characters.

People in human resources are becoming interested in theft prevention. Niehoff and Paul (2000 p 61) offer ten guidelines:

Procedural guidelines
1   Install security systems and implement internal accounting controls for any process involving money or company assets.

2   Use integrity tests in selection process, but only if you can assure that such tests are valid.
3   Conduct background checks as thoroughly as the laws allow.
4   Review and revise, if necessary, any job or organizational information presented to prospective employees, assuring that all information is accurate and consistent.
5   Conduct orientation programs that discuss the company's code of ethics and formal procedures to be followed in case of problems.

Interactive guidelines
1   Initiate and model a culture of honesty in the organization, with clear reinforcement for honesty and punishment for dishonesty (including for all levels of management).
2   Provide support or encouragement for employee personal and skill development.
3   Contract with an employee-assistance program for counselling troubled employees.
4   Review compensation and benefit packages for internal and external equity.
5   Get to know employees through effective communication and implement programs that create bonds between employees and the company.

Theories of theft

Inevitably the perceived cause of the problems leads to an appropriate strategy for prevention. Most researchers in the area, like Greenberg and Barling (1996), recognize that different forces together impact on when, how and why theft takes place. Their simple model is shown in Figure 4.6.

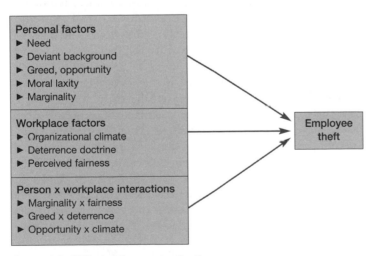

Figure 4.6 **Different forces on theft**
Source: Adapted from Greenberg and Barling 1996.

There appear to be three types of theories of theft based on different levels:

1 *Personal:* This focuses on the personality, demographic and criminological profits of the individual whose background and morality lead to their thieving. Impulsive, excitement-seeking, people with poor moral development and education are the most common types.

2 *Social:* This focuses on theft as both/either a response to unfair treatment/violation of psychological contract *and/or* a compliance with organizational norms that support, endorse and even require thieving. The focus is not on the individual's personality but his/her feelings of betrayal, distress, injustice, revenge and retaliation after being badly treated.

3 *Systemic:* This focuses on two features with theft as compensation for perceived poor (inequitable) pay and poor control systems that allow individuals to get away with it.

There are many factors involved in employee theft. Greenberg and Barling (1996) suggest that they can be grouped into three types:

1 *Person theories:* these are concerned with the essentially psychological problem of explaining why some individuals (and not others) are involved with pilfering and theft:

   A *Financial needs.* The idea is that stealing occurs as a function of financial need. But others' needs are implicated, such as social or belongingness needs, because people may steal in order to obtain goals/money that allows them to become a 'club member'. It is a weak theory as it does not distinguish the origin or type of need (for example drug addiction, gambling, sick relatives).

   B *Deviant personality/background.* The concept is that there is a person type who is more vulnerable to opportunities to steal as well as personally more likely to rationalize stealing behaviour. The theory is weak and tautological – people who steal are the stealing type – stealing types steal!

   C *Greed/tempted opportunities.* The idea is that people are inherently greedy and steal when they can: they are inherently untrustworthy. However, it fails to explain why there are systematic differences in greed.

   D *Moral laxity.* Here the theme is that some groups (especially young people) do not possess the same ethical standards or trustworthy qualities as other groups. Again the argument is poor: it is tautological and does not explain individual differences.

   E *Marginality.* People who are marginal have less static jobs with no tenure or social standing and steal as a way of expressing grievances. Because they have had no opportunities to develop commitment – they steal.

Each of these theories is profoundly problematic for the same specific reasons.

2   *Workplace theories* emphasize rather different factors:

A   *Organizational climate:* In effect this refers to a moral atmosphere than can even endorse dishonesty or at least turn a blind eye towards it. The idea is that the prevailing climate sends clear messages to employers about whether, what, which and when dishonest behaviours are acceptable or not.

B   *Deterrence doctrine:* This refers to the existency, explicitness and retributive nature of company antitheft policies and the perceived certainty and severity of punishment, as well as the visibility of that punishment. The idea is simple: get tough with deterrence and theft will be reduced.

C   *Perceived organizational fairness:* This 'theory' suggests it is exploitation by the employer that causes pilferage. Note that it is perceived unfairness on the part of the organization that is the crucial factor. Pay cuts in particular lead to this activity.

There is also possibly the interaction between personal and workplace factors. There must be opportunity but it is the combination of person characteristics and workplace characteristics that probably predicts theft most accurately. Thus a morally lax individual in a morally lax workplace that offers opportunity for stealing would be an extreme case. Equally a greedy, opportunistic individual who works in an organization he/she believes to be exploitative is also a situation likely to lead to theft.

In a recent study Greenberg (2002) showed that the moral development of an individual and the actual victim of a theft (individual vs. organization) actually determine when and why people steal money. That is, it is the particular interaction between the person and the job that leads to thieving.

Dissatisfaction, injustice and theft

Many researchers have tried to understand theft at work in terms of theories of injustice and justice (distributive justice, equity justice). The idea is simple. People are in a *social exchange relationship* at work: they give and they get (inputs and outputs). They 'sell' their time, expertise, labour and loyalty and, in return, get a salary, pension, paid holidays and so on. Where the 'equation' is balanced all is well. Where not, people are motivated to re-establish it. Thus people can, if they believe they are inappropriately rewarded, ask for a raise, leave, work less hard, go absent *or steal.*

People who feel frustrated, cheated, humiliated or undervalued often steal as revenge and to right a wrong. This is not to say that all dissatisfied people thieve. But there is evidence that thieving is often a *restitution and retaliative* response to perceived unfairness. People steal partly because of the way they are treated. People *strike back* with reciprocal deviance if they feel poorly or unfairly treated:

> In summary, it appears that employee theft is more than simply an attempt to restore a mathematical balance between outcomes and inputs. Such inequities appear to be necessary for theft to occur, but may not always be sufficient. What needs to be added to the formula for employee theft is improper social treatment – variously called social insensitivity, lack of dignity, rudeness, disrespect, or lack of compassion. Although inequitable outcomes may be necessary to instigate employee theft, they may be insufficient to do so. Showing social insensitivity to those outcomes may also be required to trigger the theft response. (Greenberg and Scott 1996 p 14)

Greenberg and Scott (1996) asked the fundamental question as to why theft at work seems so widely acceptable. They believe there is a *cycle of employee theft acceptance* based on three factors: people's willingness to harm (particularly big) organizations; organizations too infrequently prosecute employees caught thieving; many employees feel complete lack of guilt over stealing.

Often large organizations are seen as very rich abusers of power, bullies of their workforce and competitors and hence just 'victims' or targets of 'Robin Hood' thieving. Companies do not prosecute, however, because of the cost, the nature of the evidence they have, the poor publicity and the effect on the other staff. And because companies do not often prosecute employees don't see the activity as necessarily wrong and hence steal happily and without guilt.

Equally supervisory norms may condone and even encourage theft. This may occur because of *parallel deviance* or *passive imitation* which simply means that people follow the lead of their bosses who they notice abusing the system and thieving. If the supervisor calls theft 'a perk' so do the staff. Next there is the *invisible wage structure* or system of *controlled larceny* which effectively means that supervisors allow, help and even organise employee theft. They often say they do this to enrich jobs and more efficiently motivate staff.

However, even more common are work-group norms that support and regulate employee theft. Becoming part of a group may involve being taught how to, when and where to steal. Indeed work-group thieving may ritualistically and symbolically be linked to becoming a successful employee. Thieving norms involve how people divide the spoils/outcomes of theft. Further, the group help 'neutralise' their acts with a raft of excuses/explanations like denials of responsibility, injury, the company being a victim, appeals to higher authority and a condemnation of the condemner. Group norms often spell out the parameters of thieving behaviour – that is, what is and is not stolen, and the worth of what has been stolen.

So how can the manager reduce employee thefts? The first thing is to *break the social norms* that accept and rationalize theft. Some companies have had success with simply printing theft statistics on the intranet. It is essential to stop employees seeing their theft as appropriate and desirable. Business ethic talks can help this, but they are insufficient and can be seen as preaching.

Profit-sharing also helps align the interests of employer and employees. Activities that lower profitability (pilfering in employee-owned companies) soon become taboo. Where this is not possible, having a clear social contract prohibiting theft may help.

If perceived (note, not actual) fairness is an issue, it is important to emphasize continually the *fairness* of the company's *compensation system*. Company hotlines for just whistle-blowing have been shown to have a significant effect. Some companies have suggested that the issue of theft should be brought into the open and employees should be encouraged to discuss how it is to be defined and treated. This helps to flag that the company is serious about theft and helps ensure employees' commitment.

Companies are now so worried about the issue that they are attempting serious preventive, proactive, rather than reactive, methods. This involves integrity testing and background checks at selection. It also involves employer publications and, more ominously, a tightening up of internal controls and security.

Most employers would prefer to avert the problem in the first place perhaps with some pre-employment screening such as giving people integrity tests. Yet Greenberg and Barling (1996) point to some severe limitations with that idea.

> Although integrity tests have been shown to predict on-the-job theft, they still need to be used with caution for several reasons: it is ironical and unreasonable to expect dishonest people to answer questions truthfully about their own attitudes toward theft and past dishonest behaviour. Attitudes about theft or personality tendencies are only moderately correlated with theft behaviours. Opportunity for theft does not necessarily lead to greater occurrences of theft. In fact, most employees in various occupations have access to money or merchandise but choose not to steal. Labelling someone a 'thief' may become a self-fulfilling prophesy and would certainly make it more difficult for that person to obtain alternative employment. Privacy issues and most importantly, this approach ignores [sic] the potential contribution of workplace factors that might lead to employee theft. (p 59)

Greenberg (1998) has argued that there are forces that both encourage and discourage theft at various levels. They work first at the level of the individual. Thus the personality and the moral development of the individual may be either an encouraging or an inhibiting force while various life pressures (for more money to fund gambling debts, secret love affairs and so on) may encourage the individual to thieve.

Individuals have to make the decision to thieve which then usually results in their justifications (to self and others) of that act. After the theft they then usually try to manage the interpretation of that action and label it according to their own ends. Many try to legitimate a clearly illegitimate act. Their personality, morality and intelligence are powerful determinants in how, when and why this is done.

At the group level there may well be peer pressure to take part in group-organized and accepted thieving. Equally there may well be peer-based pressure not to take part in any or specific types of theft. Paradoxically some organizations encourage theft by tacitly accepting it as an invisible wage structure. Most say that they (or indeed try to) induce inhibiting forces by a mixture of a code of ethics, ethical leadership and having a non-bureaucratic structure.

All organizations attempt to weaken forces that seem to encourage theft and equally strengthen those that try to inhibit it. Greenberg and Barling (1996) have argued that some deterrent actions nearly always seem successful and should be recommended always to reduce theft. These include treating employees with dignity and respect; getting them involved in what is defined as theft; opening and regularly communicating the cost of organizational theft and making sure that no one (particularly leaders) is a role model for unethical behaviour.

Less successful methods include reducing bureaucracy, using preselection screening, rotating group membership constantly and having assistance programmes for people in financial trouble.

Recent research into employee theft

▶ *Employee theft is the cause for one out of every three business failures in this country*

▶ *87% of those surveyed admitted to falsifying time sheets because they regularly stole time from their employers and were paid for hours they did not work*

▶ *19% of firms in the UK with fewer than 15 employees have experienced staff fraud, this figure more than doubles to 48% for businesses with over 36 staff*

▶ *In German retail companies 22.5% of shrinkage is the result of employee theft; in Ireland it is 32%*

▶ *Workers who help themselves to software, hardware and other office equipment are costing Britain's small businesses £1.2 billion a year*

▶ *Fraudulent activities such as submitting false expense claims and making long-distance phone calls from the office cost UK businesses £831 million a year*

▶ *30 US-based retail chains – with sales of $355 billion – caught 73,326 dishonest employees in 2000, a 10% increase over the 1999 figure*

▶ *Employee theft costs US businesses over $53 billion annually and affects every type of organization. The majority of unexplained inventory losses involve employee theft*

▶ *70% of all corporate fraud and theft problems are caused by employees – and not outsiders. When outsiders are actually involved in defrauding a business, you can bet they've got a partner working at the company*

▶ *It is estimated that 95% of all businesses experience employee theft and management is seldom aware of the actual extent of losses or even the existence of theft*

Fraud

The difference between employee theft and fraud is largely about scale. In the previous section 'petty' theft of cash, goods on shelves or in cupboards has been discussed. Here the theft is more determined and larger scale.

Fraud is defined by David Davies (2000 p 2) in one of the standard works on fraud as:

All those activities involving dishonesty and deception that can drain value from a business, directly or indirectly, whether or not there is a personal benefit to the fraudster.

> *Merrill Lynch was plunged into fresh controversy yesterday when allegations emerged that a former energy trader had embezzled $43 million from the firm.*
>
> Guardian 12 August 2003

There is also an issue about position in the company. Theft and pilfering are done by blue collar less well-paid workers; fraud is something usually done by white collar workers. The only purpose for the distinction between the two is that their motivations may be different.

Fraud comes in various forms. PricewaterhouseCoopers, in its 2003 report on economic crime, identifies seven different forms of fraud:

1 Asset misappropriation
2 Financial misrepresentation
3 Corruption and bribery
4 Money laundering
5 Cyber crime
6 Industrial espionage
7 Product piracy.

Not all are committed by employees, but most of those identified in the list above are perpetrated by those inside the organization.

On 14 September 1999 *People Management* (the magazine for the Chartered Institute of Personnel and Development – CIPD), quoting from a report commissioned by Business Defence Europe, revealed that the £5 billion of serious fraud every year in the UK is the tip of the iceberg and that the majority of fraud is committed by middle management (p 11).

PricewaterhouseCoopers (PWC) has for three years produced an Economic Crime Survey. In 2003, it found that well over a third of respondent companies worldwide (37%) said they had suffered from one or more serious frauds during the previous two years. While there were regional differences, the impact was wide-

> *According to a recent joint report by the Australian Institute of Criminology and PricewaterhouseCoopers, the problem costs Australia about $3.5 billion a year. Many see this estimate as conservative.*

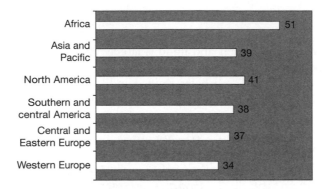

Figure 4.7 **Percentage of companies suffering serious fraud**
Source: Investigations and Forensic Services Department of PricewaterhouseCoopers 2003.

spread. The percentage of respondents who reported serious fraud in each region is shown in Figure 4.7. The research also showed which sectors were most vulnerable (Figure 4.8).

Of those companies which PWC surveyed and which had suffered fraud, the average loss was over $2 million. But the report recognizes that this figure is partial. Many companies knew they had been the subject of fraud but could not quantify the cost.

Fraud or embezzlement is not restricted to companies. In 2003 a former UN official in Kosovo went on trial in Germany. Joe Trutschler, 37, admitted to stealing $4.3 million

> **Norwich acts on '£1.5m fraud'**
>
> *Simon Bowers* Guardian *Thursday 19 June 2003*
>
> *Norwich Union, the insurance firm owned by Aviva, confirmed yesterday that it had filed a high court claim against a former employee and a number of people outside the firm over allegations that £1.5m had been illegally siphoned out of company coffers in a decade-long fraud.*
>
> www.guardian.co.uk

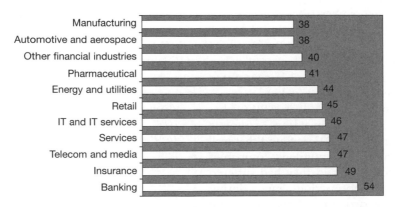

Figure 4.8 **Victims of fraud worldwide**
Source: Investigations and Forensic Services Department of PricewaterhouseCoopers 2003.

from the Kosovo Electricity Company and depositing the money in private accounts in Gibraltar. Initially, he claimed that he had been setting the cash aside to secretly raise the salaries of Kosovo's energy workers (*France Presse* 16 June 2003).

In 2000, Paul van Buitenen, an official in the European Union, went public with details of corruption, cronyism and abuse of power in the Commission. The entire team of 20 commissioners, headed by then president Jacques Santer, resigned in a symbolic gesture to demonstrate their commitment to cleaning up the Commission's act.

Buitenen was eventually forced to leave his job and return to his home town, Breda, in The Netherlands. The story however continued as Marta Andreasen, former chief accountant of the European Union, has reported that the Commission's systems failed to meet even the most basic accounting standards. In August this year, a leaked report from the EU Court of Auditors found that the £63 billion a year budget was open to fraud and abuse. The report warned that the EU systems were 'out of control' with 'obvious risks as regards liability'. Ms Andreasen said she believed that a lack of security left the system open to fraud at any time which could not be traced (www.news.bbc.co.uk 3 October 2002).

Increasingly fraud cases have an international dimension. In the UK the Serious Fraud Office (SFO) is responsible for investigating and prosecuting cases:

> This can require our investigators to obtain evidence from abroad, interview witnesses in other countries or sometimes deal with an extradition, all of which requires liaison with the authorities in foreign jurisdictions.

Examples of cases with a foreign dimension

R v Roger Crow and James Lovat

Crow was a senior manager at the London branch of the Hungarian International Bank. Lovat ran a printing company that provided services to the bank. Both defendants conspired to steal over £½ million from the bank. Crow manipulated the bank's payments system to disguise the purchase of a printing press for the benefit of Lovat's company by debiting the sum from a dormant account not subject to internal scrutiny. The fraud was uncovered when the bank went into voluntary liquidation. Thirty-five days into the trial, on 29 January 2003, the defendants pleaded guilty to the charge of conspiracy to steal. On the following day both men were sentenced to 21 months' imprisonment, suspended for two years.

R v Christopher Freeman and Alan Hodgkinson

The defendants were charged in January 2002 with conspiracy to defraud, fraudulent trading, false accounting and forgery in connection with Universal Bulk Handling Ltd of which they were directors. The business went into receivership in February 1999 with debts of £10 million. Freeman pleaded guilty on 7 November 2002 to fraudulent trading, false accounting and forgery. Sentencing of Freeman was held over, pending the outcome of proceedings against Hodgkinson and a third defendant.

R v Roddam Twiss

In July 2001 Twiss was charged with theft, conspiracy to steal and conspiracy to defraud. He was acting for The Grosvenor Trust. The allegation is that funds held by the Trust on behalf of investors for the purpose of high-yield investment schemes were not applied for investment purposes. Instead the funds were transferred to Twiss and another person (Emile Coury) and disbursed by them. Coury is awaiting extradition from Switzerland to the UK and it is intended to join him on the same indictment as Twiss. The trial is scheduled for March 2004.

SFO 2002/03 report pp 24–30

Davies (2000 pp 23–4) identifies 22 common indicators and risk factors when considering the potential for fraud in an organization:

▷ Autocratic management style
▷ Mismatch of personality and status
▷ Unusual behaviour
▷ Illegal acts
▷ Expensive lifestyles
▷ Untaken holidays
▷ Poor quality staff
▷ Low morale
▷ High staff turnover
▷ Compensation tied to performance
▷ Results at any cost
▷ Poor commitment to control
▷ No code of business ethics
▷ Unquestioning obedience of staff
▷ Complex structures
▷ Remote locations poorly supervised
▷ Several firms of auditors
▷ Poorly defined business strategy
▷ Profits well in excess of industry norms
▷ Mismatch between growth and systems development
▷ Poor reputation
▷ Liquidity problems

According to Davies (2000) people commit fraud for a whole variety of reasons: pressure to perform (for example to reach targets); personal pressures (gambling); the joy of beating the system (alienated hacker); greed, boredom and revenge. Fraudsters, he believes, come in four types: the boaster, the manipulator, the deceiver and the loner.

Davies (2000) clearly paints the picture of organizations that provide a fertile field for fraudsters. The downsized, delayered organization, eager to

Table 4.2 Fraud-watch chessboard

STRATEGY	Nepotism	High staff turnover	Ethical dilemmas not dealt with	Structure conflicts with risk management	Complex structures	Poor learning from other businesses	Overly aggressive targets
Weak strategy	Skills gaps	CULTURE and ETHICS	STRUCTURE	Defensive business units	Multiple audit relationships	Poor communication of fraud and ethics policies	Core business processes not clearly defined
Poor implementation plans	Inappropriate career moves	Cultural confusion	Dysfunctional board	Front and back office skills and status mismatch	REWARD STRUCTURES	FRAUD RISK MANAGEMENT	Gaps in processes and controls not identified
Poor communication of strategy	Low morale	Cultural pressures	Confusion between chairman and chief executive	Structure does not fit strategy	Impact of bonus and other structures not recognized	No antifraud strategy	Low focus on areas most vulnerable to fraud
Strategic drift	Low level of fraud awareness	Sub-cultures	Confused reporting lines	Centre and business units in conflict	Risks relating to earn-outs not managed	Fraud implications of business strategy not assessed	FRAUD RESPONSE
PEOPLE	Untaken holiday	Need-to-know culture. Concentrations of power	Management structure not aligned to reward structures	Poor role definition	Relative disparities in pay-to-market rates	No fraud risk profiling	No fraud policy
Weak recruitment screening	Lifestyles inconsistent with salary	Business units not assimilated into culture	Special reporting arrangements	Responsibilities for managing fraud risk poorly defined	COMMUNICATIONS	Fraud risks not matched with controls	Poor fraud reporting channels and protections
Prior business relationships	Autocratic management style	Weak ethical code and values	Lack of expertise to operate structure	Low status of finance	Poor organizational learning	Performance measures manipulated	No fraud response plan to follow up fraud incidents.

Source: Davies 2000.

outsource and in a state of constant flux and change, is typically where fraud occurs. A command-and-control organization with a blame culture and highly aggressive targets and a dysfunctional board is where fraud occurs most.

To illustrate the sheer number and complexity of variables in this issue he provided a wonderful fraud-watch chessboard, shown in Table 4.2.

But how are we to really manage this growing blue collar, highly counterproductive behaviour? Davies (2000) maintains the first task is to persuade the board – usually by showing the cost of fraud – *the cost of not doing anything*. He believes an antifraud strategy has five components. *First*, being very clear about ethics, values, standards and what is and is not acceptable behaviour. The message is clear: there are rules that are logical and fair and those who break them cheat the company and the shareholder.

Second, human resource policies need to be developed for serious screening – the morally desirable in and the undesirable out. They need to monitor work patterns and holidays, attempt fair appraisals and do regular surveys to identify issues and problems early. *Third*, they need a fraud reporting channel that people will not be frightened to use and they need a fraud response plan. *Fourth* they need to put in place a good fraud awareness programme to make managers more vigilant about the causes and manifestations of fraud. *Fifth*, managers need to be taught how to incisively but successfully interview/ interrogate their staff to find out the 'who, when and why' fraud at all levels is occurring.

Fraud is in many ways similar to petty thieving. Whilst successful fraud may involve the loss of many millions by clever trained professionals, the reasons why people steal are much the same. It is only the methods and values that differ, usually as a function of opportunity. Resentment, greed, opportunity are key ingredients in fraud. Indeed, fraud and petty theft are controlled in much the same way, which underlines the fact that they result from similar causes.

Deceit

Estimating the costs of this kind of fraud is difficult, not least because some deceptions are not motivated by personal gain but are designed to enhance or maintain a person's reputation. Some of the great names in science have been guilty of falsehoods. For a thousand years astronomers credited Ptolemy with theories about the positions of planets. Historians now believe that his writings were based on the observations of an earlier astronomer, Hipparchus of Rhodes. Newton is suspected of actively trying to discredit his competitors as well as falsifying or massaging data to fit his existing theories. Mendel was so convinced of the correctness of his theories he made the data fit his hypothesis perfectly.

Fraud in the field of science and medical research in particular, is surprisingly frequent and at least in the last 30 years reasonably well documented. In 1981 the US House of Representatives investigated scientific misconduct. Al Gore, Chairman of the Committee on Science and Technology, opened the hearing with these words: 'We need to discover whether recent incidents are merely episodes that will drift into the history of science as footnotes, or whether we are creating situations and incentives ... that makes such cases as these "the tip of the iceberg"'. The reaction from the scientific community was hostile. Phillip Handler, President of the National Academy of Sciences, called the issue 'grossly exaggerated' (Lock and Wells 1996 pp 5, 6). But the evidence of consistent and prevalent fraud and misconduct is strong.

Lock collated details of 71 case histories broken down between the following countries: Australia 4, Canada 1, UK 14, and US 52. They include some extraordinary examples, including the notorious case of William Summerlin at the Sloan-Kettering Institute, New York, who faked transplantation results by darkening transplanted skin patches in white mice with a black felt tip pen (Lock and Wells 1996 pp 15–28). In 1997 a German investigative committee uncovered evidence that two biomedical scientists had falsified data in as many as 37 publications between 1988 and 1996.

Lock himself conducted a small survey in 1988 of 80 people in the medical research fields and in a response rate of 100% (itself an indicator of the interest people have in the subject) found that over half knew of some instance of fraud or misconduct. His colleague Frank Wells was responsible for reporting 26 cases to the General Medical Council in the UK.

In Australia cases of deceit have taken on a high profile. In 1991 Dr William McBride faced 15 complaints brought against him by the Health department. He admitted publishing false and misleading data, claiming it was 'in the long-term interests of humanity'. He was found guilty and struck off. The Medical Tribunal said his 'acts demonstrated a course of premeditated deception in the field of medical research and indicate a serious flaw or defect in his character, a trait of dishonesty' (Lock and Wells 1996 p 135).

Professor Michael Briggs was dean at Geelong University and worked in the field of oral contraceptives. He was a man with a quick wit, and an ability to attract large sums of money from drug companies. In the early 1980s there was considerable controversy over his research, culminating in his resignation and move to Marbella in Spain. The *Sunday Times* in London drew a partial admission from him of generalizing from a small amount of data (Lock and Wells 1996 p 130).

Husson et al. (1996 p 211) identify three types of fraud in clinical and medical research:

1 Falsification of data
2 Concealment of data
3 Creation of data.

But the detection and prevention are still fraught with problems. There is some movement to bring the approach in the western world to fraud together and to show consistency.

C. Kristina Gunsalus distinguishes two types of deceivers, the straightforward crooks and the 'jerks'. The latter tend to be 'bright but without social skills; are aggressively competitive; are idiosyncratic; drive each other hard and have a variety of unclassified characteristics including corner cutting, self delusion, and incompetence' (Lock, in Lock and Wells 1996 p 30).

The theme of self-delusion or self-deception is taken up by William Broad and Nicholas Wade: 'Self-deception is so potent a human capability that scientists, supposedly trained to be the most objective of observers, are in fact peculiarly vulnerable to deliberate deception by others' (Broad and Wade 1985 p 116).

Deviant, dysfunctional, counterproductive behaviour takes place in many organizations. Universities are one such place. Brockway et al. (2002) showed how student cynicism may well lead to variable behavioural problems among cynical students. Interestingly they distinguished between policy cynicism, academic cynicism, social cynicism and institutional cynicism. Jackson et al. (2002) also found personality factors in fact predicted student cheating behaviour at university.

Cizek (1999) noted how prevalent misconduct is. He also noted typical reasons students give. These include:

▷ The instructor assigns too much material.
▷ The instructor left the room during the test.
▷ A friend asked me to cheat and I couldn't say no.

Table 4.3 Top five circumstances related to planned and spontaneous cheating

Rank	Circumstances that increase cheating	Circumstances that decrease cheating
	Planned cheating	
1	Student perception that instructor doesn't care about cheating	Punishment for cheating (for example expulsion)
2	Student financial support depends on grades	Essay examination format
3	Student perception that test is unfair	Student perception of high instructor vigilance during examination
4	Student perception of low instructor vigilance during examination	Student perception that test is fair
5	Direct effect of course grade on student's long-term goals	Course material highly valued by student
	Spontaneous cheating	
1	Student financial support depends on grades	Punishment for cheating (for example expulsion)
2	Student perception that instructor doesn't care about cheating	Essay examination format
3	Direct effect of course grade on student's long-term goals	Student perception of high instructor vigilance during examination
4	Student perception of low instructor vigilance	Students seated far apart during examination
5	Student perception that test is unfair	Student perception that test is fair

Source: Adapted from Cizek 1999.

▷ The instructor doesn't seem to care if I learn the material.
▷ The course information seems useless.
▷ The course material is too hard.
▷ Everyone else seems to be cheating.
▷ In danger of losing scholarship because of low grades.
▷ Don't have time to study because I am working to pay for school.
▷ People sitting around me made no attempt to cover their papers.

He noted the circumstances where cheating occurs and these are shown in Table 4.3.

Deception is also frequent in business. In the late 1990s Roger Eden and Geoffrey Brailey – former directors of Corporate Services Group plc – dishonestly caused and permitted the company's financial statements for 1997 to be prepared in such a way as to overstate the true extent of its profitability and sought to do the same in 1998. In 1997, the overstatement amounted to just over £3 million. In 1998, the accounting irregularities came to light before the statements could be published. The potential overstatement of profit for 1998 is estimated to exceed at least £25 million (Serious Fraud Office press release 17 September 2003).

Information leakage (citizenship espionage)

Information itself is a commodity which can be sold or used to damage a company or organization, though in some cases the perpetrators can reasonably claim that their action was for the public good. Although the individuals will feel they are giving a fair account of what has happened, or of the data, this is often disputed and sometimes there is no attempt to tell the truth. In most cases of information leakage a third party has to be involved. The questions to be asked are: did the employee know he or she was passing useful information, did the employee deliberately seek out a third person or did the third person seek out the employee?

It is also possible for individuals to take information away from an organization for their personal use later. Whenever anyone moves job, they take with them information and experience which will help them make better judgements as they make decisions in their new job. They might, for example, decide to pursue (or not) a particular client because they know what they need from earlier experience with the former company. For the purposes of this section we are concerned mainly with those employees who pass information to another, as this is what causes the real damage.

> 'Gossip is the cement which holds organizations together,' said Ms Doyle.
>
> 'Providing communal space, such as coffee areas or lunch rooms, allows employees to share information, knowledge and build relations that benefits both the company and the employee.'
>
> A study by the Industrial Society reported by www.bbc.co.uk 20 November 2000

Information leakage, which is the responsibility of employees, as opposed to external stealing, can be for the following six reasons:

1 *Accidental.* The loss of papers or electronic data, which might be found by other interested parties. It might also be the result of indiscreet comments made over the phone or overheard in a bar. The person concerned does not intend to cause damage.
2 *Casual gossip.* A conversation motivated by the individual's desire to discuss either other people's private lives or the company's business.
3 *Deliberate gossip* or bad-mouthing. This is the result of an individual feeling hurt or resentful about something which has happened in the office, which they feel is unfair.
4 *Deliberate passing of information* to expose some wrongdoing in the company or organization (whistle-blowing).
5 *Deliberate and clandestine passing of information* (orally or in paper or electronic format), which benefits the business of the third party. In this case the individual benefits, usually financially, but stays in the company.
6 *Taking confidential information* on departure from an organization that will be of direct benefit to that individual in his or her new employment.

Accidental loss can be put down to carelessness and the responsibility of the individual. The employers would have to accept some responsibility if they had not trained the individuals concerned sufficiently or were working them so hard that mistakes begin to happen out of tiredness or out of having too much to do.

Can one man's journey be responsible for kickstarting America's textile manufacturing industry? At least one American president thought so. Heralded as the father of the American Industrial Revolution by President Jackson, Samuel Slater's decision to emigrate to the United States had consequences far beyond his own life. Derbyshire born Slater gained his expertise in the textile industry as an apprentice to Jedediah Strutt in one of his mills at Milford. To reach America, he betrayed his employers, deceived his family and broke the law. However, the rewards were rich; on his death in America, his fortune was worth $1,200,000.

www.bbc.co.uk/legacies

A chief executive who sent his staff an email accusing them of being lazy and threatening them with the sack has seen the share price of his company plummet after his message was posted on the internet.

In the three days after publication of his outburst – which gave managers a two-week ultimatum to shape up – stock in the American healthcare company dropped by 22 per cent over concerns about staff morale. It is now trading at more than a third less than it was before the email was sent. Neal Patterson, head of the Cerner Corporation, based in Kansas City, has spent the past three weeks trying to assuage investors.

His email to managers read: 'We are getting less than 40 hours of work from a large number of our EMPLOYEES. The parking lot is sparsely used at 8am; likewise at 5pm. As managers, you either do not know what your EMPLOYEES are doing or you do not CARE. In either case, you have a problem and you will fix it or I will replace you.'

His email read: 'NEVER in my career have I allowed a team which worked for me to think they had a 40-hour job. I have allowed YOU to create a culture which is permitting this. NO LONGER.' He added that 'hell will freeze over' before he increased employee benefits. He wanted to see the car park nearly full by 7.30am and half full at weekends. He wrote: 'You have two weeks. Tick, tock.'

A week later, the email appeared on a Yahoo financial message board and Wall Street analysts began receiving calls from worried shareholders.

Daily Telegraph 6 April 2001

People at work spy on their bosses. They may betray their colleagues, their bosses or the company as a whole. They may even become a traitor by committing treason. Countries have laws about treason, espionage, sedition and mutiny to discourage their enemies.

The enemy within can be a thief but is often worse: a betrayer of trust. They are the sorts of industrial or organizational spies that tend to be portrayed in novels: they tend to be in some sense outside conventional society; they are somehow invisible; their attachment to others is superficial; they are fascinated with the power of secrecy and they are individualistic (autonomous, self-reliant). The enemy within, the citizen spy, is often caught only after selling trade secrets.

Eoyang (1994 pp 85–6; emphases in original) believes that classically there is a behaviour chain or typical sequence of events that occur:

> The chain begins with *intention*, which is some level of interest and motivation in violating security. Next is the formulation of *plans* either along or with others to transform the intentions into concrete actions. The third essential step is to gain access to locations, persons, or sources that retain restricted information. Once access has been achieved, the actual *acquisition* of the information must be effected. Since most perpetrators of espionage wish to minimize the risks of their trade, they typically engage in deception to hide their activities and their responsibility for it. As most consumers of espionage products are governments, spies must have *contact* with some foreign agency to whom they can confer the stolen information and from whom they can receive their compensation (*exchange*). The actual transmittal of the information may take many forms, some of which have been celebrated in innumerable spy novels. Although the rewards of espionage are rarely munificent, the consumption of the gains from espionage can sometimes arouse suspicions when it shows as unusual or unexplained affluence. Finally, it may be necessary for spies to flee (escape) to avoid capture and punishment or to enjoy the fruits of their clandestine endeavours without retribution.

Table 4.4 Possible countermeasures used to catch spies in the organization

INTENTION	Clearances	Training, education	Leadership/counselling, Situational matching
PLANNING/ CONSPIRACY	Periodic reinvestigation, polygraph	Informants search warrants	Personnel rotation
ACCESS	Clearances	Compartmentalization	Position vulnerability
ACQUISITION	Special access programmes	Classification management, document control	Need to know
DECEPTION	Periodic reinvestigation, polygraph	Inspections	Group cohesion, integrity
FOREIGN CONTACT	Periodic reinvestigation, alien prohibitions	Surveillance	Continuing assessment
EXCHANGE	Periodic reinvestigation, polygraph	Punishment	Sting operations
CONSUMPTION	Periodic reinvestigation,	Tax enforcement	Employee assistance
ESCAPE	Travel checks	Travel restrictions	Plea bargaining, double agents

Source: Eoyang 1994.

He also notes possible countermeasures used to catch spies in the organization, as shown in Table 4.4.

Morris and Moberg (1994) note how work organizations are often excellent contexts for betrayal. People need to be, and are, trusted at work for various specific reasons. Many work tasks are ambiguous and dynamic so organizations can prescribe how they are done. They have to trust the employee to do his/her best. Also, inevitably, many work behaviours are difficult to observe and therefore the employee has to be trusted to do them. Often the work outcomes are difficult to assess, so organizations have to balance the mixture of putting in place (expensive) control systems and of trusting individuals. Certainly in some jobs the trust factor is less important than in others.

Trust is a two-way street: a contract. The person puts trust in the organization and vice versa. A victim who feels that they have intentionally and individually been harmed by the organization with little opportunity for adequate redress is ripe for betrayal. Morris and Moberg (1994 p 187) note:

> From the standpoint of managerial practice and policy, the themes that we have developed here yield few revelations, but they do support much of what is already accepted as sound, if well-worn, advice. First, hire people who are believed to be trustworthy. Recognize the three particular features of work that make interdependent people vulnerable to one another's actions and the need for personal trust that such situations require. Respond to these situations by encouraging the emergence of internal control systems to support and sustain personal trust between functionally dependent members – but only after ensuring that what is possible has been done to reduce the need for personal trust in the first place. We hope we have made clear that personal trust between interdependent workers can

be crucial to getting the job done; but when alternatives are available, it is wrong for organizations to freeload on personal trust between their members because it is the members themselves, and not necessarily the organization, who may be victimized by violations of such personal trust. In addition, no matter how irrational such acts may seem we can only wonder how many crimes or other transgressions against organizations were precipitated by unredressed breaches of personal trust between individual members.

Hogan and Hogan (1994) make four important observations about organizational betrayal by citizenship espionage. First, it is rare (a low baserate phenomenon) and therefore very hard to predict. Second, the greatest danger to organizations comes from those within them (not without). Third, people who are as used to competition as opposed to cooperation at work are experts in deceptive communication. Those who take part in treachery and betrayal are often unusually socially skilled (charismatic, charming, intelligent, socially poised and self-confident).

From their research Hogan and Hogan (1994) suggested that there are four characteristics of the ideal or prototypic betrayer. They are attractive, interesting, charming and past-masters at flattery and ingratiation. However, they also have unusual degrees of egocentrism, self-absorption and selfishness. These people are, however, privately self-doubting, unhappy and unsure about their self-worth. Finally, they are particularly prone to self-deception – in short they lie to themselves. The betrayer an essentially hollow man or woman – retains only the mask of integrity.

Whistle-blowing

Very few people attempt to defend stealing from, or sabotage in, an organization by an employee. Whilst it is conceivable to do this, say in times of war or in other exceptional circumstances, these behaviours are normally deviant and considered both morally and legally wrong.

Whistle-blowing, however, has begun to have a rather different reputation. Indeed there are now on the web numerous international sites that purport to help (and encourage) whistle-blowing. Whistle-blowing is, or at least should be, about organizational wrongdoing. It is where, often, many senior people conspire to do things which are illegal, immoral, and dangerous but benefit themselves.

What constitutes wrongdoing is very questionable. One study (Keenan 1990) categorized actions into three categories: *minor fraud* (that is, fiddling expenses, stealing office supplies), *harm to others* (discrimination, violating health and safety rules), and *serious fraud* (bribery, overtime abuse). That study also found:

1   the great majority (70%) work in organizations without a formal written policy for suspected dishonest and fraudulent activities that includes a description as to what is to be done if wrongdoing is observed or suspected

2   a sizeable number (37%) are uncertain about the adequacy of their com-
    pany's protection of employees who report illegal or wasteful activities within
    company operations
3   a sizeable number (21%) believe that there is an unfair and inconsistent
    treatment of wrongdoing in their organizations because of the position held
    by the suspected wrongdoers or length of service; and
4   fear of retaliation is a major factor influencing perceptions about company
    encouragement of whistle blowing and having enough information on where
    to blow the whistle. (p 233)

Consider four examples:

*1   An engineer believes the plans for a building are wrong and would lead
     to an unsafe construction that does not follow industry guidelines. He
     reports this first to his boss, then the CEO, then his professional body.
     None acts so he contacts the media.*

*2   An employee from an ethnic minority has noticed that the rejection to
     acceptance rate of applicants from his particular racial group is higher
     than that of the dominant group. He reports this to his boss and then the
     head of human resources who both deny any form of racial discrimin-
     ation. The individual is unconvinced and turns to the Commission for
     Racial Equality, the media and activists at the same time.*

*3   A person working in the pharmaceuticals business finds out that,
     contrary to the organization's public statements, some of its materials
     are tested on animals. She reports this to a director who denies it and
     challenges that evidence. She believes she is right and, met with further
     denials, phones the local antivivisection group.*

*4   A loyal worker gets passed over for promotion a number of times. She feels
     that this is unfair and age discriminatory. She therefore waits until a
     voluntary severance programme goes embarrassingly wrong before
     leaking it to the media as a revenge for her frustration.*

So what is whistle-blowing? The term supposedly arises from sport where
referees blow a whistle to indicate foul play. As we shall see, whistle-blowing
can take many forms. It appears to have three components. First, that an
individual or group working, or recently working, in an organization
perceive something 'morally amiss'. That is, they believe organizational
policy, practices, acts or intentions to be morally wrong. Second, they
communicate that information to people outside the organization: these
may be journalists, competitors, the police. Third, the perception by at 'least
a number' of people inside the organization is that the communication
should not have been made.

There are three 'actors' in every whistle-blowing case: the wrongdoer,
the whistle-blower and the recipient of the information. From a legal
perspective, whistle-blowing is warranted if the person believes in good faith

the wrongdoing has implications for public policy. From a philosophic perspective, the question arises whether the act is ethical. However, from an auditor's perspective the central question is whether the wrongdoing is sufficient to pursue the problem. Whistle-blowers need to decide between internal and external channels for complaint, which are clearly very different in outcome. They also need a reasonable supposition of success in that they believe their action will lead to the wrongdoing being stopped.

Near and Miceli (1996) in an extensive review considered two myths. First, that *whistle-blowers are crackpots*. The results of numerous studies, though not entirely consistent, seem to indicate the precise opposite. Compared to 'silent, inactive' observers, whistle-blowers tend to be older, more senior, better educated, with better job performance and commitment and believe they have a role responsibility to report wrongdoing through appropriate channels:

> To date, empirical evidence has shown that whistle-blowing is more likely in organizations that support whistle-blowing in various ways, but not including incentives for it, and where whistle-blowers report greater value congruence with top managers. Organizations with higher rates of whistle-blowing seem to be high performing, to have slack resources, to be relatively non-bureaucratic, and tend to cluster in particular industries or in the public rather than private or not-for-profit sectors. Finally, group size is positively related to whistle-blowing, while quality of supervisor is not. (pp 512–13)

Researchers have questioned whistle-blowers' morality and loyalty. The latter naturally questions who the loyalty is to. Near and Miceli (1996) conclude that there is no evidence for the crackpot myth and that most whistle-blowers simply have the opportunity to observe the wrongdoing because of the nature of their jobs.

NHS inspector praises whistle-blowers

Patrick Butler
Wednesday 15 November 2000

Staff who blew the whistle on poor standards of hospital care have been praised by the government's health standards regulator for their courage in attempting to alert the authorities to care abuses.

Peter Homa, chief executive of the Commission for Health Improvement (CHI), criticized North Lakeland NHS trust in Cumbria for not acting after abuses were reported by staff in 1996, and blamed that failure for further alleged mistreatment of patients in 1998.

Mr Homa today praised the 'courage' of whistle-blowers who battled to expose mistreatment of elderly mentally ill patients at North Lakeland.

www.society.guardian.co.uk

Second that *all whistle-blowers suffer retaliation*. Despite looking at all sorts of factors (personal characteristics of whistle-blowers that predict retaliation, situational factors such as organizational structure and culture) the authors found little evidence and:

> can only conclude that: a) retaliation against whistle-blowers is not universal (and perhaps not even widespread); b) retaliation, when it does occur, may take many forms (ranging from less severe to more severe), all of which are highly subject to personal interpretation by the whistle-blower; and c) whistle-blowers claim that it does not deter them, either currently in the future cases, although fear of retaliation may cause them to seek external channels for whistle-blowing, to the obvious dismay of the organization. To date, however, most state and federal legal statutes have been written with the primary goal of preventing retaliation under the assumption that retaliation will deter future whistle-blowing – despite empirical evidence to the contrary. (p 523)

When are whistle-blowers effective? Most, it seems go public once organizations attempt to cover-up wrongdoing and retaliate against the whistle-blower. Where whistle-blowers are powerful, with unique skills, resources and secrets the organization needs (and cannot easily replace), they are more

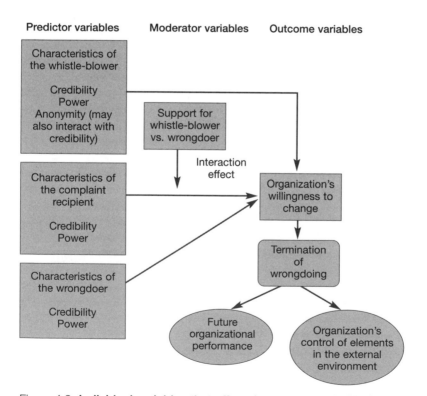

Figure 4.9 **Individual variables that affect the outcome of whistle-blowing**
Source: Near and Miceli 1995.

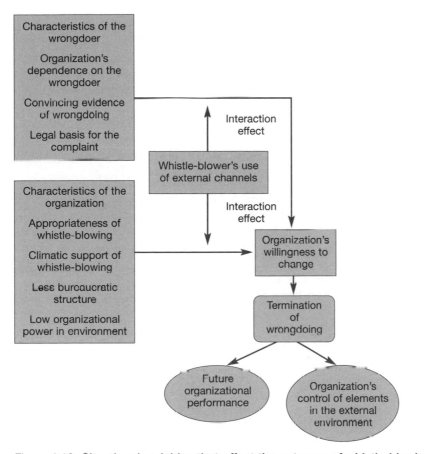

Figure 4.10 **Situational variables that affect the outcome of whistle-blowing**
Source: Near and Miceli 1995.

likely to succeed. The more competent, confident, credible and objective they seem, the more they are listened to. Experts with legitimate power are likely to be more effective particularly with internal whistle-blowing.

Near and Miceli (1995) have done an excellent job in looking at the characteristics that predict effective whistle-blowing. They divide these into individual and situational variables and present two explanatory flow charts (Figures 4.9 and 4.10).

This model is based on 12 simple but crucial propositions. Whistle-blowing effectiveness is enhanced when managers, co-workers and the compliant recipient see the whistle-blower as credible and relatively powerful in the organization and when the whistle-blower identifies him/herself at the outset rather than looking for anonymity. Effectiveness increases when the compliant recipients are supportive of the whistle-blower's actions and when the wrongdoer has little power and credibility.

They assert that the greater the dependence of the organization on the wrongdoing the less likely internal and the more likely external whistle-blowing will be. The more evidence provided and the more unambiguously illegal the acts, the more likely the effectiveness. Further, the whistle-blower needs to be seen to use appropriate channels and means. Naturally, effectiveness is enhanced in organizations where the climate discourages wrongdoing and actually encourages whistle-blowing and discourages retaliation. It is most effective in organizations with bureaucratic structures but only where there are formal and operating mechanisms to encourage internal whistle-blowing. Finally, effectiveness will be enhanced in organizations that have low power in their environment particularly if external channels of reporting are used.

The problem for the organization, the researcher and the law is to determine the *real motive* of the whistle-blower (Casal and Zalkind 1995; Miceli et al. 1991; Somers and Casal 1994). The disgruntled, passed-over, vengeful employee may take to whistle-blowing to 'get even'. Hopefully close investigations of whistle-blowing accusations can help determine just from unjust whistle-blowers. But the reputation and legal cost to an organization falsely accused can be enormous. It can break organizations as well as individuals.

Some whistle-blowers feel guilty and do so because by 'telling the truth' they feel in part able to redeem themselves for their complicity, collusion and participation in the wrongdoing.

From the top-down perspectives in organizations, the whistle-blower is disloyal, a traitor, one who indulges in tittle-tattle. From the bottom-up perspective, whistle-blowers can be seen as heroes: courageous, fighters for truth. Some of the lionized whistle-blowers talk of personal sacrifice (the retaliation) for a noble cause; acting because they had no choice; being unable not to act knowing what they know. There is a lot of talk about identification with victims, a sense of collective guilt and shame (working for the company), even being a part of history. Seeking revenge or the limelight is never discussed.

It is quite simply too easy to be a whistle-blower: media experts explain how frequently they are called by people with all sorts of impossible stories and little evidence to support them. Their motives are often a curious mix of the personal and the political. Justice, ethics and fairness are concepts that are bandied about with abandon.

Rothschild and Miethe (1999 p 107) did a survey of whistle-blowing in the US and found:

> data the authors collected on whistle-blowers and on silent observers that shows a) whistle-blowing is more frequent in the public sector than in the private: b) there are almost no sociodemographic characteristics that distinguish the whistle-blower from the silent observer; c) whistle-blowers suffer severe retaliation from management, especially when their information proves significant; and d) no special method of disclosure or personal characteristics can insulate the whistle-blower from such retaliation. Furthermore, the authors found that retaliation was most certain and severe when the reported misconduct was systematic and significant – when the practices exposed were part of the regular, profit accu-

mulation process of the organization. The authors conclude from their interviews that the journey to exoneration that follows a whistle-blower's disclosures often alters the whistle-blowers identity, leading them to see themselves as people who resist hurtful or criminal conduct in the workplace.

The question then is, essentially, when is whistle-blowing justified? This may refer to the manner as well as the reasons for it. Those who believe whistle-blowing to be both a good thing and a safety valve talk of the suppression of dissent and give advice on how to be an effective resister. It has been portrayed as an effective anticorruption device. Some organizations, clearly worried by the threat of whistle-blowing, often more euphemistically referred to as 'raising concerns at work', actually have policies and procedures to deal with it. Thus they may have a job entitled 'Whistle-blowing Champion' and set out who to contact, how 'the investigation' is dealt with by internal inquiry, and what occurs if this is not satisfactorily dealt with by the organization according to the whistle-blower.

In surveys, it has been shown that the overwhelming majority of people support the concept of legal protection for people who report corruption. A clear majority say they would probably or definitely not report corruption without legal protection. Clearly job loss and other reprisals are seen to be the major deterrent to reporting corruption. Where people have faith in the management who will respond to reports not by shooting the messenger but investigating and confronting the problem, the need for whistle-blowing is significantly reduced.

It is, however, sensible for the organization to put into practice whistle-blower procedures that state the issue of malpractice is both serious and will be dealt with firmly. It must accept the right to raise issues confidentially and without fear of repercussions. It needs also to have guidelines and time limits for the consequent investigations. Perhaps most wisely of all, its procedures should specify the consequences and penalties for making false and malicious allegations in the first place.

Some countries pass legal statutes. For example, The British Public Interest Disclosure Act gives legitimate whistle-blowers legal protection against reprisal, victimization and, usually, dismissal. This Act applies to those who have 'genuine concerns' about such things as criminal activity, civil offence, and breaches of health and safety regulations, miscarriages of justice, environmental damage, and so on.

The Act states that whistle-blowers must have an honest and *reasonable suspicion* that a malpractice has/is likely to occur and have made a *disclosure/representation* to their employer. The Act protects them if they reasonably believe they would be victimized if they raised concerns with senior people *internally* or with the *prescribed regulator*; that evidence would be concealed or destroyed if raised internally; or that they believed the disclosure was of an exceptionally serious nature.

Whistle-blowing is a serious act. The 'just' whistle-blower needs to be completely sure of his/her facts and have evidence sufficiently reliable and robust to stand up in a court of law. They may be advised to seek legal help first. They need to follow current procedure, be prepared to compromise and take advice.

So when is whistle-blowing justified? This refers to the manner and matter of disclosure as well as to the reasons/motives behind the whistle-blower. Various criteria may be set:

1 *Utilitarianism*
   This is about working out the harm/good, ends/means ratio. There are nearly always positive and negative consequences of whistle-blowing. Whistle-blowing might cause a company to fail and innocent employees to lose their jobs. If the end is not justified by the means it probably means it is not justified at all. There are those who are not utilitarians and absolutists who believe that the *truth must be known* whatever the cost. It is a supposedly virtuous and moral necessity whatever the consequences.

2 *Correcting and preventing wrongdoing*
   If an act of whistle-blowing is disinterested in prevention but only seeks restitution (and revenge), it may be a sign of insincerity. Pessimists who talk of 'the system' claim it cannot be changed, will always be corrupt and no, even altruistic, act can change that. On the other hand, if the whistle-blower seems genuinely interested in seeking that this event could (and should) not re-occur, it may be a sign of justifiability.

3 *'Responsible whistle-blowing'*
   It may seem oxymoronic to some and quite natural to others that a code of conduct should be followed. To be responsible means things like: getting facts correct without distortion, exaggeration or fabrication; avoiding personalizing or vindictiveness; avoiding hurt, pain or embarrassment to innocent parties; consulting colleagues and relevant others before acting; choosing the appropriate time, manner and target for the whistle-blowing. Of course all these rules must be seen in context and balanced. But the extent and reason for why they are broken gives a good insight into the real motives of the whistle-blower.

4 *Channels exhausted*
   All organizations have policies and procedures about 'complaints'. The sincerity and honesty of a whistle-blower may be judged by the extent he/she gave the organization warnings and a chance to rectify wrongs. It is true that within some organizations channels for complaints, disciplinary procedures and grievance may be absent, or biased, or negative, dealing only with complaints and not prevention. Whistle-blowers often say it is dangerous, even suicidal, to try the 'official' route but that is something they must prove themselves in order to justify their actions.

Sabotage

Sabotage is not exclusively the domain of a lunatic with explosives or a weapon. It is the cold calculation of a person intent on revenge and there are many manifestations. Sabotage can have a wide and very specific meaning. It has, most often two distinct connotations: the intention to damage company property and/or subvert company operations. This involves, quite simply the destruction or tampering with (but strictly speaking not theft of) machinery and goods as well as attempting to stop, or slow down production. The reasons for sabotage are manifold: protect one's job; protect family/friends from a boss or simply employ the principle of an eye-for-an-eye.

Faking application forms and shrinkage seem almost trivial compared with industrial sabotage. Chemical products (medicines, foods) can easily be 'tampered' with. A virus can be introduced into a company's vital computer destroying all records and files. Large crucial mechanical equipment can be 'disabled' so preventing a whole series of jobs being done. Perhaps the most widespread and growing forms of sabotage involve the web: sabotaging others' computer files. All sorts of industries seem vulnerable and have been targeted. They include food and drink processors, cosmetic companies, supermarkets and restaurants and other high-tech organizations. Sabotage takes place during strikes. It is often seen by psychologists as the cathartic destruction of property.

Crino (1994) has defined sabotage as work-related behaviour specifically designed to 'damage, disrupt, or subvert the organization's operations for the personal purpose of the saboteur by creating unfavourable publicity, embarrassment, delays in production, damage to property, the destruction of working relationships, or the harming of employees or customers' (p 312).

An examination of the sabotage literature suggests commonly five predominant motives (Ambrose et al. 2002):

1 A reaction to powerlessness where people feel they have no freedom or autonomy at work. It is an attempt to attain control for its own sake.
2 Chronic and acute organizational frustration that originates from such things as inadequate resources to do the job.
3 To make work easier to accomplish like breaking rules, restructuring social relationships. It may involve non-sanctioned means to achieve sanctioned ends.
4 Boredom: entertainment and fun can certainly be had when things go wrong.

> *Still stinging after the violence of last June's anticapitalist riots in the City, police are taking seriously the threat of sabotage from anarchists who may try to infiltrate big companies to coincide with this year's protests, planned for May 1. Last week, they issued a warning to companies in the country's financial heart to be on their guard against temporary workers who may come to work with a hidden agenda.*
>
> Guardian Monday 17 April 2000

5　Evening the score through a sense of injustice typically generated by disrespect, being passed over for promotion, given additional responsibilities without power.

In the world of anarchism and terrorism which exists today there is a sixth reason – that of the terrorist or anarchist infiltrating organizations to sabotage key business or public services.

It is quite impossible to get valid sabotage statistics for two reasons. First, organizations do not always know when it has occurred. Second, where they do, for obvious reasons of poor publicity they do not report it.

Sabotage was the tool of labour movements in the nineteenth century. However, in the twenty-first century increased technological complexity of products and greater customer demand for quality and safety have meant sabotage is both more important and difficult to detect. For some writers saboteurs tend to be characterized as hostile, angry, vengeful, impulsive, narcissistic, paranoid or psychopaths (Klein et al. 1996).

Indeed sabotage has different aims: destroy machinery or goods, stop production or reduce the work being done. It should not be assumed that sabotage is exclusively the lot of *workers*. There is also *management* sabotage: indeed they are often in a better position to be more successful at it. management sabotage has been shown to be caused by things like the perception of uneven work distribution, arbitrarily made investments, wages being unrelated to productivity and unfair promotions.

Sabotage has different goals but many refer to simple retaliation. There are also different targets – managers, machinery, customers. Usually the target is the same as the perceived cause of the injustice and frustration. The severity of the injustice is also important: the amount, type and source of perceived injustice or unfairness relates logically to the severity of the injustice (Ambrose et al. 2002).

Further, one can distinguish between *instrumental* and *demonstrative* sabotage. The former is aimed at achieving demands or changing the power structure, while the latter is about castigating management, protesting about injustice or simply showing one's rejection of company values and policies. Sabotage may be a 'publicity stunt' aimed primarily at spoiling a company's image.

Saboteurs may be vengeful, defensive, lazy or self-promotional. Some are retaliative and try to 'get even' while others are more involved in self-presentation trying, somewhat bizarrely to meet perceived expectations or requirements or organizational success.

Using interesting examples Crino (1994) listed a number of motivations for sabotage.

1　To make a statement or send a message. They hope to gain maximum publicity and sympathy for their position which may be based on political, moral or religious beliefs.

2　To prevent or encourage corporate change. Some want to stop mergers or stock sales by scaring off bidders. Others sabotage old equipment forcing a company to buy new machines.

3   To establish personal worth or simply be the centre of attention. They may want to increase their status or join particular subcultures. This is rarely politically motivated sabotage but more likely pathologically motivated sabotage.

4   To gain a competitive advantage over co-workers. They may destroy others work or, withholding or lying about important information, losing important documents; compromising others reputation (rumour, blame, altered records) or encouraging them to take part in self-defeating behaviours. The idea is to enhance one's own reputation at the expense of others.

5   To gain revenge against management and co-workers. Workers who have been shown disrespect, passed over for promotion, given added responsibility but no commensurate reward, or not been given support from colleagues become disgruntled. Arson, bomb threats and attempted poisoning is not unusual for these saboteurs.

6   To have an impact in a large, faceless, distant bureaucracy. People are loyal to their local group and resent the interference by anonymous people from head office often many miles away. Curiously sabotage can increase a sense of control: they (personally) can slow down production, make errors, let faulty products leave the factory. It allows them to think, quite negatively, that they can make a difference.

7   To obtain thrills and satisfy a need to destroy. Bored sensation seekers love a fire, a line of cars with slashed tyres, a building with broken windows. Sabo tage is a game and an exciting one at that. One can beat the system and out smart pompous authority figures.

8   To avoid responsibility for failure, incompetence or to avoid work. Sabotage can refocus attention away from them. It can also be used to intimidate or implicate others or even encourage them to conspire to avoid work.

9   For personal gain. Sabotage may well create conditions for additional compensation, compromising data, setting up good jobs with competitors Clever IT sabotage can lead to access to data on managed funds, customer records, and so on.

10   To vent anger created by one's personal life. The disappointed, disillusioned and frustrated may take out their anger at work quite simply because they spend a lot of their time there. The acts are random, unplanned and gratuitous aimed simply to vent anger and feel more control.

One study gathered data from 44 HR managers and 164 supervisors in 10 American companies (Di Battista 1991, 1996). It attempted to discuss the forms, reasons for and best ways of reducing the risk of sabotage. They listed 15 forms of sabotage, later made up to 30.

1   Doing 'personal work' on company time with company supplies and telephone.

2   Writing on company furniture and walls.

3   Flattening tyres and scratching company cars.

4 Stealing to compensate for low pay and poor work conditions.
5 Self-creating 'down time'.
6 Switching paperwork around the office.
7 Snipping cables on word processors.
8 Passing on defective work and parts to the next station.
9 Calling OSHA representative as a scare tactic.
10 Altering the time on the punch clock.
11 Punching someone else's time card.
12 Calling upon the union to intervene.
13 Setting up the foreman to get him/her in trouble.
14 Pulling the fire alarm and bomb threats.
15 Turning on a machine and walking away, knowing it will crash.
16 Instructing others to engage in activities which will be harmful to the company.
17 Altering or deleting data stored in computer databases.
18 Falsifying information on company records.
19 Disclosing secret information to competitors.
20 Allowing defective parts to pass inspection.
21 Lowering the quality of the product by purposely using lower quality parts.
22 Altering company records.
23 Placing a false order.
24 Wrecking the office of an executive you don't like.
25 Damaging someone else's work.
26 Insulting customers.
27 Losing important files and papers.
28 Ruining relations with other companies.
29 Lying to management about important data.
30 Interrupting mail so that it fails to get to people on time.

Some of these seem more trivial than others and some people do consider poisoning products or serious luddite destruction of machines quite acceptable. Over 200 people came up with 10 reasons for sabotage:

1 Self-defence
2 Revenge
3 Pressure of the work environment
4 To protect oneself from boss/company
5 To protect friends or family from boss/company
6 To protect one's job
7 The foreman/company deserved it
8 Just for fun/laughs
9 No one was hurt by the action
10 Frustration with employee situation.

However, being HR professionals, they seemed better at listing attempts to reduce sabotage. They came up with eight interpersonal approaches and ten structural or 'organizational' approaches:

Interpersonal approaches
1 Manage the suggestion system.
2 Monitor the flow of written and oral messages.
3 Improve interviewing skills.
4 Encourage feedback from subordinates.
5 Develop workable communication programmes.
6 Let subordinates know the direction in which they make progress in the organization.
7 Provide a record for assessment of the department or unit as a whole and show where each person fits into the larger picture.
8 Insist, for certain employees, that improvement is necessary.

Structural approaches
1 Setting up a quality circle.
2 Implementing job enlargement programmes.
3 Setting up autonomous production groups.
4 De-emphasizing the corporate role in decision making.
5 Expanding strategic planning to cross-functionally develop key employees.
6 Storing copies of data at another site.
7 Using biometrics devices as ID cards for workers. These machines can scan voice reflections and handprints.
8 Using antiviral programs to detect viruses.
9 Prohibiting employees from loading contested software into the system.
10 Encrypt data and program the computer to accept calls only from authorized phones.

Di Battista (1996) argues that sabotage crises move through various stages: *pre-crises* (where small warning signs can be detected), *acute crises* (when the event has just occurred and demands swift, sure management) and *chronic crises* (when the crises are not resolved) and the *crisis resolution* stage. He believes management can forecast the effect by considering five factors:

1 Intensity of consequences
2 Scrutiny to the normal operations of the business
3 Interference to the normal operations of the business
4 Damage to the public image
5 Cost both in hard (profits, ROI) and soft (morale, stress) currency.

In a study of 121 American HR managers, he found that of the actual sabotage events reported by the respondents:

▷ 3% escalated in intensity
▷ 24% were subject to close scrutiny
▷ 15% were subject to close government scrutiny
▷ 82% interfered with normal business operations
▷ 62% damaged the company's bottom line

▷ 18% damaged the company's public image.

Di Battista (1996 p 51) concluded:

> Research shows that organizations can no longer look to prevent sabotage occurrences, but rather to anticipate and manage the event to a quick resolution. It is in management's best interest to avoid the acute and chronic stages of an event. At these stages, the organization may find the event to escalate in intensity, to fall under close media and governmental scrutiny, to interfere with the normal operations of business, to jeopardize its public image, and to damage its bottom line. Therefore once management can admit that an act may occur, it can access the impact of it on the organization and its public. With this combination of assessing an impact assuming a probability, management has developed a forecast procedure that it can make as part of a comprehensive plan to manage risk.

Some researchers have become very interested in very specific sabotage. Logan (1993) looked at product tampering which frequently triggers 'an avalanche of false alarms, copycat cases, tampering threats and falsified reports of suspected tampering' (p 918). A favoured method is placing cyanide in food such as cakes and also in toothpaste, fresh produce and drinks. Interestingly, threats of tampering are much more common than actual tampering. Motives have been found to vary from sociopolitical, malicious mischief and revenge to economic terrorism.

Logan (1993 p 925) concluded:

> The extent of tampering crime, and the potential for its expansion, highlights the vulnerability of the food, drink, and drug supply to tampering, and the potential economic and social consequences that this crime or even its threat has. It is evident that the public has a morbid fascination with this type of public safety threat, as evidenced by the deluge of reports to the authorities following even a single documented episode of tampering. The potential for hysteria is very high and underscores the need for responsible reporting in the media and tactful handling of information by public health agencies. Manufacturers and food, drug and produce suppliers need to be keenly aware of the threat when planning marketing and packaging strategies for their products. The public needs to be educated in the importance of inspecting the tamper evident packaging at the point of sale, and prior to consuming or storing food, and to accept that part of the responsibility for protection from adulterated products is their own. The penalties for product tampering need to be more widely publicized, possibly through the use of warnings on food and drug packaging material, similar to alcohol warnings. Perversely however, heightened warnings regarding product tampering could lead to new outbreaks.

Recommendations at reducing sabotage are not fundamentally different from those causing other types of problem. Many are obvious (Crino 1994).

1   Assess job applicants carefully, verifying particularly job history, especially frequent changes in jobs and the reason why this occurred. One should look for signs of persecution feelings (multiple claims of maltreatment at work) and whether they have all the requisite skills. Integrity testing may be used most beneficially.
2   Train employees to minimize disorientation and frustration particularly in times of change. Training should make the employee feel important and valued and worthy of investment. Job enrichment and having self-managed teams can prevent alienation.
3   Create an atmosphere of fairness, justice and trust by equitable award and appraisal. Employees need to be kept informed and consistent, ethical not political, standards need to be set up. Regular, honest, supportive performance appraisals can go a long way to reduce feelings of bitterness and revenge. All disciplinary action needs to match the offence. Managers need to keep their word.
4   Stress the compatibility of employee/employer interests. If employees believe they personally suffer when sabotage takes place they are naturally less likely to do it or condone it. Companies need to ensure workers feel supported and that demands of work and family are nicely counterbalanced.
5   Take security seriously because carelessness and patchy security provide perfect options for the saboteur. Employees need to be made accountable for security issues which need to be seen as part of the job that interferes with real work. Security issues can easily be introduced to job descriptions, orientation and appraisal to attempt to create a real security culture.
6   Limit access to facilities, information and production, particularly through computer networks. Through usual techniques of passes, passwords, identification badges, it is possible to reduce 'easy' sabotage.
7   Improve the ability to trace sabotage. Saboteurs do not want to be caught. Video cameras, authorized (and traceable) computer and building access can ensure that authorities know where people are and what they are doing.
8   Assume sabotage will occur and plan for it. Limiting the impact of behaviour is important. This may mean having backup programs and databases offsite as well as running antiviral programs. Companies need to have a plan for recalling products, informing the public, handling media interest and managing liability when necessary.

Resignations

Few companies or organizations offer young people a career for life. The emphasis from career advisers and in recruitment agencies is to move jobs regularly in order to develop talents fully. Retention of their talented, knowledgeable and hard-working employees is therefore becoming an endemic problem for employers.

Recent Hay studies reveal that about one-third of employees surveyed worldwide plan to resign in three years. In the previous five years, employee attrition surged by more than 25%. The Hay Group report showed that for companies with revenues of $500 million the loss could amount to 4% of revenues amounting to 40% of profits, assuming those companies earned 10% on revenues. The report gives an example from a consumer products group which recruits 100 executives a year, a quarter of whom leave within 12 months. The average direct cost of recruitment and training was $6.25 – if they could have held on to 10 of those 25 they would have saved $2.5 million per year (Hay Group 2001).

In the UK, a survey in 2001 showed that 22% of doctors intended to quit direct patient care in the next five years. In 1998 the figure was 14%. The principal reason was a reduction in job satisfaction (Sibbald et al. 2003 p 1). The cost of recruitment throughout the UK was estimated by Simon Howard in 2002 as £7 billion, 'which is a lot of money in anyone's book' (Howard 2002 p 58).

There has been a great deal of research on employee turnover: why, when and how employees choose voluntarily to leave organizations. What have all these studies demonstrated? In their exhaustive meta-analysis Griffeth et al. (2000) came to the following conclusions:

▷ There are *proximal* and *distal* causes that lead to the decision to leave which takes place over time in a fairly well-described dynamic process. The general decision to leave is usually initiated by job dissatisfaction. This leads to a search for an alternative. The distal factors that have been consistently shown to be important are: job content, stress, work-group cohesion, autonomy, leadership, distributive justice and promotional chances. These affect commitment and satisfaction which leads to ideas about leaving.

▷ The turnover rate in companies is not necessarily a powerful factor determining whether any one individual will leave.

▷ The turnover rate for women is quite similar to that of men.

▷ Companies that have merit-based reward systems tend to keep people longer. Where collective reward programmes replace individual incentive, their introduction seems to increase turnover.

▷ Organizations (like the military) that have specific compulsory contracts to discourage resignations in a fixed period certainly experience far less turnover and a more stable workforce.

▷ Personality factors – specifically neuroticism and conscientiousness – do predict turnover over and above other factors.

Resignations form the most frequent and perhaps the most innocent reason for staff turnover, but are often a manifestation of discontent and the one which costs most. And so many could be avoided!

Conclusion

This chapter has looked at some of the very specific types of CWBs. There is a separate research literature on these topics: theft, fraud, deceit, information leakage, whistle-blowing, sabotage and excessive turnover. Yet many similar themes occur. These CWBs occur in a variety circumstances most of which are predictable and preventable. Certainly specific characteristics of individuals seem related to the particular CWB. A rather different sort of individual chooses to become a saboteur as opposed to a whistle-blower, though they may be motivated by very similar circumstances.

Opportunity, work-group norms, and management practices are the factors that most obviously account for specific CWBs. Theft, petty and serious, may be condemned by junior management; deceit may be the norm in some settings, and mass turnover after expensive training and selection a common reaction to particular circumstances.

Integrity researchers in those specific areas offer similar advice. They maintain, with good empirical evidence, that those CWBs can be significantly reduced (though probably never eliminated). They all talk of more careful selection better management practices and the introduction, where appropriate, of surveillance equipment. Organizations have gone (and will go) out of business because of the preventable CWBs of their employees. No matter how good the product or service, or how hungry the market for it, if the employees are disgruntled and vengeful because of the way they are treated the organization may yet fail.

Hence the importance of taking the dark side of work behaviour seriously. CWBs are damaging; they affect profits and productivity. But disloyalty and indifference can be turned round and, with the right policies and management organizations, one can create a workforce that is loyal and committed.

5 Bad-person Theories

Introduction

This chapter is about individualistic, person-centred explanations for counterproductive behaviour. Psychologists have long talked about the *fundamental attribution error*, which is essentially the idea that people like to explain behaviour by using personality trait, internal or dispositional causes rather than external or situation causes. Thus asked to explain why someone is frequently absent or has many accidents they prefer to explain the former behaviour in terms, say, of hypochondria or laziness and the latter behaviour in terms of clumsiness or simply accident proneness. Most people ignore or underplay the many other external and situational factors that might play a role. Thus a person may be frequently absent because of a dying parent or accident prone because of poor factory layout, machinery or safety rules in an organization.

There are bad, conscienceless, psychopaths who commit serious and petty organizational crimes. We can explain their behaviour primarily in terms of their pathology, but they are the exception not the rule. They may be high-profile in media stories but are, mercifully, very rare. They are, as statisticians say, a low-base-rate phenomenon. As we have consistently noted, by far the most common motive for organization deviancy is the way people feel they have been treated by the organization.

How to explain lying, stealing and cheating at work? This section lists typical *internal* personal, 'bad person' type explanations given by psychiatrists, psychologists, journalists and ordinary people who are victims or simply observers of 'nasty' people in the workplace. Whilst there are clearly occasions where the stealing, cheating and other CWBs are attributable primarily to the characteristics of individuals – namely their personal pathology – it is nearly always the case that CWBs are not performed by 'sick', 'deranged' or 'wicked' individuals but rather by those who for one reason or another are pushed over the brink.

Personality disorders

Over the past 100 years, psychiatrists have described ten or so personality disorders. They are characterized by being chronic, difficult to treat and, where the pathology is pervasive, integrated into the personality.

They can be divided into three groups. The first constitutes the dependent, histrionic, narcissistic (and antisocial) personalities, and is characterized by relatively coherent, non-conflicted behaviour. Whether oriented toward or against other people, such individuals tend to function in comparatively effective ways:

▷ *Antisocial personality*. This is by far the most important personality disorder to explain CWBs. It is characterized by the chronic manifestation of antisocial behaviour in a person who is typically amoral and impulsive. They are self-obsessed and have an inability to delay gratification or deal effectively with authority. Distress usually occurs only as a result of immediate frustrations and relationships are at best shallow. Antisocial personalities display both an excessive need for stimulation and a lack of response to standard societal control procedures. The chronic nature of the pattern is reflected in a failure to profit from experience and is related to the inability to delay gratification. The pattern is already apparent in adolescence or even early childhood, and the disorder spans a broad performance spectrum, including school, vocational, and interpersonal behaviours.

▷ *Dependent personality*. They have a great need to cling to stronger personalities who will make a wide range of decisions for them. They may even change their beliefs to come into accord with a dominant personality. They are naive and docile but suspicious of possible rejection: they show little initiative in any area, following stronger others. They are very likely to commit CWBs.

▷ *Histrionic personality*. They are intensely emotionally reactive and rather flamboyant, often called hysteric. Their dramatic behaviour is attention seeking, and they are extremely demanding of others interpersonally. Although hysterics often promise some reciprocal response, they seldom provide one.

▷ *Narcissistic personality*. This new category describes people who have an inflated sense of self-worth and care little for the welfare of others despite occasionally making pretence of caring. They are asocial rather than antisocial; most of their behaviour is designed to boost their self-image.

Second, come the compulsive, passive-aggressive, schizoid and avoidant disorders. These personality traits are either ambivalent about interpersonal relationships (compulsives and passive-aggressives) or virtually isolated from external support. None is likely to manifest CWBs:

▷ *Compulsive personality*. They can be described as 'workaholics without warmth'; compulsive personalities are overly controlled emotionally. They find it hard to express warmth or caring. They are formal and perfectionist, and they place inordinate value on work and productivity, yet they are surprisingly indecisive.

▷ *Passive-aggressive personality*. Passive-aggressive personalities show a pattern commonly encountered in clinical practice. They live life as a double message, engaging others in dependency-oriented relationships but then expressing much resistance and hostility in the relationship. They are stubborn and inefficient, often procrastinate on deadlines and resort to threats or pouting if confronted with their inconsistent and unhelpful behaviour.

▷ *Schizoid personality.* Schizoid personalities are asocial, shy, introverted, and significantly defective in their ability to form social relationships. They have difficulty expressing hostility and are usually described as cold loners.

▷ *Avoidant personality.* They tend to be shy, inhibited. They have low self-esteem despite being desirous of interpersonal relationships. They appear unwilling to tolerate any risk in a relationship, and they easily come to feel rejected.

At the lowest level of personality integration fall the borderline, paranoid, and schizotypal disorders. Profound difficulties with interpersonal relationships are common in these disorders, and characteristic behaviour patterns include overt hostility and/or confusion. Occasionally these types can be very difficult at work:

▷ *Borderline personality.* Borderline personalities are moody and emotionally unstable and appear very liable to further personality deterioration. They are irritable, anxious, and occasionally spontaneously aggressive but have difficulty being alone. They are interpersonally intense and may show identity problems similar to those with the depersonalization.

▷ *Paranoid personality.* They are suspicious, envious, rigid in emotions and attitudes, authoritarian and hyper-alert for intrusions into their psychological world. They project blame for problems in their psychological world on to others and tend to be, particularly in the US, litigious and legalistic.

▷ *Schizotypal personality.* Schizotypal personalities are similar to schizophrenics. They are isolated interpersonally, somewhat suspicious, and illogical. Whereas the schizoid's behaviour remains rather constant, the schizotypal person may, under stress, decompensate into actual schizophrenia.

There are many possible origins of these disorders: genetic, psychological, hormonal, poor learning, bad parenting. But what is important here is the suggestion that some, if not most, people at work who thieve, deceive, take part in sabotage or other counterproductive behaviours are genuinely 'suffering' from a psychiatric illness, namely one of the personality disorders. It is assumed that this, in and of itself, explains (away) why people do what they do.

The antisocial personality, the psychopath or moral imbecile

The personality disorder most obviously implicated in the 'dark side of behaviour at work' is the psychopath – now called the antisocial personality.

Are those who lie, steal or cheat mentally deranged? We know that around a third of all people in prison can be diagnosed as antisocial people. Are they psychopaths who seem to have no moral control over self-destructive, anti-social behaviour? Antisocial people or psychopaths' most conspicuous and dangerous signs include an absence of guilt, conscience or anxiety about the future; lack of feeling of affection for others; impulsivity and inability to control behaviour in the light of probable consequences, although those are known and fully understood.

The psychopath is both overtly antisocial yet has superficial charm. They are superficial, grandiose, and manipulative. They lack empathy, long-term goals and remorse. They are both personally irresponsible and refuse to take responsibility for their behaviour. If good looking and intelligent, they can be lethal with their superficial charm.

Furnham (2003 p 18) reinterpreted the latest US psychiatric manual (Diagnostic and Statistical Manual (DSM) IV) for the psychopath – now called the antisocial personality into (hopefully) everyday language:

Psychopaths show a disregard for, and violation of, the rights of others. They often have a history of being difficult, delinquent or dangerous.

1   They show a failure to conform to social norms with respect to lawful behav-
    iours (repeatedly performing acts that are grounds for arrest, imprisonment
    and serious detention). This includes lying, stealing and cheating.
2   They are always deceitful, as indicated by repeated lying, use of aliases, or
    conning others for personal profit or pleasure. They are nasty, aggressive, con
    artists – the sort who often get profiled on business crime programmes.
3   They are massively impulsive and fail to plan ahead. They live only in, and
    for, the present.
4   They show irritability and aggressiveness, as indicated by repeated physical
    fights or assaults. They can't seem to keep still – ever.
5   They manifest a terrifying reckless disregard for the physical and psycholog-
    ical safety of others – or the business in general.
6   They are famous for being consistently irresponsible. Repeated failure to
    sustain consistent work behaviour or to honour financial obligations are their
    hallmark.
7   Most frustrating of all, they show a lack of remorse. They are indifferent to,
    or rationalize, having hurt, mistreated, or stolen from another. They never
    learn from their mistakes. It can seem like labelling them as antisocial is a
    serious understatement.

Controversy surrounds this concept of psychopath (pathopatic personal-ity and sociopath are sometimes used synonymously). Some believe this categorization is vague, contradictory and used by psychiatrists as a sort of wastebasket category for people too difficult to diagnose. But the condition has become well known since the famous book by Cleckley (1976) called *The Mask of Sanity*.

The following are typical characteristics:

1 Thrill-seeking behaviour and disregard of conventions
2 Inability to control impulses or delay gratification
3 Rejection of authority and discipline
4 Poor judgement about behaviour but good judgement about abstract situations
5 Failure to alter behaviour punished in the past
6 Pathological, shameless and constant lying
7 Asocial and antisocial behaviour.

They have been called hollow – their relationships are superficial and they have no loyalty to any except themselves. They have little sense of who they are and have no value-system or long-range goals. Most of all they cannot bide time. They like the here and now and an exciting one at that. They eschew stability and routine. They like lots of excitement. Further, they often seem devoid of anxiety.

Psychopaths have nearly always been in trouble with the law. What gets them into trouble is impulsiveness. They are not planners and think little about either the victim of their crime or the consequences for themselves. Crimes are often petty, deceitful and thefts but are most often fraud, forgery and failure to pay debts.

The first response to being caught is to escape, leaving colleagues, family or debtors to pick up the pieces. They do so without a qualm. The next response is to lie with apparent candour and sincerity even under oath and to parents and loved ones. They behave as if social rules and regulations do not apply to them. They have no respect for authorities and institutions.

They are at the mercy of their impulses. Whereas neurotics tend to be overcontrolled, the psychopath shows inadequate control. They are childlike in their demands for immediate gratification. They also seek thrills, often associated with alcohol, drugs, gambling and sex.

They never learn from experience, consistently repeating illegal and immoral acts. They maintain their lying, swindling, thieving and deserting despite being frequently caught and punished because they tend to be careless about being caught. They make poor efforts to conceal wrongdoing believing they have special protection, privileges or immunity to punishment.

They have to keep 'on the move' because they get to be known in the community. Their geographic and vocational mobility is indeed a good index of their pathology.

Curiously, when asked about justice and morality in abstract, they tend to give 'correct' conventional answers. They just don't apply this knowledge of right and wrong to themselves. This is particularly the case when their judgement conflicts with their personal demands for immediate gratification.

Psychopaths have problematic relationships. They seem incapable of love and deep friendship for several reasons. They manifest a near complete absence of empathy, gratefulness and altruism. They are selfish not self-sacrificial. They appear not to understand others' emotions. They seem completely ungrateful for the help and affection of others. It is difficult to have a good relationship with a self-centred, selfish, egocentric individual. Others are seen as a source of gain and pleasure irrespective of their discomfort, disappointment or pain. Others' needs are too trivial.

Lack of empathy and vanity means the psychopath finds it difficult to predict how others will behave and which of his or her own many behaviours will lead to punishment. Psychopaths are in essence completely amoral. They accept no responsibility for their actions and therefore no blame, guilt, shame or remorse. They are able to mouth trite excuses and rationalizations for the benefit of others. Indeed they often have a convincing façade of competence and maturity. They can appear attentive, charming, mature and reliable – but have difficulty maintaining the façade. They can do so long enough to get a job or even get married but not to sustain either. The restless, impetuous, selfishness soon emerges.

The first question is why they are attracted to certain jobs and they to them. They seem attracted to entrepreneurial, start-up business or those in the business of radical change such as when delayering. It is when businesses are chaotic that they are often at their best.

Industrial psychopath

Babiak (1995) presented the case of Dave who worked for a highly profitable US electronics company.

Dave was in his mid-thirties, a good looking, well-spoken professional, married for the third time with four children. He had a degree from a large university and had been hired into a newly created position during a hiring surge. Dave interviewed well, impressing his prospective boss as well as the department director with his creative mind, high energy level, and technical expertise. Routine reference checks seemed positive as did a security check. Dave had come across as such a perfect fit with the organization that Frank was surprised when things started to go wrong.

During his second week of employment Dave stormed into Frank's office and demanded that the department secretary be fired because she had not demonstrated sufficient respect for him. According to her, Dave had been rude and condescending, and was upset that she would not drop everything to cater to his requests.

Although Dave often arrived early and stayed late, making a positive impression on everyone in the office, the quality and quantity of his work was actually less than it first appeared. Frank discovered that Dave's first major report included plagiarized material. When questioned, Dave brushed aside the concern, commenting that he did not think it a good use of his time and talents to 'reinvent the wheel'. Subsequently, Dave would 'forget' to work on uninteresting projects, claimed that he was being overworked, and frequently complained that some projects were beneath him.

Disruptive behaviours included verbal tirades during staff meetings, to which he often showed up both unprepared and late. He frequently left during the middle of meetings in order to make 'important' phone calls, and denounced meetings as a waste of time, preferring to conduct all of his business in one-on-one conversations. When assigned to a task force he dominated the discussions and verbally bullied other team members into supporting his ideas. However, he would alternate berating others with compliments, begging for forgiveness, and promising to return favours.

After three months Frank spoke with Dave about his inability to get along with others in the department, his inappropriate emotionality, and unwillingness to assume a greater number of assignments. Dave acted surprised that anyone thought there was a problem and denied causing any disruption, adding that fighting and aggression were necessary in order to achieve greater things in life. By the fourth month of Dave's employment, Frank was warned by a colleague who was leaving the organization to 'watch out for Dave' (pp 177–8).

Dave was frequently described as taking advantage of the organization and many of its members. Dave once convinced a manager to lend him an expensive piece of equipment swearing that he would lock it up before going home. The equipment was found by security that evening in an open hallway. On three occasions Dave attempted to take specialized tools and equipment home at the weekend without authorization. In each instance he argued with the security guard insisting that he was too well known in the company to need a property pass and his work was too important to be questioned.

There were several individuals in the company whom he was said to have 'wrapped around his finger'. These included a middle-aged staff assistant through whom Dave interacted with the company grapevine, a young female security guard who worked at the entrance of the building in the early evening, and a professional in another department who was described by some as Dave's 'soul mate' and by others as the person who was really completing Dave's assignments. Dave frequently showed up at this person's office in an agitated state and she would allegedly 'counsel' him. All made positive, glowing comments about Dave, and one described him as a nice guy, 'an artist who was misunderstood'.

Some of the stories told about Dave were humorous. One secretary reported a time when he knelt down at her desk to beg for something he wanted. Another reported that her boss asked her to change his own travel itinerary so that he did not have to fly on the same plane as Dave. Several people said that Dave saw himself as a 'ladies' man'. Dave offered a co-worker a drink, and then tried to leave without paying for it. The woman reminded him of his offer and Dave caused a scene by arguing with the waitress over the price of the drink (p 179).

In reviewing Dave's credentials several discrepancies were discovered. Dave had listed four major fields of study on his resumé, application blank, and other documents. When confronted, he dismissed the discrepancies with a comment that there was nothing wrong in using different major designations for different purposes because he had taken courses in these subjects. (He did not possess a degree in the field for which he was hired.) Further investigation revealed expense reports containing numerous undocumented charges. When confronted, Dave became irate and stated that the request for receipts was a symptom of a sick organization. This writer was also shown a memo from the purchasing manager warning Dave to stop ordering merchandise and supplies directly from vendors, without authorization (p 180).

Dave consistently made favourable first impressions. Over time, however, the perceptions of some organization members grew increasingly negative. The discrepant views in organization members' perceptions seemed to vary as a function of the frequency of interaction with Dave and the finesse he used to influence them based on their current utility to him (p 182).

Babiak (1995) found five characteristics in the many studies of industrial psychopathy:

> Comparison of the behaviour of the three subjects observed to date revealed some similarities: each (a) began by building a *network of one-to-one relationships* with powerful and useful individuals, (b) *avoided virtually all group meetings* where maintaining multiple facades may have been too difficult, and (c) *created conflicts* which kept co-workers from sharing information about him. Once their power bases were established, (d) *co-workers who were no longer useful were abandoned* and (e) *detractors were neutralized* by systematically raising doubts about their competence and loyalty. In addition, unstable cultural factors, inadequate measurement systems, and general lack of trust typical of organizations undergoing rapid, chaotic change may have provided an acceptable cover for psychopathic behaviour. (pp 184–5, emphases added)

One of the most important ways to differentiate personal style from personality disorder is flexibility. There are lots of difficult people at work but relatively few whose rigid, maladaptive behaviours mean they continually have disruptive, troubled lives. It is their *inflexible, repetitive, poor stress-coping responses* that are marks of disorder.

Personality disorders influence the *sense of self* – the way people think and feel about themselves and how other people see them. The disorders often powerfully influence *interpersonal relations* and *work*. They reveal themselves in how people 'complete tasks, take and/or give orders, make decisions, plan, handle external and internal demands, take or give criticism, obey rules, take and delegate responsibility, and cooperate with people' (Oldham and Morris 1991 p 24). The antisocial, obsessive, compulsive, passive-aggressive and dependent types are particularly problematic in the workplace.

People with personality disorders have difficulty expressing and understanding emotions. It is the intensity with which they express them and their variability that make them odd. More importantly they often have serious problems with self-control.

Bad bosses

Just as there are problem or sick employees there are sick bosses. They too can suffer the kind of personality disorder described in the previous sections, but in addition they can be subject to their own kind of syndrome. The effect can be far more wide reaching. A single employee might make life hell for those in his or her immediate vicinity. A boss's influence can affect many more. If anything is going to turn a worker from a passive condition of alienation (see Chapter 8) to more active aggression and revenge, the cultures created by these people will ensure it.

Narcissism

Students of personality disorders have long implicated narcissism in management derailment. Thus some have argued that narcissistic personality disorder explains a lot of counterproductive behaviours at work. Penney and Spector (2002) have shown that narcissism is both directly and indirectly related to CWBs.

Essentially the difference between a narcissistic person and those with high self-esteem (sometimes described as vain) is that for the latter positive self-evaluation is grounded in reality. The narcissist on the other hand has an inflated or grandiose self-image that is unstable, uncertain and in need of constant support. Narcissists unrealistically expect to be dominant, successful and admired in all situations. If this is not forthcoming, the way they traditionally maintain their (bizarre) self-image is to express aggression, anger, violence and disdain towards those who threaten their self-view. Expressing anger to the ego-threat from others potentially serves different functions. It punishes, discourages further negative feedback/evaluations and signifies dominance over another.

Thus the narcissist, not grounded in reality, is likely to experience many work-situated challenges to their (inappropriately inflated) self-appraisals. These ego-threatening challenges lead to frequent outbursts of anger, frustration or hostility that are manifest as constant aggression.

In the workplace various constraints (time, money, equipment) often obstruct or reduce successful job performance which affects the ability to do the job and are therefore ego-threatening. Narcissists are particularly sensitive to any indication that they are not better than everyone else and therefore hypersensitive to constraints which lead to anything from manifestations of minor annoyance to great rage.

In their study, Penney and Spector (2002) found exactly what they hypothesized. Narcissists experienced more anger, more frequently and engaged more in CWB. It fits well with the theory of threatened egoism. Job constraints were important: when a non-narcissist experienced job constraints it did not lead to CWBs but for a narcissist the more perceived job constraints, the more CWB. In this sense, people respond to the same levels of constraint differently. Thus personality factors (traits and disorders) seem to be effective predictors of CWB under difficult, trying or stressful work circumstances.

The bullying boss

The idea of the manager as a bully is a much more common lay explanation for why workers may react badly at work. Very occasionally sabotage or stealing, or some other dark-side behaviour, is the direct result of the bullying behaviour of one or more supervisors or boss. The dark-side behaviour is usually the attempt of a deeply frustrated individual or group to have their revenge for the humiliation, hurt and powerlessness that they have felt at the hands of a bullying boss.

Often the vengeful act may be directed particularly to the individual. Their car tyres may be let down, their computer 'infected', their office set on fire. Malicious, possibly exaggerated or untrue rumours may be spread. However, frequently the vengeful act can be less specifically targeted at the bully him/herself than at the wider organization either because of the inability to take revenge only on the individual or else because the bullied see the bully as acting with the approval of the organization as a whole.

Indeed, some organizations or parts of them may approve, even require a bullying culture. That is, it is normative to bully. So, what is workplace bullying? There are no agreed definitions but all share certain themes. First, it is inappropriate, repeated and unreasonable behaviour that is experienced as demeaning, humiliating, insulting, intimidating, offensive and even physically painful.

It is possible to distinguish between personal bullying, which can range from teasing, practical jokes, rumour-mongering to persistent targeted criticism. There is also procedural, corporate-culture bullying which may involve excessive workloads, unreasonable and unfulfillable demands, and paranoid monitoring of work.

The list of bullying behaviours specified by the literature in the area is indeed long. It includes:

▷ Verbal abuse; name-calling, rudeness, screaming, profanities.
▷ Ridicule via insults, slander, belittling or patronizing comments.
▷ Malicious teasing, pranks and practical jokes.
▷ Unwanted and inappropriate physical contact.
▷ Consistent criticism, accusations and blame.
▷ Isolation, ignoring or giving the person the 'silent treatment'.
▷ Unreasonable/impossible targets, deadlines, tasks, pressure.
▷ Assigning meaningless, pointless, dirty-work tasks.
▷ Devaluing work efforts, giving no credit for effort/outcome.
▷ Withholding and distorting work-related information.
▷ Refusing reasonable requests for training, equipment.

▷ Introducing unexplained, unnecessary, erratic changes.
▷ Constant threats of job loss.
▷ Tampering with a worker's individual property or work equipment.

Bullying is a difficult problem because it can be so subjective. One man's firm and directive supervision is another's bullying. To this extent it is in the eye of the beholder. Jokes can be seen as insults; promotion refusal attributed to bullying rather than poor progress.

The law tends to side with the person who is complaining and if the employer fails to deal adequately with the complaint, a worker may be able to resign and claim constructive unfair dismissal. If the bullying is serious, the worker may also be able to bring a civil or criminal claim (Kibling and Lewis 2000 p 241).

It has been argued that some people have a 'victim mentality', with widespread anxieties, fears and uncertainties, and experience practically everything as bullying. Equally, in a struggling organization that has had to radically change and restructure some resentful or inadequate individuals may table reasonable and necessary requests as bullying. It could therefore be argued that it is better and more cost-effective to invest in teaching coping skills and stress resilience in the workforce than trying to catch, punish and rehabilitate bullies.

This renders 'statistics' particularly problematic. Thus self-report surveys show anything from 3% to 93% of people report some form of workplace bullying taking place over the past month/year. However, it does seem that some groups are more vulnerable than others: older and younger people, casual/temporary staff; low status/few skills/poorly educated staff; those with impairments/disabilities; and those with minority beliefs/lifestyles.

What is clear is that perceived or real (if distinguishable) bullying has powerful consequences on the bully, the bullied and the work group. Usually the most manifold consequences of bullying are on the health and well-being of the bullied. But there are usually noticeable increases in absenteeism and staff turnover and a decrease in productivity.

Some researchers have attempted to count the costs and benefits of taking action such as the introduction of prevention and redress measures. Much of this is about creating awareness and providing employee support systems as well as managing incidents well.

A central question is why some managers bully? Is it a result of the personality, leadership style or lack of skill? Is it because of different expectations or even an awareness of their behaviour on others? Are bullies simply people with low social/emotional intelligence and an inability to influence and persuade? And as a result should they be punished or helped or both?

This book is not about the causes of bullying but possible reactions to it. Some people who feel bullied simply resign; others retreat; some complain; others take revenge. It seems logical that dark-side behavioural revenge against individuals and organizations can be significantly reduced by developing both a healthy workplace culture and a sensitive and sensible set of procedures to deal with bullies.

Corporate cultures that condone bullying, explicitly or inexplicitly, in a sense invite revenge. Certainly all organizations can experience problems particularly at times of change and restructuring. Handled well, the incidences of reported bullying should decrease as well as some of the negative consequences of those who feel bullied.

The toxic boss

Another person-explanation in lay terms rather than psychobabble is the idea of the toxic boss. Results from studies on the origin of delinquency and criminality make depressing reading. As does coming across young children in a clearly toxic family; one feels they really have so little chance of growing up as healthy, responsible, adaptable individuals. The antisocial personality has often had a miserable upbringing which, alas, he or she often perpetuates, producing a cycle of misfortune, neglect, unhappiness and crime.

Reading the list of typical characteristics of the dysfunctional parent in the toxic family, it is not difficult to see why children from these families end up as they do. Moody, egocentric, uneducated, immoral 'care givers' give little care. Instead of providing a loving, stable environment, they do the opposite, which can have a disastrous long term effect on the child.

And the same can happen at work. Dysfunctional managers create toxic offices. They manage, often in a brief period of time, to create mayhem, distrust and disaffection. And even in stable adults this can have long-term consequences. That perfidious issue of 'stress at work' and its more serious cousin the nervous breakdown are often caused by the dysfunctional manager.

To many, especially young people, a manager is in loco parentis. They can have considerable influence over one's health, happiness and future. They can create an environment that allows employees to give of their best. They can stretch their staff by setting reachable but challenging goals and they can give them support in doing so. They can be helpful and encouraging and consistent – or not.

But there are some seriously poor managers who create a working environment at the precise opposite end of the spectrum. What are the symptoms of the dysfunctional manager? Check the list:

▷ *Inconsistency and unpredictability:* this is often the hallmark of the type. They are unpredictable to staff, to clients and to customers – even to their family. You can never be sure about what they will say or do. They are fickle and capricious. The job of a parent and manager is often to create stability in a world of chaos, a sense of security in an insecure world, not the opposite. A dysfunctional manager is often more than inconsistent in that they give contradictory and mixed messages that are very difficult to interpret.

▷ *Low tolerance of provocation and emotional sensitivity:* dysfunctional managers fly off the handle. They are known for their moodiness. One has quite literally to tread around them very gently. Jokes backfire – unless, of course, they make them. They take offence, harbour grudges and can show great mood swings, especially when stressed.

▷ *Hedonism and self-indulgence:* the dysfunctional manager is no puritan: they like pleasure. The golf round on a Friday afternoon, those expensive meals, that overpriced office furniture are all ways of a dysfunctional manager pleasing himself or herself. Further they are often deeply selfish about them. There can be real problems if their pleasures are addictive, which so often they can be. The hedonistic, addictive personality is a real nightmare not only from a financial point of view.

▷ *Nowness and no long-term planning:* the dysfunctional parent and dysfunctional manager live every day as it comes – not for religious reasons, but because they cannot or will not plan for the future. They have never understood postponement of gratification. Hence, they experience serious setbacks when unexpected things happen. Saving for a rainy day is not part of their repertoire. They can't or won't plan for future eventualities.

▷ *Restlessness and excitement seeking:* the dysfunctional manager is always on the go. They get bored easily, can't pay attention. They look as if they have an adult form of ADHD. They look as if they need thrills and variety to keep them going. And, inevitably, they find themselves in situations that are commercially, even physically, dangerous. They chop and change all the time. They can not sit still and rarely pay attention to others.

▷ *Learning problems:* dysfunctional managers do not learn from their mistakes. In fact, they do not like learning at all. The skill-based seminar is not for them. Outward bound perhaps, but not the conference centre. Many have few educational qualifications. They don't value them in their staff or themselves. Hence, they do not encourage learning of any sort, often pooh-poohing the educated staff member.

▷ *Poor emotional control:* they let feelings hang out. Dysfunctional managers are the opposite of the stereotypic reserved and controlled Englishman. They shout and weep, sulk and gush with little embarrassment or control. This is not the result of some California-based therapy: in fact, they have poor self-control. They become well known for their outbursts.

▷ *Placing little value on skill attainment:* the dysfunctional manager is unlikely to have an MBA. They despise attempts of their staff to upgrade their skills. They talk about gut feelings, experience or, worse still, luck. They are loath to invest in training on the job.

▷ *Perpetual low-grade physical illness:* dysfunctional bosses always seem to be ill. They get coughs, colds, chills – whatever is going around. They certainly are not health conscious, and are very liable to absenteeism.

The dysfunctional boss, like the delinquent child, may have come from a dysfunctional home or socialized in a dysfunctional organization. Management consultants often talk about management practices they have come across that are little short of startling. They cause unhappiness and reduce productivity and morale, which, over time, can lead to the breakdown of the staff.

It has been observed by the business guru Manfred Kets de Vries that whole organizations can become toxic because of the character of senior managers. Toxic senior managers see the world in a particular way, which influences their selection, self-perception and style.

The workplace can become psychologically as well as physically toxic. The dysfunctional manager is a sort of Typhus Mary of stress and incompetence, taking the disease around with them wherever they go. Worse, they model dysfunctionality to young staff, who may consider such behaviour normal. The cure, alas, is often not worth the candle. Dysfunctional managers need more than counselling: they really need cancelling.

Conclusion

This section has concentrated on various 'within-person' explanations for counterproductive behaviour. They tend to describe the thief, liar, saboteur or whistle-blower as sad, bad or mad. Further the 'pathology' or personality of the individual is sufficient to explain his or her often outrageous, immoral or illegal behaviour.

Whilst it is no doubt true that for select individuals this type of explanation is important, the evidence suggests that a great deal of counterproductive behaviour at work is not committed by angry, sick or evil individuals. The vast majority of people who take part in counterproductive acts are neither immoral nor insane. They react in a series of circumstances that confront them. They might feel aggrieved or wronged by clear injustice; they might be part of a group that not only condones but enforces thieving; or they may be driven by personal circumstances to act in the way that they do.

Indeed, whistle-blowers are often portrayed as highly moral people acting with courage and integrity. Equally, some possibly less hard-working staff have accused their boss of being a bully, toxic and incompetent when all that he or she is doing is ensuring that productivity reaches an acceptable and necessary standard.

Bad-person theories are too often the easy option for employers or employees to 'explain away' bad behaviour. They do not take into sufficient consideration the complexity of forces acting on individuals when they commit counterproductive behaviour at work. The theories may be 'psychologically satisfying' but they are often misleading. As we have pointed out elsewhere, many different forces have to be implicated to explain the sort of behaviours we are dealing with in this book.

6 Measuring Dark- and Bright-side Attitudes, Beliefs and Behaviours

Introduction

Both the behavioural scientist and the astute manager want to measure CWBs: the former for research, the latter for decision making. As a result various people have tried to develop questionnaires that supposedly measure CWBs. They make interesting reading because they give an insight into the attitudes, beliefs, behaviours and values of those who commit CWBs.

Of course, the central question for all parties is their validity. Do they measure what they say they are measuring? Most crucially do they have predictive validity; that is do scores on the test actually relate to CWB in the organization? To develop a well-psychometrized test is a long and expensive business. Researchers need to show a test is reliable and valid. This is particularly difficult in some areas such as CWBs because the topic is taboo. Few people are happy to admit doing CWBs and there is always the possibility of faking and distortion. Nevertheless, there has been a recent concerted effort to develop such questionnaires.

Researchers have, however, been more active in measuring 'bright-side' attitudes such as job commitment and engagement. By looking at the opposite of a phenomenon one can often get an insight into the issue itself. The question is whether alienation and detachment are the opposite of commitment and engagement or qualitatively different. Frequently the absence of something does not imply the presence of another. It may, then, not be possible to measure the dark side by testing the bright side – or vice versa.

Measuring CWBs by questionnaire

To develop a good, sensitive and psychometric measure of CWBs is difficult. It must be compressive but parsimonious: all relevant CWBs must be included but not those which are marginally or only very occasionally CWBs. It must also be sensitive to distinctions made earlier: severity, target, anonymity. Ideally it could be used across a wide variety of job categories, sectors and organizations.

Marcus et al. (2002) developed and tested a German language questionnaire with eight factors. They found intelligence (cognitive ability) was not related to CWB but self-control and integrity were. Self-control, defined as the general tendency 'to avoid acts whose long-term costs exceed the momentary benefits', was the best predictor of not getting involved in CWBs. This may be seen as deferment of gratification or simply being 'grown-up'. The second best predictor was integrity as measured by an integrity test.

Their 74-item scale details typical CWBs. The first 20 items are shown in Table 6.1.

One possibility is to group these CWBs into, say, *property deviance* (theft, sabotage) and *production deviance* (tardiness, alcohol abuse). Another approach is to talk about *CWB towards the organization* and CWB towards other *organizational members*. It also should be noted that some acts are *public* (that is, absence) others are private (theft).

Another way to think of CWBs is to think of their *opposite* which may be called organizational citizenship, or pro-social, behaviour (OCB): supporting the organization, persistence, diligence, dutifulness. It is quite possible that a set of organizational variables (good management, fair appraisal system) lead to citizenship behaviour and their opposite to CWBs. Citizenship behaviour can be measured at the individual level in terms of the support people at work give to others (peers, subordinates, boss), the organization as a whole and

Table 6.1 Typical counterproductive work behaviours

1	I argued with people from outside the organization (for example customers or visitors).
2	I left my workplace during working hours without permission.
3	I stayed away from work without excuse.
4	I was intoxicated during working hours.
5	I intentionally worked slowly or carelessly.
6	I sought revenge from colleagues.
7	I came to work late or went home early.
8	I've got physically rough with other employees (co-workers, colleagues or superiors).
9	I exceeded a break for more than five minutes.
10	I spread rumours about the firm.
11	There were occasions when I skipped work.
12	I worked less in the absence of my supervisor.
13	I had drunk too much during working hours.
14	I arrived at work at least 10 minutes late.
15	I talk within the firm to shirk working.
16	I presented ideas of colleagues as my own.
17	I shirked unpleasant tasks.
18	I stayed away from work, although I was actually healthy.
19	I overheard discussions of co-workers to take personal advantage of it.
20	I pretended to work to avoid a new work order.

Source: Adapted from Marcus et al. 2002.

their level of persistence with extra effort despite difficult conditions (see Organizational Citizenship later in this chapter). Give people a reasonable and equitable workload in a relatively conflict-free environment and you are likely to achieve OCBs. On the other hand, frustrate them with few or poor resources, restricting and unreasonable rules and procedures, interruptions and poor training and you get CWBs (Miles et al. 2002).

One question for both the researcher and the manager is the relationship between CWBs and OCBs. Thus are they opposites? Is the absence of one an indicant of the presence of the other? Could people be low on both? Or could they swing wildly, being high on both. One study (Kelloway et al. 2002), which measured both on two short scales (see Table 6.2), found they were unique constructs. In this sense, they are not opposites. Presumably, the factors that may control the one (particular personality traits, special organizational circumstances) may be quite different from those that control the other. However, much must depend on the nature of the job. Where jobs are very well structured and rule bound (such as working on a manufacturing conveyor belt), OCBs might be distracting and, paradoxically, lead to lower performance.

Table 6.2 Items comprising the OCB and CWB measures

OCB	
1	Helping other employees with their work when they have been absent.
2	Volunteering to do things not formally required by the job.
3	Taking the initiative to orient new employees to the department even though it is not part of your job description.
4	Helping others when their work load increases (assisting others until they get over the hurdles).
5	Assisting supervisor with his/her duties.
6	Making innovative suggestions to improve the overall quality of the department.
7	Punctuality in arriving at work on time in the morning, and after lunch and breaks.
8	Exhibiting attendance at work beyond the norm. For example, I take less days off than most individuals or less than allowed.
9	Giving advance notice if unable to come to work.

CWB	
1	Exaggerated about your hours worked.
2	Started negative rumours about your company.
3	Gossiped about your co-workers.
4	Covered up your mistakes.
5	Competed with your co-workers in an unproductive way.
6	Gossiped about your supervisor.
7	Stayed out of sight to avoid work.
8	Taken company equipment or merchandise.
9	Blamed your co-workers for your mistakes.
10	Intentionally worked slow.

Source: Kelloway et al. 2002 p 150.

Table 6.3 Twenty of the 80 CPI items selected for the CPI scale as an example

True

20	I have had very peculiar and strange experiences.
26	It's a good thing to know people in the right places so you can get traffic tickets, and such things, taken care of.
44	Sometimes I feel like smashing things.
77	When I get bored I like to stir up some excitement.
101	I must admit that I often do as little work as I can get by with.
145	I have a tendency to give up easily when I meet difficult problems.
164	My parents have often disapproved of my friends.
191	I can remember 'playing sick' to get out of something.
203	When things go wrong, I sometimes blame the other person.
250	I must admit I find it very hard to work under strict rules and regulations.

False

14	I always follow the rule: business before pleasure.
68	I am embarrassed by dirty stories.
69	I would disapprove of anyone's drinking to the point of intoxication at a party.
96	I take a rather serious attitude toward ethical and moral issues.
230	I would rather be a steady and dependable worker than a brilliant but unstable one.
254	I have never deliberately told a lie.
276	I have very few quarrels with members of my family.
278	If I get too much change in a store, I always give it back.
286	I have never done anything dangerous for the thrill of it.
380	I am known as a hard and steady worker.

Source: Hakstian et al. 2002.

Another way to devise a self-report measure of CWBs is to take an established questionnaire and see which items related to CWB. This is what Hakstian et al. (2002) did. Using a student sample they first created a CWB that measured nine factors (see below). Then they derived an 80-item scale based on a well-established measure called the Californian Personality Inventory (CPI). The respondent simply puts true or false against each. To give an example of this measure 10 true and 10 false items are displayed in Table 6.3. This means if you put true to all true items and false to all false items you would get the maximum score.

The authors in an excellent example of how to validate a psychometric measure showed how their measure was significantly and logically related to such things as personality traits (that is, high neuroticism, low conscientiousness, low responsibility, low self-control) and all of the above measures on student CWBs, as well as to supervisor ratings of trustworthiness, the work ethic, use of time, desire to improve and overall performance.

The following nine scales were devised statistically. An example of a single questionnaire item is in brackets behind the label of the CWB. They show how various behaviours are grouped systematically into specific areas:

1 *Cheating:* (During an exam, quickly looked at, and got information from a classmate's paper).
2 *Substance abuse:* (Used more than one recreational drug at a time, for example alcohol and marijuana).
3 *Low personal standards:* (Turned in work that was of poor quality – lower than your true potential or ability).
4 *Property theft:* (Borrowed or took money from employer without approval).
5 *Duplicity:* (Falsely claimed having suffered some medical illness, for example flu, in order to avoid penalty for missing exam).
6 *Misrepresentation:* (Handed in an assignment and/or project that contained passages, for example sentences or paragraphs, that had been copied from someone else).
7 *Work avoidance:* (Used sick leave when not sick).
8 *Petty personal gain:* (Allowed yourself to be reimbursed more money than you actually spent on expenses).
9 *Indolence:* (Did not do your share of the work in a cooperative group project).

Some of these questionnaires have been developed to be 'user friendly'. Thus Jones et al. (2002) developed and reported the validity of a measure (Applicant Potential Inventory) which can be administered by fax, internet, personal computer and telephone. It measures:

1 *Honesty:* Attitudes to theft and previous theft-related behaviour.
2 *Drug avoidance:* Likelihood to sell or use drugs.
3 *Employee relations:* Tendency to cooperation and courteousness.
4 *Safety:* Safety consciousness.
5 *Work values:* Attitude to work and work habits.
6 *Supervision attitudes:* Likelihood of appropriate responses to supervision.
7 *Tenure:* Likelihood not to quit after a short time.
8 *Customer service:* Attitudes to and understanding of customers.

Clearly this is a general commercial instrument that only in part attempts to measure CWBs.

Others have attempted to see whether these instruments 'travel well' not only across work sectors but also across countries. Fortmann et al. (2002) provided reasonable evidence of this, contrasting South African and Latin American data collected on people at work.

Can you assess a potentially counterproductive person at interview? Interestingly, Blackman and Funder (2002) have shown unstructured interviews to be better at detecting CWBs. Why? Mainly because they appear to both parties as more informal and relaxed which reduces the candidate pressure to fake 'good'. They see the interviewer more as a 'social partner' and are likely to let down their guard. However, it seems good interviewers get more out of structured interviews because they can 'get at' and probe better. But detection at interview depends on:

1 *The good judge:* Socially skilled extraverts seem best, particularly those motivated to detect the decent.
2 *The ideal target:* It is more difficult to detect the decent in the inconsistent, erratic and unstable. Indeed inconsistency of any sort (that is, between verbal and non-verbal behaviour, between emotional states, between action, beliefs and deeds) is a good indicator of bad news.
3 *The particular trait:* Some personality traits are easier to see than others. Extraversion, neuroticism and agreeableness are easier to see in interview than conscientiousness, which previous employees see very evidently. You cannot see the trait of counterproductivity in an interview but you can see its correlates.
4 *Good information:* The more information collected from different sources over time is clearly best.

The interview may not be the best way of catching potential liars, cheats, thieves and saboteurs but, under specific circumstances, they can do rather well.

The typological approach

Questionnaires attempt to derive scores on particular dimensions. Another, older approach is to categorize people into types. Without doubt the most interesting work in this field has been that of Gerald Mars. In his thoughtful and very well-researched book looking at the anthropology of work crime, Mars (1984) looks at a typology of rewards at work.

Table 6.4 A typology of work and its rewards

	Official	Unofficial	Alternative
Legal	*1* *Formal rewards* Wages, salaries, commissions, overtime	*3* *Informal rewards* Perks, tips, extra work, consultancy	*5* *Social economy rewards* Domestic production, barter, exchange, 'do-it-yourself'
Extra – legal or illegal	*2* *Criminal rewards* Returns from professional crime, prostitution, and so on	*4* *Hidden economy rewards* Pilfering, short-changing, overcharged expenses, overloading and underdropping	*6* *Black economy rewards* Unregistered production and service organizations, moonlighting

Source: Mars 1984.

He notes that in the hotel and catering industry a waiter will receive basic and formal pay from Box 1 in the form of wages and overtime payments. This will be supplemented by informal rewards from Box 3 – the tips he receives and the perks of 'free' meals and 'free' accommodation. From Box 4 he or she may well be allowed to indulge in pilfered food or be afforded a 'winked-at-facility' to short-change or short-deal customers. The contents of Box 4 are usually allocated on an individual basis through an individual contract with a specific contract-maker – usually a first-line supervisor. It is the receipts from Boxes 1, 3 and 4 which, in their entirety, comprise a person's total rewards from work.

It is therefore not only meaningless to compute an individual's income entirely from Boxes 1 and 3, let alone exclusively from Box 1 – it is also grossly misleading. It distorts policy making. For instance, by directing attention from the concerns of the really low paid towards those whose claims are not as well justified.

Boxes 5 and 6, though not the central concerns of this book, distinguish the rewards that derive from alternative economic activity; they are distinct from official rewards, are allocated outside the official system and do not appear in official returns. They often involve a higher degree of social satisfaction than is derived from the same activities carried out for formal rewards and located in Box 1. At the same time, the economic component of this reward is often less than would be expected from work derived from Box 1. When people obtain rewards from Box 5 it is likely to involve an element of reciprocity – a doing of favours, a swapping of services – so that high expense or scarcities or bureaucratic complexities inherent in obtaining official provision can be overcome by mutual cooperation. It may also be characterized by an exchange of obligation or increased prestige in return for economic benefit.

They attribute this to the growing inadequacy of official provision particularly of services utilizing cheap capital goods such as hand tools. This reflects a shift in formal production towards high technology at high wages and a reduction in services provided formally which, being labour-intensive, cannot compete. Box 5 covers much of the small-scale alternative technology and alternative food production that has flourished in recent years as well as reciprocal neighbourly exchange such as when a neighbour fixes my car in return for my decorating his bedroom.

Box 6 is concerned with rewards from the black economy. As with the two pairs already described, this box also represents the extra-legal or illegal of a continuum – the social rewards of Box 5 blending into the unregistered production of Box 6. A group of cooperating artisans might well decide, for instance, to build themselves houses by working for each other at cost. If, however, they then extend their activities on a business basis by working for cash, not paying taxes and employing unregistered, non-union or moonlighting labour, then they will have gravitated to the black economy. It is Box 6 that is expanding, and the building industry that regularly provides a sizeable constituent of this increasing total. It is estimated, for instance, that a quarter

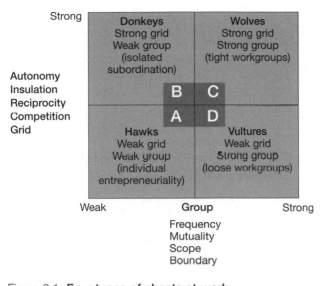

Figure 6.1 **Four types of cheats at work**
Source: Adapted from Mars 1984.

to a third of Italy's total production is now black and that a consistent 100,000 houses a year are built by this method, which has amounted to over a million illegal houses produced in the last ten years (Mars 1984 pp 8–10).

Mars (1984) described four types of cheats at work, also defined by a two-by-two grid (Figure 6.1).

Type A, Hawks (weak grid and weak group) relates to occupations that emphasize individuality, autonomy, competition. The control that members have over others is greater than the controls exercised over themselves. They emphasize entrepreneuriality, where the individual's freedom to transact on his or her own terms is highly valued. Individual flair is at a premium. Success is indicated by the number of followers a person controls. Rewards here go to those who find new and better ways of doing things and where the drive for successful innovation is paramount. Hawks are individualists, inventors, small businessmen. They are hungrily 'on the make'.

Hawks are typically entrepreneurial managers, owner businessmen, successful academics, pundits, the prima donnas among salesmen and the more independent professionals and journalists. Hawkish entrepreneuriality is also found in waiters, fairground buskers and owner taxi drivers. Alliances among hawks tend to shift with expediency and a climate of suspicion is more common than one of trust.

The need for innovative, corner-cutting operators on the one hand, and the need to maintain rules on the other, represent the dual dilemmas of groups or organizations based on science, technology and innovation. They have to be skilled at manipulating people, procedures and paperwork; by being powerful enough to obtain a reduction in the targets and by speeding up or even increasing essential supplies to ensure that targets are achieved.

They are experts in beating the system's inherent rigidities, and dealing principally in information. They are vital to the system, though the system tries
to ignore them.

Workers in *Type B, Donkeys* (strong grid and weak group) are characterized by both isolation and subordination. An example today may be a 'live
in' nanny to a wealthy household with many children.

Donkeys are in the paradoxical position of being either or both powerless or powerful. They are powerless if they passively accept the constraints
they face. They can also be extremely disruptive, at least for a time. Resentment at the impositions caused by such jobs is common and the most typical
response is to change jobs. Other forms of 'withdrawal from work' such as
sickness and absenteeism are also higher than normal. Where constraints are
at their strongest, sabotage is not infrequent as a response, particularly where
constraints are mechanized.

People dislike being treated like a programmed robot and fiddling makes
a job much more interesting; it gives new targets and a sense of challenge as
well as hitting the boss where it hurts.

Type C, Wolves (strong grid and strong group) is the home of those 'traditional', rapidly disappearing, working-class occupations such as miners and
longshoremen. These are occupations based on groups with interdependent
and stratified roles (garbage collection crews, aeroplane crews) and stratified
groups who both live and work in 'total institutions' such as prisons, hospi-
tals, oil rigs and some hotels. Where workers do live in or close to the
premises in which they work, group activities in one area are reinforced by
cohesion in others. Such groups then come to possess considerable control
over the resources of their individual members. Once they join such groups
individuals tend to stay as members. There is no place here for the independent individualist: teamwork is vital and highly valued both for success and
for security.

Type D, Vultures (weak grid but with a strong group).Vulture jobs
include sales representatives and travellers of various kinds, like driver
deliverers, linked collectively by their common employer, common work-
base and common task, but who have considerable freedom and discretion
during their working day. These are jobs that offer autonomy and freedom
to transact but where this freedom is subject to an overarching bureaucratic control that treats workers collectively, employs them in units.
Workers in these occupations are members of a group of co-workers for
some purposes only and they can and do act individually and competitively
for others. They are not as free from constraint as are hawks, but neither
are they as constrained as donkeys; the group is not as intrusive or controlling as are wolfpacks.

There are fewer professionals among vultures, more craftsmen and most semi-
skilled. Fiddle 'fiefs' are likely to be allocated with normal work – by and
through the administrative collusion of management (at least of those at lower
levels) – and to be exploited by proven individuals. To prove themselves to their

managers brings competition into the vulture group. Problems arise when bureaucratically imposed changes which often come from higher level management disturb the fiddle earnings of all members of a group rather than involving a single individual. Where all members are affected there is likely to be a collective reaction which focuses on some generally acceptable cause, and which avoids direct reference to the real cause of the trouble. When a managerial change affects only an individual's access to fiddles, rather than the group's access as a whole, then group reactions are more likely to be absent. This is one of the important distinctions between vultures and wolves. In the latter, an attack on one is seen as an attack on all. In the former, managements find it relatively easy to discipline or scapegoat individual workers and frequently do so to discourage the others. (Mars 1984 p 33)

The typological or categorized approach outlined by Mars is a way of categorizing CWBs by type rather than dimension. It seems from this perspective that it is the nature of the job, and the very specific opportunities that it provides, which most often determine the nature of the CWBs. Further, this approach seems to imply that the dark-side behaviours are normative in those particular jobs.

This is an interesting approach but one that may seem a little crude and dated. Further, it does not fully explain individual differences within jobs. Some people cheat; others do not.

Alienation, engagement, commitment, citizenship and attachment

How do people feel toward their boss, their organization and their work? It has been said that people join organizations but leave bosses: that they are attracted to the values and images of organizations but leave because of the way they are treated by individuals.

People can feel alienated in and by organizations. Equally they can be deeply committed to them, sacrificing a great deal so that the organization survives or prospers. There are three different research areas that deal with these related issues. There is a literature on the concept of *alienation*, much discussed by sociologists, political scientists and others. There is a smaller, but growing literature on *attachment* that looks at how attachment to others may be in part a function of early attachments to care givers. There is also a fairly extensive literature on organizational *commitment*.

Researchers have distinguished, and tried to measure, work alienation at one end of the continuum and work commitment, involvement and attachment at the other. Commitment is seen as a broad attitude towards one's employing organization – especially loyalty, acceptance of goals and values and desire to be a member. Job attachment is a more focused concept, being an attitude to one's job rather than towards the organization as a whole. Other related concepts are organizational identification and loyalty.

Work alienation

For centuries theologians used the word alienation to talk about alienation from God. Then, in the nineteenth century, Karl Marx and other sociologists focused on alienation in two senses: workers feel they cannot influence what or how they produce things (alienated from the products of labour); and workers having no ownership or control of their factories and equipment (alienated from the means of production).

Philosophers have noted that alienation is associated with disappointment and isolation. Looking for some sort of personal integration the alienated person feels inconsistent and deficient in their various roles of workers, spouse, parent and manager. The alienated report difficulties in thinking, reasoning and judging. They feel they have lost their spontaneity and are emotionally flat. In essence, they feel inauthentic, not their real selves.

People can experience both *social* and *self*-alienation. Social alienation occurs when the person finds the department organization or society in which they live to be oppressive or incompatible with their values: they are socially estranged. The self-alienated person loses contact with inclinations or desires that are not in agreement with prevailing social patterns and feels incapable of controlling their own actions.

The loyal, proud worker is one who derives satisfaction from the job activity and/or the output of work. Hence the job satisfaction found among craftsmen. One can derive satisfaction or be alienated from the work itself or the job function, or both.

There are many questionnaires (for example Seemann 1959) that attempt to measure work alienation and they appear to tap into the following issues:

▷ Whether people feel they have enough authority to do their job well
▷ Whether people at work value and respect one's expertise, experience and training
▷ Whether one's work gives a sense of pride and accomplishment
▷ Whether work offers an opportunity to make independent decisions when carrying out tasks.

Below is a more extensive list of questions and statements devised to ascertain the extent to which people feel alienated at work (Shepherd 1972). They give a good insight into what is meant by alienation:

▷ *Powerlessness.* To what extent can you vary the steps involved in doing your job? To what extent can you move from your immediate work area during working hours? To what extent can you control how much work you produce? To what extent can you help decide on the methods and procedures used in your job? To what extent do you have influence over what happens to you at work?
▷ *Meaninglessness.* To what extent do you know how your job fits into the total work organization? To what extent do you know how your work

contributes to company products? To what extent does management give workers enough information about what is going on in the company? To what extent do you know how your job fits into the work of other departments? To what extent do you know how your work affects the jobs of others you work with? To what extent do you know how your job fits in with other jobs in the company?

▷ *Normlessness.* To what extent do you feel that people who get ahead in the company deserve it? To what extent do you feel that pull and connection get a person ahead in the company? To what extent do you feel that to get ahead in the company you would have to become a good 'politician'? To what extent do you feel that getting ahead in the company is based on ability?

▷ *Instrumental work orientation.* Your job is something you do to earn a living – most of your real interests are centred outside your job. Money is the most rewarding reason for working. Working is a necessary evil to provide things your family and you want.

▷ *Self-evaluative involvement.* You would like people to judge you for the most part by what you spend your money on, rather than by how you make your money. Success in the things you do away from the job is more important to your opinion of yourself than success in your work career. To you your work is only a small part of who you are.

Other questionnaires look at related issues such as the propensity to leave as well as organizational frustration. The latter looks at things such as people believing there are too many petty and arbitrary rules at work; that work is boring, monotonous and unfulfilling and that people feel trapped in the job.

Alienated workers may be passive or aggressive but most likely passive-aggressive. Whilst they may not become actively involved in betrayal by theft or whistle-blowing it may be that they do not report others they know doing so or even encourage them.

Most researchers agree that people at the bottom of hierarchies are most likely to feel alienation from their work. However, the work role, the group or department and the organizational context all have an effect on alienation. It is often a clear function of the social controls that people experience at work.

One way to try to understand the concept of work alienation is to see how researchers have tried to measure it. One group (Aiken and Hage 1966) differentiated alienation from work (disappointed with career, professional development and inability to fulfil professional norms) and alienation from expressive relations (dissatisfaction with social relations, supervisors and fellow workers). Eight questions were posed to get at this concept.

Alienation from work

1 How satisfied are you that you have been given enough authority by your board of directors to do your job well?

2 How satisfied are you with your present job when you compare it to similar positions in the state?

3 How satisfied are you with the progress you are making towards the goals that you set for yourself in your present position?
4 On the whole, how satisfied are you that (your superior) accepts you as a professional expert to the degree to which you are entitled by reason of position, training and experience?
5 On the whole, how satisfied are you with your present job when you consider the expectations you had when you took the job?
6 How satisfied are you with your present job in the light of career expectations?

Alienation from expressive relations
7 How satisfied are you with your supervisor?
8 How satisfied are you with your fellow workers?

But is the alienated worker one who is likely to steal, cheat or partake in sabotage? Often proactive acts such as stealing, sabotage or whistle-blowing are the result of anger. At the heart of alienation is passivity, withdrawal and inaction. The alienated are certainly more likely to go absent and follow commands to strike. They are likely to 'work to rule' and be unproductive but are not likely to be active participants in counterproductive practices at work.

It could be argued that alienation if not 'the mother of deviance' is certainly a cousin. That is, most organization deviants feel alienated from their organization. How they come to feel that way can take many forms. However, it may be true that alienated employees are more likely to become disengaged than destructive. There seem at the heart of the concept of alienation notions of apathy, of withdrawal and of passivity rather than pro-activity. The alienated may be differentiated from the angry, though it is possible that there is stage-wise process with the two strong emotions preceding one another.

Organizational commitment and attachment

This concept refers to positive feelings towards the organization. Commitment is not the same as satisfaction: it refers to the extent to which employees identify with, are involved with, and are unwilling to leave their organization. Commitment is generally viewed as a broad but very relevant attitude to one's employing organization and is about loyalty, endorsing of values and acceptance of goals. People at work have multiple commitments: to their work group, their supervisor, top management and the organization as a whole. The committed worker is embedded in the organization. Attachment is focused more on the particular job than on the organization as a whole. Job commitment is related to low levels of absenteeism and voluntary turnover. More importantly perhaps, it is related to a high level of willingness to share and make personal sacrifices to benefit the organization as a whole. In short, commitment is highly desirable.

		Commitment to boss/work group	
		Low	High
Commitment to top management and organizations	Low	Uncommitted	Weakly committed
	High	Globally committed	Committed

Figure 6.2 **Comparison of the work group and the top management on commitment**

There are many similar constructs in this area: occupational commitment (strength of motivation to work in a chosen career role), organizational commitment (strength of identification with and involvement in a particular organization), job involvement (state of psychological identification with the job), and work involvement (work attitudes about the job in general). Hackett et al. (2001) believe they are related thus: work involvement determines job involvement which predicts both occupational and organizational commitment which in turn predicts people's intention to withdraw from the job.

Researchers have distinguished between the focus of commitment and the bases of commitment. Consider first the focus of commitment that is about who you are committed to within the organization. One can have quite different feelings of commitment to top management, boss or supervisor, colleagues and clients, the union, support staff, and so on. Figure 6.2 is a useful way of thinking about these differences.

It is not unusual for people to be 'locally committed'. They feel loyalty and affection to their boss and colleagues and their local department but care little for the organization as a whole. Propinquity or frequent contact are the real determinants of affection and thence commitment.

Organizational commitment may be differentiated into different types. First, there is *investment* commitment. Over time people invest in organizations not only through buying shares and compulsory pension plans but also through their hard work and knowledge. People talk of 'having given their best years' to an organization knowing that beyond a certain age their chances of employment become reduced. They make a cost–benefit type judgement and conclude that leaving the organization is more costly than staying in it.

Second, there is *value* or *goal congruence* and commitment. This essentially means that people perceive that their personal goals are nicely aligned to that of the organization. These values may be about a wide range of issues but lead some people to being committed to organizations that are not widely popular.

Third, there is *social* commitment. For many colleagues, friends at work are very important. One's entire social network may be built around the workplace. Social identity, social support and social contact are latent benefits of the work experiences. It is not unusual for the major source of a person's commitment to be other people in the organization.

Essentially organizational commitment has three separate but related components:

1 Acceptance of the explicit and implicit goals and values of the organization
2 A willingness to work on behalf of, and exert effort for the organization
3 Having a strong desire to remain loyal to, and affiliated with the organization.

There seem to be both personal and organizational factors that are related to commitment. Naturally these are related to job characteristics, (jobs with responsibility, opportunity to demonstrate skills), nature of reward (salary, profit sharing schemes), alternative employment opportunities (one's worth in the job market), treatment of newcomers and so on. There are a number of personal factors that appear to relate to commitment:

▷ Older employees with a service of loyalty ethos seem more likely to feel commitment
▷ Length of service is quite naturally a predictor but it is not certain if this is strictly linear
▷ Those with fewer personal financial difficulties seem more committed
▷ People who are sent abroad and are properly prepared for overseas sojourn seem more committed to their parent company at home
▷ Engineers and scientists seem less committed than other occupational groups
▷ Government/public sector employees seem less committed than employees in private, entrepreneurial organizations.

The organizational factors are relatively easy to predict:

▷ The most important is the employees' perception of how committed they felt their organization was to them
▷ The more people felt their managers and colleagues supported them the more committed they feel
▷ The more diverse or heterogeneous the workforce, the lower the commitment
▷ Curiously, the more women in the work group, the lower the commitment among the men, but the more men in the work group, the higher the commitment of women.

Similarly there are a whole range of questionnaires on organizations' commitment. Many have questions divided into sections that attempt to measure identification with the organization (adopting as one's own the goals and values of the organization), job involvement, loyalty (feeling of affection for and attachment to the organization), willingness to uphold the norms and rules of the organization, and dedication to continuing commitment. The questions refer to pride in the organization, a desire to stay working there, and feeling part of the organization.

How does one measure commitment? Fortunately there is no shortage of questionnaires that have been well tested. Porter and Smith (1970) saw commitment as a stable, affective reaction that means people are willing to give something of themselves in order to contribute to their organization. They see commitment to have three factors: a strong belief in, and acceptance of, the organization's goals and values; a readiness to exert considerable effort on behalf of the organization; and a strong desire to remain a member of that organization. Their questionnaire has 15 attitude statements:

1 I am willing to put in a great deal of effort beyond that normally expected in order to help this organization be successful
2 I talk up this organization to my friends as a great organization to work for
3 I feel very little loyalty to this organization ®
4 I would accept almost any type of job assignment in order to keep working for this organization
5 I find that my values and the organization's values are very similar
6 I am proud to tell others that I am part of this organization
7 I could just as well be working for a different organization as long as the type of work is similar ®
8 This organization really inspires the very best in me in the way of job performance
9 It would take very little change in my present circumstances to cause me to leave this organization ®
10 I am extremely glad that I chose this organization to work for, over others I was considering at the time I joined
11 There's not too much to be gained by sticking with this organization indefinitely ®
12 Often, I find it difficult to agree with this organization's policies on important matters relating to its employees ®
13 I really care about the fate of this organization
14 For me, this is the best of all possible organizations for which to work
15 Deciding to work for this organization was a definite mistake on my part ®

Responses: Strongly disagree; Moderately disagree; Slightly disagree; Neither disagree nor agree; Slightly agree; Moderately agree; Strongly agree; scored 1 to 7 respectively. ® is a reverse item

Buchanan (1974) devised a 23-item, three-factor scale to measure commitment defined as 'a partisan, affective attachment to the goals and values of an organization, to one's role in relation to goals and values, and to the organization for its own sake, apart from its purely instrumental worth' (p 533).

A few researchers have attempted to measure *job attachment*. Koch and Steers (1978) defined attachment as congruence between one's actual and ideal jobs, an identification with one's chosen occupation, and a reluctance to seek different employment. Their measure had just four questions:

1   If you were completely free to go into any type of job you wanted, what would your choice be?
    Want the same type of job you now hold; Want to retire, not work at all; Prefer some other job to the kind you have; scored 5, 3 and 1 respectively.
2   How often have you thought very seriously about making a real effort to enter a new and different type of occupation?
    Very often; Once in a while; Hardly ever; Never; scored 1, 2, 4 and 5 respectively.
3   Check one of the following statements that best tells how you feel about changing your job.
    I would quit my job now if I had anything else to do; I would take almost any other job in which I could earn as much as I am earning now; My job is as good as the average and I would just as soon have it as any other job, but would change jobs if I could make more money; I am not eager to change jobs, but would do so if I could make more money; I do not want to change jobs even for more money, because the one I have now is a good one; scored 1 to 5 respectively.
4   How well would you say your job measures up to the kind you wanted when you first took it? Is it very much like the kind of job you wanted? Somewhat like the job you wanted? Not very much like the kind you wanted?
    Very much; Somewhat; Not very much; scored 5, 3 and 1 respectively.

Organizational citizenship

As we discussed earlier, there is yet another concept in this area, which is known as organizational citizenship behaviour (OCB) and which is commonly defined as exceeding job requirements. It is, however, not clear where the boundary is between in-role or extra-role behaviour or in other words between the formal job requirements and extra activities. It is also not clear what sort of behaviours might make up this list. For instance Morrison (1994), in a study of daytime clerical employees in a large US medical centre, specified 20 possible citizenship behaviours:

1   Covering for co-workers who are absent or on a break.
2   Helping others who have heavy workloads.
3   Helping orient new people even when not asked.
4   Helping others with work when they have been absent.
5   Giving time to help others with work-related problems.
6   Volunteering to do things without being asked.
7   Helping people outside department when they have a problem.
8   Helping patients and visitors if they need assistance.
9   Arriving early so you are ready to work when shift begins.

10 Being punctual every day regardless of weather, traffic, and so on.
11 Not spending time on personal telephone conversations.
12 Not spending time in non-work-related conversation.
13 Coming to work early if needed.
14 Not taking excess time off, even if you have extra sick days.
15 Attending voluntary functions that help the medical centre's image.
16 Attending voluntary meetings considered important.
17 Helping organize departmental get-togethers.
18 Keeping up with changes and developments in the medical centre.
19 Reading and keeping up with organizational announcements.
20 Using judgement to assess what is best for the medical centre.

Interestingly many of these employees saw these behaviours as in-role rather than extra-role in the sense that they were expected.

In another study Organ and Lingl (1995) measured 18 citizenship behaviours:

1   Always follows the rules of the company and department.
2   Demonstrates concern about the image of the company.
3   Always treats company property with care.
4   Attends and participates in meetings regarding the company.
5   Respects the rights of others.
6   Never abuses his or her rights and privileges.
7   Stays informed about the company.
8   Maintains a clean workplace.
9   Helps others who have been absent.
10 Helps others who have heavy workloads.
11 Helps make others productive.
12 Offers suggestions to improve operations.
13 Helps orient new people.
14 Shares personal property with others to help their work.
15 Attendance at work is above average.
16 Gives advance notice when unable to come to work.
17 Is always on time.
18 Always completes work on time.

They found that these 18 behaviours broke down into three factors they labelled generalized compliance, altruism and time/attendance. They found as predicted that the more satisfied employee tended to take part in most citizenship behaviours. They also found that the personality variable of conscientiousness was directly related to citizenship behaviours.

What do companies do to enhance commitment?

Companies who are aware of, interested in and indeed committed to increasing commitment in their staff try to facilitate the process by such things as:

▷ Making the workforce dependent on the company.
▷ Increasing the opportunity costs of job transfer.
▷ Providing an attractive, integrated, remuneration including housing, transportation and so on.
▷ Improving and integrating of skill, part of which is not transferable.
▷ Offering job security and growing stability of employment.

In a sense what organizations want to do is reduce job mobility while making people highly specialized. Making it difficult to leave is, of course, not the same, as making it attractive to stay. Commitment is an affective and emotional as a well as a rational issue. It is also a moral one. All organizations want employees who feel a moral responsibility to stay because of a series of reciprocated, subtle, mutual obligations and rights that bestow particular privileges but also specific commitments.

The committed employee has trust in the organization: trust that good-will, loyalty and hard work will be recognized, rewarded and reciprocated.

What sorts of factors may influence commitment? The following are possibilities:

1 *Size of the organization:* On the one hand, big organizations tend to be very impersonal and possibly bureaucratic but, on the other hand, they do seem to offer more possibility of advance by promotion.
2 *Age of the organization:* Better established, more stable organizations may both attract a different type of person and keep them. Those who adapt to the working conditions are more likely to feel committed and more likely to stay.
3 *Location of the organization:* This may reflect on urban–rural difference or simple opportunities to change job. Thus, if the organization is located in an area where there are many other jobs available this fact may reduce an individual's commitment.
4 *Wage structure:* If there is an internal labour market that favours insiders and if wage differentials are thought to be equitable, these factors may well facilitate commitment.

It has been the central message of this book that commitment and loyalty can be managed but that the process is continuous and begins at selection and only ends at the exit interview.

Conclusion

This chapter has been about measurement. It first examined self-report questionnaires and measures of integrity, or the lack of it. It is indeed interesting to note that integrity is nearly always measured by its opposite. The assumption in absence of CWB implies integrity, which is clearly not the case.

Psychometricians tend to prefer using questionnaires that attempt to measure behavioural dispositions along specific dimensions. Others, like the anthropologists, prefer the typological approach which prefers to categorize types of deviants. One of the most interesting insights from the latter approach is that it implies it is the nature of the job and the very specific CWBs that are important.

The second section of the chapter looked at the measurement of concepts related to integrity. The first was alienation, which is a passive form of disillusionment and may be a stage that occurs before an employee chooses to get involved in CWBs. However, to understand disloyalty it is equally important to look at measures of organizational commitment and attachment as well as at citizenship behaviour. Rather than focus on the dark side they do the opposite, looking at beliefs and behaviours of the attached, committed, loyal and highly desirable employee.

Two conclusions are important: the absence of CWBs does not imply loyalty any more than the absence of commitment implies disloyalty. Most people probably feel neither extreme, though they can be managed or mismanaged in either direction. Second, dark- and bright-side behaviours do not occur by chance. They can, and must be, managed; it is possible to turn-around people and organizations to foster loyalty and commitment where they (or even their opposite) did not exist.

7 Integrity Testing

Introduction

For over 50 years psychologists dreamt of devising robust and reliable tests to measure the integrity of people – a notion that has been very attractive to many employers. The idea of having a good (cheap and efficient) way of testing honesty and integrity has been a holy grail. Fifty years of test development and evaluation have led to the following conclusions:

> There is now a reasonable body of evidence showing that integrity tests have some validity for predicting a variety of criteria that are relevant to organizations. This research does not say that tests of this sort will eliminate theft or dishonesty at work, but it does suggest that individuals who receive poor scores on these tests tend to be less desirable employees. (Murphy 1993 p 215)

> Thus, a large body of validity evidence consistently shows scores on integrity tests to be positively related to both a range of counterproductive behaviours and supervisory ratings of overall performance. However, virtually all the research has been done by test publishers, leading sceptics to question whether only successes are publicised. (Sackett 1994 p 74)

> Intentional distortion on self-report measures is often assumed to be a serious threat to criterion-related validity of such measures. The preponderance of evidence to date suggests that it may not be as serious a problem as is often thought. Indeed the evidence suggests that validity if it is affected at all, is affected only modestly. Though more research is needed, this conclusion may be more accurate for moderately subtle tests, than for overt, obvious tests. In general, however, the evidence indicates that integrity test scores can be trusted. (Hough 1996 p 103)

Estimates of the use and growth of integrity tests come almost exclusively from the US. The following are typical estimates from the 1980s and 90s:

1 Around 5000 companies use pre-employment integrity tests to screen around 5,000,000 applicants
2 Between 5 and 20 per cent of all US companies use some form of testing for some forms of job (highly sensitive jobs in particular)
3 There are 40–50 commercially available tests in the market as well as various in-house measures developed for very specific purposes.

Every organization would prefer to have honest, dependable and trustworthy employees. In some organizations such as police forces, banks, and the military it is essential. Hence they often invest a lot in techniques for assessing honesty and integrity and detecting deception to be used in selection. Equally, these techniques can be used to 'vet' people in the organization or attempt to establish guilt after the event. However, it is in the area of pre-employment screening that they are most used.

Integrity testing at work

Integrity tests, also called honesty tests, are pencil-and-paper questionnaires designed to assess a very wide variety of work-related behaviours. These include:

▷ Dishonesty and general untrustworthiness: unauthorized use of company information; forgery.
▷ Alcohol/drug abuse: selling, using on the job, coming to work with a hangover/intoxicated.
▷ Deception and deliberate misrepresentation; tax fraud and cheating; bribery.
▷ Violent behaviour: physical assault on others at work.
▷ 'Maladjustment': blackmail.
▷ Job instability/excessive absenteeism, turnover/time theft, coming late to work; using sick leave when not sick.
▷ Theft of cash, merchandise and property: misuse of discount privileges; embezzlement.
▷ Poor conscientiousness/prudence; no work ethic; intentionally going slow or doing sloppy work.
▷ Failure to implement company policy.
▷ Alienation attitudes: the opposite of commitment and engagement.
▷ Inattention to safety rules; causing preventable accidents.
▷ Ludditism and damage to property; wilful damage and waste; vandalism.
▷ Poor time keeping; having unauthorized work breaks.
▷ Sabotage.
▷ Sexual harassment.

Anyone examining this list will be struck by two things: first, these behaviours go far beyond the simple concept of integrity and, second, the list contains diverse and unrelated issues. Depending on your view alienation attitudes are somewhat different from sabotage! The idea, however, is that integrity/honesty is relevant to all of these behaviours because, in some sense, they all reflect a level of dishonesty.

Historically, self-reported honesty tests contain items of few different types:

▷ Confessions – admissions of illegal, disapproved, prohibitive or antisocial behaviour.

▷ Attitudes/opinions – about the above types of behaviour.
▷ Self-descriptions of personality and thought patterns around illegal activities and moral issues.
▷ Reactions to hypothetical situations.

Some tests try to veil or disguise their purpose. Others assume low integrity is associated with thrill seeking, non-conformity and low conscientiousness. Many tests have traditionally been used: either to screen out undesirable applicants; to investigate crimes for current employees, to vet those being considered for promotion or transfer or just to assess the current moral beliefs of people within the organization. Integrity tests were typically used with supervisory-level personnel especially in retail and financial companies.

The sorts of options people have to do honesty testing include: the lie detector (polygraph); reference checking or background investigations; drug testing; use of application forms (biodata); integrity interviewing; and personality testing.

There has been a great growth of interest in, and use of, integrity tests. However, personality and other similar tests have been used since the 1930s to identify 'agitators, malcontents and thugs' (Zickar 2001). The US data suggests as many as 6000 companies employ one of the 50 or so tests on the market using 25–5,000,000 tests per annum (Miner and Capps 1996). There seems both demand and supply: the test publishers respond to the market need.

Popularity is put down to various specific but predictable issues:

1 *Increase in theft:* though initially it was lower-level blue collar workers, typically in supermarkets, that were considered for testing, more interest has been given to white collar employees. Surveys in the US have yielded the following statistics: arrests for fraud have doubled in most western countries. Reasonable estimates of the value of theft stand at $100 billion (£70 billion). Also a quarter to a third of employees (depending on sector) get involved in theft every year.

2 *Alcohol and drug problems:* reduction in the cost of alcohol, and its acceptance in the society has no doubt affected consumption in and out of work. The same applies to a range of illegal 'recreational' and hard drugs. It is estimated that random drug testing with younger people would reveal that about 10% were taking drugs which probably affects their productivity and can lead to addiction.

3 *Workplace violence and bullying:* frustration due to stress and other factors, including a corporate culture which condones it, means that violence in the workplace, especially serious physical assault, as well as psychological bullying, appears to be on the increase.

4 *Legal liabilities:* the cost of dishonesty, especially law suits brought against a company, means companies see honesty as a good investment. Where a company is found negligent, the compensation fee to aggrieved

workers can be astronomical. Having honest employees and managers with integrity makes good financial sense.

5   *The difficulty of sacking:* most employers will describe how difficult it is to 'discharge' a poor or problematic employee. More and more seriously problematic employees find it convenient to argue that their dismissal is based on sex, age, race, religion, handicap, sexual orientation, and so on.

Another reason for the growth in integrity testing is quite simply the fact that the use of the lie detector/polygraph has become more problematic (see below). So with a favoured method less available and respectable and evidence of increasing counterproductive behaviours at work it seems natural to resort to any integrity tests on the market.

'Honesty' screening

An employer interested in 'honesty' screening has a number of different options:

1   *Polygraph/lie detector.* These come in different forms. The old ones measured blood pressure, pulse, sweat gland activity and breathing. Newer models measure the electrical activity in the brain or voice stress analysis. Once popular in the US its use has never taken off so much in other countries and there is now serious doubt about its validity. It seems popularly accepted that eliciting an accurate confession depends more on the skills of the examiner than the characteristics of the testee. Legislation in the US and elsewhere has significantly reduced its usage.

2   *Vetting.* This is also called reference checking or background/biographical investigations. Essentially this involves checking up on what applicants have said or written about themselves and their past work, education and reward. Typically, referees are contacted by phone but so are educational establishments, banks, even medical staff. The latter course is expensive and may require detective agencies. However, the former is common. Indeed people are often happy to say things 'off the record' which they would be much less happy to put on paper. Issues around slanderous (spoken) or libellous (written) communication have made people very conscious about defamation and hence 'informers' are far less forthcoming, making this problematic.

3   *Drug testing.* Taking urine and blood samples is useful and legal but some companies prefer not to do it because of the sort of impression that it conveys and also because of charges of invasion of privacy. Also, these tests cannot always pick up those likely in the future to have addictive problems.

4   *Application form/biographical data research.* This method seeks retrospectively to look at the differences between honest and dishonest employees for signs of future possible problems. A weight is given to

certain answers and if that score exceeds a specific number they are screened out. Consider the following characteristics found to predict CWBs in US supermarket employees:

▷ Does *not* want relative contacted in case of emergency.
▷ Substandard appearance on application.
▷ Does not own their own car.
▷ Applicant recently consulted a doctor.

There are well-known problems with this method. It openly discriminates against certain groups and the weights/scores often seem very unreliable, that is, highly specific to the organization.

1 *Integrity interviewing.* This is often little more than a structured interview that asks obvious and predictable questions and seeks to observe verbal, vocal and non-verbal signs of lying like higher voice pitch, speech errors, increased blinking, frequent swallowing, fast and shallow breathing and false smiles. It does require some considerable expertise. The jury remains out on the validity of these methods.
2 *Personality tests and assessment.* These come in very many forms, for instance: *graphological* analysis which has little or no evidence of validity; *projective* tests where people tell stories about pictures they see and project their personality (motives) into those stories but are still thought of as highly unreliable; *personality* tests around issues of morality, conscientiousness. We will discuss these in detail.

Reactions to integrity tests

How do people react when asked to do an integrity test? Are they offended, insulted or accepting? One study looked at *student* reactions to honesty testing as an abstract concept (Ryan and Sackett 1987). They found:

▷ 68% felt it was appropriate for an employer to administer such a test.
▷ 10% would refuse to take such a test.
▷ 25% would enjoy being asked to take such a test.
▷ 42% felt this type of test was an invasion of privacy.
▷ 46% said if they had two comparable job offers, they would reject the company using such a test.
▷ 26% would resent being asked to take such a test.
▷ 59% felt that a test such as this is sometimes an appropriate selection procedure.
▷ 33% believe that administering a test such as this reflects negatively on the organization.
▷ 42% indicated that being asked to take such a test would not affect their view of the organization.
▷ 56% indicated that tests such as this are routinely used in industry.

In a more realistic study with *job applicants,* Jones (1991) found:

▷ 90% felt it was appropriate for an employer to administer such a test.
▷ 4% would refuse to take such a test.
▷ 63% would enjoy being asked to take such a test.
▷ 11% felt this type of test was an invasion of privacy.
▷ 2% said if they had two comparable job offers, they would reject the company using such a test.
▷ 3% would resent being asked to take such a test.
▷ 82% felt that a test such as this is sometimes an appropriate selection procedure.
▷ 5% believe that administering a test such as this reflects negatively on the organization.
▷ 80% indicated that being asked to take such a test would not affect their view of the organization.
▷ 80% indicated that tests such as this are routinely used in industry.

One recent study looking at seasonal student employees found, as predicted, that those who were given clear advance notification of work monitoring, and thought it fair, were much more likely to return to the organization the following year compared to those with no warning or who thought it unfair (Hovorka-Mead et al. 2002). The central question is whether these tests measure loyalty or the opposite.

The issue is that there is a thin line between what may be seen as benign and what as intrusive/invasive monitoring technologies. Zweig and Webster (2002) found that employees' acceptance of monitoring systems was a function of their perceived usefulness, fairness and privacy invasion which, in turn, were dependent on the precise characteristics of the monitoring system involved and the justification for its use. They argue:

> There is a delicate balance in the line between benign and invasive. People form expectations about the degree of personal information they will communicate with others in their daily lives. Often, there are shared expectations that are respected by all and serve to guide social interactions among them. When these expectations are violated, people can experience feelings of discomfort, embarrassment and even anger. From these studies, it was suggested that when awareness systems are put in place, employees might be unsure about the expectations guiding their own and others' behaviours. That is, awareness systems appear to cross this line and are considered invasive. Thus, we believe that the notion of boundary violations represents a key construct in explaining employees' reactions to technologies such as awareness systems. Awareness systems violate boundaries for sharing personal information with others, constrain employees' ability to control how they present themselves to other, and are construed as unfair. Even if attempts are made to respect individuals through manipulations of the system's characteristics, overall violations of psychological boundaries can lead to rejection. (pp 627–8)

What would be particularly interesting would be to compare these results with those from other tests. Would people be happier to complete ability or personality tests than honesty tests? Are people simply wary of tests in general? It seems many people tend to accept tests are job relevant and many even find them enjoyable.

Much, no doubt, depends on the type of test used, the way it is presented, the candidate's previous experience of testing as well as their personality and values. Certainly, results appear to indicate that neither extreme view is correct: people neither happily embrace the idea of being tested, nor find the whole idea irrelevant, immoral and offensive.

Self-report tests of integrity

There have been pencil-and-paper tests for over 50 years that have attempted to measure integrity. Those have tended to grow over the past decade or so as issues with integrity appear to have increased. These tests are fairly varied but appear to concentrate on the following four areas. First, direct, explicit admissions of dishonest behaviour (lying, cheating, stealing, whistle-blowing). Second, opinions/attitudes about the acceptability of dishonest behaviour (prevalence in society, justification of causes). Third, traits, value systems and biographical factors thought to be associated with dishonesty. Fourth, reactions to hypothetical situations that do or do not feature dishonest behaviour.

Hogan and Hogan (1989), for instance, describe the design and validation of a personality questionnaire that predicted individuals who engaged in various counterproduction behaviours at work. It also predicted the opposite: that is, persons who were liked by co-workers and supervisors. Murphy and Lee (1994) showed that the trait of conscientiousness was powerfully correlated with integrity – as one may expect. Conscientiousness is associated with dependability, perseverance and achievement orientation while integrity is about honesty so these are not interchangeable measures but they are logically related. Marcus et al. (2000) noted integrity related to three personality variables: agreeableness, conscientiousness and emotional stability.

Often these self-report measures can be distinguished in terms of whether they are overt, explicit, 'clear-purpose' tests or personality-based, 'veiled purpose' tests. The sorts of issues that an overt test examines include: honesty attitudes/admission of previous dishonesty; substance abuse, drug avoidance; personal past achievements; service orientation, customer relations; work values; clerical, mathematical, verbal skills, abilities and aptitudes.

On the other hand, the 'veiled purpose' tests are more likely to try to measure conscientiousness, dependability, prudence; hostility to rules and regulations; impulsivity, thrill seeking, disinhibition; alienation and lack of commitment.

Recently Bennett and Robinson (2000) devised such a measure. This inevitably involves defining specific items that make up deviance. Table 7.1 shows 28 items from an earlier measure (Bennett and Robinson 2000).

Table 7.1 Deviant workplace behaviours

Item		Participation rate %
1	Worked on a personal matter instead of work for your employer	84.3
2	Taken property from work without permission	51.8
3	Spent too much time fantasizing or daydreaming instead of working	77.4
4	Made fun of someone at work	77.8
5	Falsified a receipt to get reimbursed for more money than you spent on business expenses	24.6
6	Said something hurtful to someone at work	55.2
7	Taken an additional or a longer break than is acceptable at your workplace	78.5
8	Repeated a rumour or gossip about your company	72.5
9	Made an ethnic, religious, or racial remark or joke at work	52.5
10	Come in late to work without permission	70.0
11	Littered your work environment	28.5
12	Cursed someone at work	50.5
13	Called in sick when you were not	57.8
14	Told someone about the lousy place where you work	58.9
15	Lost temper while at work	78.8
16	Neglected to follow your boss's instructions	60.6
17	Intentionally worked slower than you could have worked	54.1
18	Discussed confidential company information with an unauthorized person	33.3
19	Left work early without permission	51.9
20	Played a mean prank on someone at work	35.7
21	Left your work for someone else to finish	48.6
22	Acted rudely toward someone at work	53.0
23	Repeated a rumour or gossip about your boss or co-workers	69.1
24	Made an obscene comment at work	48.4
25	Used an illegal drug or consumed alcohol on the job	25.9
26	Put little effort into your work	64.0
27	Publicly embarrassed someone at work	33.9
28	Dragged out work in order to get overtime	26.0

Note: Responses ranged from 1 (never) to 7 (daily). N = 226.
[a] Percentage of respondents who indicated that they had participated in the behaviour at least once in the last year.

Source: Adapted from Bennett and Robinson 2000 p 352.

In the end they developed a two-part question: one part measuring *organizational* deviance (behaviours directly harmful to the organization) and the other *interpersonal* deviance (behaviours directly harmful to individuals). They also provided validity data for their questionnaire. Again what strikes one is the variability in behaviours from nearly trivial to very serious; from everyday to rare; from generally condoned to quite unacceptable. This is an important issue. The assumption is that honesty/integrity is a stable 'trait' that informs *all* behaviour at work. Some looking at these items may say those who are 'grumpy' or 'emotionally volatile' or who have significant responsibilities outside the workplace are unfairly labelled as lacking in honesty.

Clearly one obvious advantage of the so-called veiled purpose test is that they are less open to faking or not admitting wrongdoing. Faking threatens test reliability. However, it has been shown to be significantly reduced when people are aware that the investigators (potential employers) have (many) other sources of information about their honesty.

There are different themes tapped into by self-report integrity tests. Further there is an assumption that the honest, reliable person with integrity acts somewhat differently from the dishonest person on this dimension. Thus:

1 *Report incidences of explicit dishonesty:* Honest people will honestly report that they have been dishonest in the past.
2 *Leniency towards dishonesty:* Honest people are likely to excuse, forgive or explain away dishonesty in others and themselves.
3 *Rationalization for thieving:* Honest people are less likely to try to excuse or provide rationalization for theft in organizations.
4 *Brooding and rumination about theft:* Honest people are less likely to even think (plan, plot, fantasize) about thieving from their organization.
5 *Rejecting dishonest norms:* Honest people are likely to question or reject dishonest behaviour of all sorts that are perceived within the organization to be acceptable.
6 *Impulse control:* Honest people are less likely to act on their impulses preferring to think through an issue before acting.
7 *Punitive attitude:* Honest people have less punitive attitudes to themselves and others.

Objections to integrity testing

Integrity testing techniques vary greatly in technology if not in purpose. These can probably be broken down into three types.

1 Physiological-based assessments like the polygraph/lie detector or those methods that seek to analyse voice stress patterns.
2 Behaviourally based assessments that look at visual and vocal concomitants of stress and deception like stuttering, nose touching and so on.
3 Self-report methods based on an analysis of interviews (tape-recorded and transcribed) as well as by questionnaire.

They are, however, all based on the premise that responses to questions about *past* attitudes, behaviours and values can be validly used to infer *future* levels of honesty. That is, the score on a test (of whatever type) is able to predict a wide range of dishonest, illegal or unacceptable behaviours.

These tests naturally cause a great deal of interest and discussion. Some reject the idea of using them at all. Others object that they are of limited worth (validity) and frequently mislabel people. If tests were totally valid people would be neatly and accurately categorized as honest or dishonest (given some cut-off score). But it is inevitable (as with our entire legal system) that guilty people are judged honest and more importantly vice versa. Some organizations argue that even if the validity is not perfect, it may be better to reject a candidate who is in fact honest than let one (or indeed many) dishonest person join the organization. Most of the debate concerns the innocent labelled guilty rather than the equally (or more) worrying situation of the dishonest being admitted to the workforce.

A *second* objection lies in the assumption that dishonesty is a stable characteristic of individuals. The one side argues that dishonesty is primary a function of the individual – their personality, values, conscience – and therefore integrity tests are in principle useful. Others argue that honesty is much less stable and a function of situational factors such as poor security, seeing others steal, being offered bribes. In this sense people may be very honest in one situation and quite dishonest in another. Thus some situations provoke dishonesty, others not. Equally, it could be argued that people are honest about some issues (their childhood, their leisure activities) but not others (tax and money issues, relationships and sex).

Over 80 years ago, psychologists found children seemed particularly variable in the honesty behaviour and a situational view presided. But later research and analysis of the data have shown stable individual differences in honesty. However, there remains sufficient substantial evidence to suggest that certain external and situational factors can influence honesty. This means that there are inevitably limits to what one can achieve with any integrity test, no matter of what kind.

A *third* objection is that paradoxically it is the more honest person who admits to dishonesty in the past. In this sense tests are better at detecting 'goodies' rather than 'baddies'. Tests assume that those who more freely admit dishonesty in the past are more likely to do so in the future or that individuals who have relatively lenient attitudes towards wrongdoing may be more likely to violate laws and policies. Indeed the opposite may apply.

A *fourth* objection is that cultural factors determine the meaning of honesty and dishonesty. A gift in one culture is a bribe in another. Traditional employment patterns in one society represent nepotism in a second. The argument is that honesty and integrity are socially defined with no absolutes. Hence it is wrong and unjust to judge a person by the dictates of a different national or indeed corporate culture. In short, integrity tests are culture dependent.

A *fifth* objection is that some people do not know the differences between right and wrong. The law makes allowance for children and certain types of mental illness. The psychopath or sociopath is, in Victorian terminology, a moral imbecile, in the sense that they do (and cannot) distinguish between right and wrong. Tests – even the polygraph – will not detect them because they feel no guilt. The implication is that there are personality factors that are associated with wrongdoing.

In the US, where these tests are most widely used, the issue of the violation of civil rights is now discussed. But tests are now becoming broader to include everything from emotional instability, through drug taking to potential for violence. Thus integrity testing is controversial. However, there is comparatively little evidence that either job applicants or incumbents find them objectionable in practice or principle.

Certainly some people do indicate 'principled dissent' to integrity testing which is seen as non-job-related and as an invasion of privacy. However, one study showed that compared with non-drug-users, drug users had stronger negative reactions to personality tests, overt integrity tests and urine analysis (Rosse et al. 1996). One may be tempted to conclude that those who 'protesteth too much' may be doing so for a good reason.

Do integrity tests work?

The most obvious and fundamental questions about honesty testing must be about *validity*. What is the evidence that they measure (only) honesty and can differentiate between the honest and dishonest? Over the past decade there have been various studious and excellent reviews. Those who are positive conclude that integrity tests are often good at detecting counterproductive behaviours as well as supervisors' ratings of good/poor performance. Others believe that the 'jury is out' and that we need more high quality, disinterested and sceptical research before making a judgement. Whatever the evidence and however it is reviewed, it is apparent that the debate for and against tests is driven by strong emotions.

Whilst validity is always the single and simply most important criterion of any test, there are others, some of which have a direct effect on validity. These include reliability, dimensionality, and so on but, perhaps the most important is *fakability*. Can clever (and dishonest) people 'beat the test' and come out looking virtuous when they are not? This problem applies to all tests but particularly to honesty tests. Results suggest that one can catch dissimulators but that there is a general, and quite understandable, trend to overemphasize honesty.

The issue of course with testing is the problem of false positives and negatives that is, classifying the honest as dishonest and vice versa. Both are equally undesirable but they do have quite different consequences. Sackett (1994 pp 75–6) reviewing this important issue concluded:

> An important aspect of the misclassification issue is that misclassification rates are only interpretable in comparison with alternatives. A test that mis-classifies, say 25% of test takers may prove dismal, or it may prove a great improvement over available alternatives.

A good example of the failure to apply this form of analysis to the misclassification problem can be found in comments made by Senator Edward Kennedy during debate about the Employee Polygraph Protection Act. Kennedy noted that even if one accepts the claims of polygraph proponents that polygraph examinations have an accuracy rate of 95%, if 1 million pre-employment polygraph exams are administered annually, a 5% error rate means that 50,000 innocent job applicants are mis-classified. Kennedy argued that any device that mis-classifies 50,000 per year should be banned. This argument reduces all personnel selection to the absurd, in that all selection devices, from tests to interviews, are certainly less than perfectly accurate, and thus should be banned by Kennedy's standards. Yet the alternative – random selection or first come, first-served – results in higher rates of misclassification than any selection device with nonzero validity.

Whilst it is not difficult to make a case for the use of integrity tests, it seems ironic that test publishers seem to make possibly fraudulent claims for the efficacy of their tests in detecting dishonest people and thence reducing theft and shrinkage problems. Honesty testing is a competitive business.

It is possible honesty testing in the future will attempt to measure very specific, rather than general, types of honesty. Further it is likely that the tests will be computer administered.

Is there evidence that these relatively simple questionnaires mean people are more or less likely to engage in dishonest, counterproductive behaviours? Can they predict who will be honest or dishonest? There are various ways of checking the variability of tests. They include:

1 The 'known' or contrast groups method. People who are known to be both honest and dishonest are given the test and the quantity and quality of the difference in response are recorded.
2 Background, biographical check. A thorough background check (number of convictions) using police, school and organizations' records are related to test scores.
3 Admissions and confessions: Separate (perhaps confidential) admissions to a wide range of dishonest behaviours from the trivial to the very serious are correlated with test scores.
4 Predictive or future method. People are tested at organizational entry and scores are related to documented (proved) dishonest behaviours over their career.
5 Time series or historic method. Before honesty tests are used in selection, all sorts of indices are collected such as loss, shrinkage. The same data is collected after tests are used in selection to see if there is a noticeable difference.
6 Correlations with polygraph or anonymous admissions of theft or absenteeism.

Each method has its limitations and failings. For instance, background checks will not show working on personal matters in company time. Predictive methods can take a decade to get results. A reduction in shrinkage (stealing) may have as much to do with the installations of a new security system as it does the use of tests. Studies have shown individual differences on integrity test faking. For instance, it seems brighter people fake better than less intelligent people (Brown and Colthern, 2002).

Certainly, tests have been validated against very different criteria – theft, faking credentials, 'counterproductive' behaviour – and they do tend to produce rather different results. Doing personal work in company time or taking long lunch breaks is called 'time theft'. Stealing office stationary (pens, paper) is strictly theft. But both of these could be considered trivial, certainly quite different from the theft of company secrets, or of valuable products used for production or the products themselves. But what is the latest thinking around these tests?

First, it is agreed that these tests are certainly useful. They are valid enough to help prevent various problems. *Second*, testing alone will not stop theft, dishonesty or sabotage as many other factors (than dishonest individuals) cause them. *Third*, integrity tests may be measuring aspects of human personality that are stable over time though it is not certain which. *Fourth*, there are problems in testing because some testing codes and standards insist that testees give informed consent on details about the test such as what it measures. Hardly the best thing to give the dishonest person. *Fifth*, there may be legal issues in how 'cut-off' scores are used and labelled. One could classify people as pass/fail or highly/moderately dangerous. How this information is used or recorded can cause expensive legal action. *Sixth*, integrity tests are used to 'select out', not 'select in'. They are designed to help people screen out high-risk applicants, not to identify 'angels'.

The issue of the validity of integrity tests and interpreting the evidence is technical. Four issues are relevant:

1 What is the criterion (or criteria) against which test scores are measured? How specific or serious is it? Is it global like job performance or specific like absenteeism or stealing?
2 What type of measure is it: is it subjective or objective? Is it recorded electronically (on camera), by others' disinterested observations or is it done by a person's own self-report?
3 What is the validation strategy? That is, is it concurrent – are things compared at the same time (test scores and cheating data) or is it predictive when scores are seen to predict behaviour forward in time?
4 Who is the validation sample of people on whom to do the study? Is it job applicants or job incumbents?

Researchers argue that studies using objective data, predictively, and job incumbents are best. Objective data is better than subjective data because of distortion. Predictive studies are best because that is how integrity tests are used: to attempt to predict behaviour ahead of time. Job applicants are the best sample precisely because they are motivated to present themselves in the best possible light.

Miner and Capps (1996) provide a masterful review of reviews more positive than negative. They conclude, as others have, that it is quite possible to construct honesty/integrity tests and this has been done, but it is essential to examine the validity evidence for each test. Yet the controversy has not gone (and probably will never go) away because the issue of using tests 'goes beyond science into values: the very use of these tests infringes certain values and beliefs.' Yet they conclude:

> we foresee a prosperous future for honesty testing. These tests serve a significant need. It is important that they be permitted to continue to serve that need, and we believe that society will have the good sense to let that happen. (p 241)

Researchers have done very extensive, critical and exhaustive reviews of integrity testing in organizations. Through a range of state-of-the-art statistical measures they have concluded the following (Ones and Viswesvaran 1998). They found them internally reliable and that they have very similar results (test-retest r = .80) on different occasions. They also looked at their validity for predicting job performance, counterproductive behaviours, training success, accidents on the job and property damage. They noted that although integrity tests were developed to predict theft they can be used to predict much more widely.

The following are quotes from their review:

> Even for high complexity jobs integrity tests display high levels of operation validity ... Those meta-analytic results lead us to conclude that integrity tests can profitably be used at all levels in organizations. (p 252)

> overall job performance and job training success are both determined by similar individual difference variables, and the personality related variable of integrity is one of them. (p 254)

> Organizations that suffer from high accident rates are likely to benefit from using integrity tests in their selection systems. (p 255)

> In general, the results from these studies indicate that integrity tests are useful in predicting absenteeism, incidents of violent behaviours on the job, and both alcohol and drug abuse. (pp 256–7)

> Hence, we conclude that integrity test operational validates are not moderated by social desirability. (p 260)

> Overall, the research reviewed above leads to the conclusion that although overt and personality based integrity tests appear to be quite different from each other, the construct of integrity that is relevant for personnel selection is captured well by both types of tests. (p 261)

> To the extent that structural interview scores correlate with integrity tests, the

incremental validity of structured interviews are likely to be diminished in a selection system including ability measures, integrity tests, and structured interviews. (pp 266–7)

It is counterproductive to argue whether individual difference predictors are more potent or whether situational predictors are more potent for predicting counter-productivity and for explaining variance in overall job performance. For a healthy and successful human resource system to operate, both situational variables and individual differences variables could be used. However as empirically shown in this paper, a successful human resource management strategy to combat counter-productivity at work and predicting job performance starts with rigorous personnel selection using integrity tests. (p 271)

Public policy

In the US in the 1980s there were both inquiries and legislation concerning the lie detector. In the 1990s the public, the media and the politicians, started to become interested in self-report integrity tests. By the early 1990s, 46 publishers and developers were identified who measured constructs such as counterproductivity, honesty, job performance, integrity and reliability. Paradoxically the integrity of integrity testers was questioned.

In 1994 the American Psychological Association (APS) listed various recommendations based on its task-force investigation of test publishers. They were, according to Camara and Schneider (1994 pp 115–19), as shown in the box opposite.

After the APS published its report, many psychologists commented on it. Their reactions can be considered under various headings:

1 *The jury is not out: tests are valid*
   Three researchers from different universities published a report that examined studies that were done on over half a million participants (Ones et al. 1995, 1996). They note:

   Firstly, integrity tests predict supervisory ratings of overall job performance with a mean operational validity of .41. This is the predictive validity that is relevant when applicants are being selected. The operational validity of .41 for integrity tests for predicting overall job performance implies that integrity tests have higher validity than some of the more accepted forms of personnel selection, including assessment centre ratings, biodata, and even mainstream personality inventories. In fact, integrity test validities for overall job performance are second only to the validities of ability tests, work sample tests, and job knowledge tests used in personnel selection.

   Secondly, integrity tests predict non-self-report broad composites of counter-productive behaviours with operational validities of .39 and .29 (depending on the type of test).

Construct validity

▶ *Each test publisher should define the construct(s) measured by the test.*

▶ *Each test publisher should provide direct evidence bearing on the test's construct validity. Such evidence should include examinations of convergent and discriminant validity moderators and alternative explanations for individual differences.*

▶ *Investigators should devote increased research attention such as whether scores from one end of the continuum are more valid than are scores from the other end.*

▶ *Correlations with other measures should be regularly sought and reported. Item analyses should be carried out routinely, with aggregate results reported at a minimum.*

Cut score use

▶ *Both test score and criterion distributions are continuous. Basing decisions on degree of risk rather than category designation reduces incidence of decision errors.*

▶ *Publishers need to provide clear and detailed information on how cutting scores (or boundaries between zones) are derived.*

▶ *Publishers need to provide evidence when the same cutting score is applied to different businesses and individual companies.*

Marketing and promotional materials

▶ *Publishers should adopt and enforce standards ensuring that the promotional claims made by each testing organization rest on a firm empirical foundation.*

▶ *Each publisher should carefully consider the aims for each of its tests, determine which aims it can support by what evidence, and then examine its promotional material to make sure that its claims are justified.*

▶ *The development of non-technical guidelines for users of all kinds of pre-employment screening tests would assist potential users in evaluating claims made on behalf of competing tests.*

Increasing openness of integrity test evaluation

▶ *Independent researchers should be given access to these tests for use in studies of honesty and related concepts, and test publishers should offer to make databases available for secondary or meta-analyses.*

▶ *Publishers should do all in their power to ensure that their tests receive adequate reviews.*

▶ *Test publishers should commit themselves to making available results of all, even negative, research on tests.*

> ▶ *Test publishers should encourage comparative studies between integrity tests, as well as other types of test, to increase understanding of the underlying constructs and incremental validity.*
>
> ▶ *Publishers should do more to ensure test users are knowledgeable about appropriate and inappropriate uses of tests and test scores. Publishers themselves should take increased responsibility for ensuring proper test use by their clients.*
>
> ▶ *Publishers should institute specific procedures for handling test materials and determining that users are in compliance with acknowledged principles for the protection of privacy.*
>
> ▶ *All publishers should undertake analyses of their instruments' compliance with published test standards.*
>
> ▶ *For foreign translations, it is recommended that (a) the equivalence of any test provided in two languages be demonstrated and (b) such a test not be distributed for use in main selection decisions before determination of its reliability and validity in each language.*

Thirdly, integrity test validities generalize across tests, jobs, organizations, and settings. (p 456)

They also believe that it is desirable that integrity tests are broad based. Further, they believe it is disingenuous to believe that test publishers' data is questionable.

2 *Classification errors are not random*
Some researchers claim that integrity tests do not measure morality but rather conventionality, conformity and traditionalism (Lilienfeld et al. 1995). In this sense rather old-fashioned, honest people can be systematically misclassified. Equally true these tests have been shown to be highly susceptible to faking or work 'coaching instructions'.

3 *Integrity, unlike ability, is changeable/mutable*
Just as criminals and delinquents can 'go straight' and even make up for past sins so those who score low on integrity can reform. But to penalize people for admissions of past misbehaviours condemns them to be 'locked in' to their past (Lilienfold et al. 1995). Dim people cannot go smart but dishonest people can go straight and, of course, the honest can easily wander off 'the straight and narrow'.

4 *Ability and personality tests do not confer value judgements or labels whereas integrity tests do*
Reike and Guastello (1994) believe that because the evidence for honesty tests is not compelling they need to be particularly carefully regulated.

The lie detector (polygraph)

The idea of having a reliable, physiologically based ways of catching liars has always appealed to people more so in the twentieth century with its love of science-fiction. The appeal of physiology is supposed that one cannot lie your way out of these test. The polygraph or lie detector has been passionately discussed and debated over this period and scientists remain divided on the issue (Lacono and Lykken 1997).

The earliest records of quasi lie detectors can be found in ancient Hindu and medieval Church methods of finding the truth. Suspects were asked to chew various substances and then spit them out. The ease of spitting and glutinousness of the spital reflected guilt. What these people had observed was that fear leads to saliva diminishing in volume and becoming viscid in consistency. Today we would say that anxiety influences the activity of the autonomic nervous system that controls salivation.

In the nineteenth century various scientists tried measuring other supposed physical concomitants of fear. These include the plethysmograph which records pulse and blood pressure in a limb, finger trembling, reaction time, word association and so on, all done while investigating suspects.

Lykken (1988) has reviewed the uses and abuses of the lie detector. He noted that William Marston, student of a famous American organizational psychologist at Harvard University, first coined the term lie detector. He wrote a book *The Lie Detector Test* published in 1938 but this was nearly 20 years after he first used the term and tried to publicize the machine. Marston was a publicist not a scientist. It was Larson, a Californian police officer, later a forensic psychiatrist, who started scientific work observing continuous measures of blood pressure and respiratory changes during interrogation. Larson wrote a book in 1932 which was in essence the first scholarly book on lying and lie detection. He was a sceptic to the end.

Two of his associates, Lee and Keeler, from the Berkley police force took up the mantle. Lee developed a portable 'field' polygraph and even a book for polygraph users while Keeler developed his own portable machine named after himself. Keeler moved to Chicago where he met others who were to proselytize this cause including John Reid, who also developed his own eponymous machine. Reid was a lawyer, developed a College of Detection of Deception and developed new ideas of polygraphic interrogation.

Up until this period (the Second World War) the favoured technique was the R/I approach which stood for relevant/irrelevant questions: one alternates between a mix of irrelevant questions (what day of the week is it?; who is Prime Minister?) to relevant ones (where were you on the night in question?; did you know the victim?). It was a poor technique because the relevant questions could and did generate stress in the innocent (see below).

Reid developed the *control question test* in which subjects were asked questions such as: have you ever stolen anything, been late for an appointment, taken credit for something you did not do? If they answered 'No', it is highly likely that they were lying. Hence one had a 'base rate' measure or standard against which the really interesting questions could be asked. He also used what were called guilt complex questions to see how the subject behaved when questioned about a similar, utterly fictitious but related crime. This was a good control question. Reid also, very controversially, listed the typical behavioural symptoms of truthful versus lying subjects.

People are asked neutral questions, relevant questions and control questions: the latter relate to the crime but do not refer to it. The main problem with the technique is that it is difficult to devise plausible questions that would ensure the eliciting of stronger reactions in an innocent person than would relevant questions relating to the crime of which he or she had been accused (Bull 1988) (see below).

Another American, Cleve Backster, introduced two important ideas. The first was the *zone of comparison* format where only the totally adjacent relevant and control questions were compared to look for the person's reactivity over the course of the test. He also developed a scoring technique to score a person's relevant response over all channels and all repetitions of the same question to get a total score. The overall verdict is based entirely on the polygraphic record and not on using case facts, behaviour symptoms and so on and, inevitably, the polygraph examines preconceived ideas.

It was not until the 1960s that the lie detector emerged from the police forensic lab into the marketplace. Operators approached all sorts of companies, especially banks and rental stores, saying their machines could screen *job applicants* to determine whether their application forms were truthful and whether they had stolen from previous employers, ever used illegal drugs, had any outstanding debts and had any undisclosed criminal records.

They also said that job incumbents could be effectively and efficiently screened for embezzlement, misappropriation of funds and theft. Soon more than two million Americans were being tested every year. It was a multi-million dollar business. Further, some serious university-based researchers seemed to endorse the technique.

But from the mid 1970s various psychologists started serious investigations into the lie detector and all condemned it. In 1988 the Polygraph Protection Act prohibited US employers from requiring or requesting that employees be polygraphed. 'Hundreds of journeymen polygraphers had to seek other employment and millions of citizens no longer had to face the humiliation of having their character vetted in an hour's time by some graduate of a six-week course in polygraphy' (Lykken 1988 p 37). However, in half of US states lie detector evidence can still be admitted. Polygraphs are now used throughout the world from Canada to Thailand, Israel to Taiwan, though their use is limited. The test is not used (at least by the government) in the Netherlands and the UK.

According to Ekman (2001) over a million polygraph tests are still given every year in the United States. Private employers, criminal investigators, the federal government, and the department of defence are the big users.

How polygraphs work

The polygraph tries to measure autonomic nervous system activity by attached sensors to different parts of the body: chest, stomach, fingers. These sensors measure changes in breathing (depth and rate), cardiac activity (blood pressure) and perspiration. It is also possible to measure brain electrical activity (event-related potentials). The indicators only show physiological changes usually induced by emotion. The machine amplifies signals picked up from sensors put at specific parts of the body. It detects not lies, but physical changes that are results of specific emotions (fear, anger, guilt) but which of these is not clear. People are asked 'hot' or relevant questions as well as 'cool' or control questions. The assumption is that for the innocent person there is no physical difference in the way he/she responds to relevant and control questions.

Problems of individual differences arise of course. Some people are more reactive than others. Drugs can be used to suppress autonomic nervous system activity and make any physiological recording inconclusive. More worryingly, people can be trained at defeating the test with a range of techniques. Tests would therefore not only be highly unreliable but counterproductive: alienating and misclassifying the innocent and letting the guilty get away scot-free.

The lie detector remains used in three different contexts: criminal investigation, security vetting and personnel selection. Some have argued the polygraph is worthless in selection because it can speak only to the past not the future. But others argue that the past indeed predicts the future. There is much less research on pre-employment screening. Some argue the base rate of liars is too low to ever be accurate. Others suggest that the test causes a poor impression. However some argue that taking the test or threatening to have to take it leads people to admitting important things they otherwise would not admit. Thus a test can have utility even without accuracy.

Ekman (2001) contends that there are many important issues associated with the polygraph such as:

▷ How the polygraph may be useful even if it is not accurate – that is, utility vs. accuracy.
▷ The base rate of lying – if there are very few liars in a group the test may easily overestimate that number.
▷ The idea that the polygraph is a deterrent – that it may successfully reduce/inhibit lying even if the procedure is faulty.

The validity of the lie detector

To be acceptable as a test a lie detector, like any other device, must minimally fulfil a number of criteria. First there must be a standardized method of administration, which is fully described, clear and repeatable. Next there must be objective scoring; not subjective, based on personal-experience scoring. Third, there must be external valid criteria – it must be shown to differentiate between truth and lies.

Critics have noted the lie detector is not a test but an interrogation device because methods are semi-standardized, it requires clinical observation and validity data is poor (Lykken 1988). Data on the lie detector comes from two sources: clinical case studies and experimental evidence.

It must be pointed out that in 'real life' cases it is often very difficult to establish validity because many crimes are never solved and confession (often false) is the only real feedback. It is possible to use laboratory studies using students. But for Lykken (1988 pp 84–5), these too have problems:

> Laboratory studies, however, have serious disadvantages for predicting lie detector accuracy in real-life criminal investigations.
>
> 1 The volunteer subjects are unlikely to be representative of criminal suspects in real life.
> 2 The volunteers may not feel a lifelike concern about mock crimes that they have been instructed to commit and about telling lies they are instructed to tell.
> 3 Compared to criminal suspects, who know they may be in real trouble should they fail the lie test, volunteers are unlikely to be as apprehensive about being tested, with respect to mock crimes for which they will not be punished, irrespective of the test's outcome.
> 4 The administration of the polygraph tests tends not to resemble the procedures followed in real life. For example, unlike real-life tests, which are most often conducted well after the crime took place, laboratory subjects are typically tested immediately after they commit the mock crime. Moreover, in laboratory research, to make the study scientifically acceptable, there is an attempt to standardize the procedure (for example all subjects are asked identical questions), a factor that distinguishes these from real-life tests.

Most of the researchers in the field have tried to evaluate the more widely known methods of lie detection. The control question technique must emotionally arouse the innocent person with the control as much as the crime-related questions otherwise it makes an error. There is rightly a tremendous concern with the innocent mislabelled or judged guilty. This may easily occur in the nervous, anxious, person particularly if he/she believes polygraphs are fallible (which of course they are) and when he/she can (often relatively easily) detect the difference between relevant and control questions. Innocent people might believe the police/polygraph operators are as fallible as are their machines or that they are unfair. Fearful, guilty, hostile, impulsive, volatile people react badly to authority figures wiring them up. Their reactions may unfairly condemn them. Further, an innocent person may be so unhappy or disturbed by a crime they did not do – but found the body, or knew the victim – that they react physiologically dramatically, seeming to show their guilt.

Vrij (2000) notes many criticisms of the control question test. The first is the possibility that innocent victims give larger physiological responses to control than to relevant questions. The next is that guilty suspects are not less concerned with control than with relevant questions. Further, examiners have to be experienced and subtle in the choice, and phrasing, of the questions. It is easy for them to frighten, embarrass and intimidate others, as well as 'leak' their own beliefs and suspicions non-verbally. Next there is the judgement problem of how to interpret the difference in response to control vs. relevant questions. It depends not only on the size of the difference in response but also the base rate for every individual: that is, a low-reactive person might show the same absolute physical differences than a high reactive person but in effect the former is much more dramatic than the latter. A related issue is that scoring polygraph charts is till a 'subjective art' rather than a 'precise science'. Finally, there are ethical and legal problems in deceiving people in some of the control questions.

The *guilty knowledge* test on the other hand works on the assumption that the lie detector operator has information about the crime exclusive to the guilty person (that is, precisely how much was stolen; the denomination of the notes). The idea is that when questioned in detail the guilty person recognizes descriptions of events, objects, people linked to the crime and this rouses him/her, which shows up on the polygraph recordings.

Of course it is not always easy to find appropriate questions and keep all details secret. Sometimes the criminal may not have noticed certain details which an innocent person at the scene of the crime might do. Problems arise in the questions and a person may have guilty knowledge without being guilty. However it is clear that experts in the area are much more likely to endorse the credibility of the guilty knowledge over the controlled question test.

As noted above, studies on the accuracy/validity of the polygraph can be categorized into two types: field studies of actual, real-life incidents and analogue/experimental studies. Both have distinct advantages and disadvantages. There is actually a rarer type called hybrid studies where the researcher arranges for a crime to occur.

Ekman (2001) reviewed 30 studies: 10 field, 14 analogue, 6 hybrid. He concluded that accuracy was better in the field studies because there was more emotional arousal, less-educated people and less certainty about the ground truth. Disbelieving-the-truth mistakes and believing-a-lie mistakes are highest in the guilty knowledge test (Figure 7.1).

Ekman (2001) notes that some critics believe the figures underestimate accuracy while some stress the precise opposite. He also believes more weight should be given to a test that shows innocence as an outcome rather than lying. Further, even when a test suggests lying, this should only be used to pursue an investigation rather than being enough evidence to proceed with a prosecution or a conviction.

Ekman (2001) believes that one cannot properly evaluate the polygraph

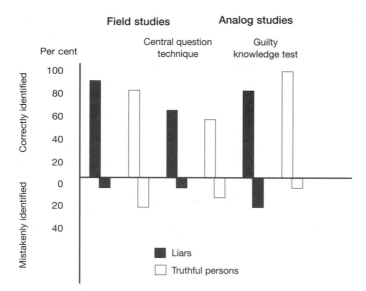

Note: The graph gives the averages, which are not always an accurate reflection of the range of research results. The ranges are as follows: For liars correctly identified: in field studies, 71–99%; in analog studies using the control question technique, 35–100%; in analog studies :using the guilty knowledge test, 61–95%. For truthful persons correctly identified: in field studies, 13–94%; in analog studies using the control question technique, 32–91%; in analog studies using the guilty knowledge test, 80–100%. For truthful person incorrectly identified: in field studies, 0–75%; in analog studies using the control question technique, 2–51%; in analog studies using the guilty knowledge test, 0–12%. For liars incorrectly identified: in field studies, 0–29%: in analog studies using the control question technique, 0–29%; in analog studies using the guilty knowledge test, 5–39%.

Figure 7.1 **Polygraph accuracy**

Source: Ekman 2001.

without understanding some fundamental concepts. Four are essential (p 192):

▷ the difference between *accuracy* and *utility* – how the polygraph might be useful even if it isn't accurate
▷ the quest for *ground truth* – how hard it is to determine the accuracy of the polygraph without being absolutely certain who the liars are
▷ the *base rate of lying* – how a very accurate test can produce many mistakes when the groups of suspects includes very few liars
▷ *deterring lying* – how the threat of being examined might inhibit some from lying, even if the examination procedure is faulty.

Vrij (2000) also reviewed various studies. Looking at laboratory studies of the control question test he found 73% of guilty people and 66% of innocent people correctly classified. Also 9% of the guilty were judged innocent and 13% of the innocent falsely accused. Laboratory studies of the guilty knowledge test were better: 96% of the innocent were correctly identified and only 4% falsely accused. Similarly 82% of the guilty were correctly classified but 18% judged innocent.

Field studies using the control question test show that 87% were correctly judged guilty and 71% innocent people judged innocent but 10%

of the guilty were incorrectly categorized innocent and 21% of the innocent judged guilty. On the guilty knowledge test, 96% of the innocent were correctly (and 4% incorrectly) judged innocent but only 59% of the guilty classified as such with 41% of misclassifications. Vrij (2000) concludes his careful review thus:

> Field studies examining the accuracy of polygraph tests have shown that these tests (both CQTs and GKTs) make substantial numbers of mistakes. The proponents of the CQT test will probably argue that this conclusion is incorrect, and they will then refer to the accuracy scores obtained by original examiners in their field studies. The problem is that independent examiners were much less accurate. This suggests that extra, non-polygraph information, known to the original examiner but not to the independent evaluator, is essential for making an accurate decision. The accuracy of the test itself can only be reliably determined by using evaluators who have access solely to the test results, and their accuracy rates appeared to be less accurate.

> Given the number of mistakes made in polygraph tests, I think that polygraph outcomes should not be allowed as a substantial piece of evidence in court ... However, polygraph tests may make a valuable contribution to the detection of deceit. Polygraph outcomes might therefore be used as an additional piece of evidence in court (as long as more substantial evidence is presented as well), or as a tool in police investigations to eliminate potential suspects, to check the truthfulness of informants, or to examine contradictory statements of witnesses and suspects in the same case.

> For this purpose, I prefer and advocate the use of the guilty knowledge polygraph tests. I do not do this for reasons of accuracy. Research has shown that control question tests can be accurate, and their accuracy rates (at least in field studies) do exceed the accuracy rates of the guilty knowledge tests. I reject control question polygraph tests, because part of the procedure involves deceiving examinees. First, deception makes the test vulnerable, as people who read about a CQT will come to know, which will probably make the test less efficient. Secondly, in many countries the use of deception in criminal investigations is illegal. For example, in both the UK (the country where I work) and The Netherlands (my native country) it is illegal to lie to suspects in criminal investigations. This makes it illegal to conduct control question polygraph tests in these countries, and impossible to use the outcomes of such tests as evidence in criminal trials. This 'deception is illegal' argument may be a typical European one.

> Before guilty knowledge polygraph tests can be widely introduced in police investigations, several issues need to be clarified.

> ▷ More field studies with GKT are needed to test its accuracy. In these tests, the multiple perception of one item technique (asking about one detail several times) instead of the multiple item technique (asking about several details) might be worth testing, because this will probably improve the

applicability of the test, as it is probably easier to design a test about one detail than a test about several details.

▷ It is important to ensure the quality of the polygraph examiners, as they have such an important role in polygraph testing. It might be a good idea to introduce university grades in polygraph testing, and only people with a 'polygraph examination degree' would then be allowed to conduct tests.

▷ Polygraph tests should be carried out by institutions that are independent of the police force. There are several reasons to support this view. First, police officers often have pre-conceived ideas about the guilt of suspects, which might influence the test. Secondly, police officers might make up polygraph outcomes in order to put suspects under pressure. This is not so likely to occur if the tests are carried out by an independent organization. Thirdly, suspects may distrust the police or may not have confidence in them. This may be particularly so with regard to innocent suspects who are falsely accused by the police of having committed a crime. It seems fair and reasonable that suspects should be given an independent test.

▷ It is necessary to check carefully confessions made by suspects after they have failed a polygraph test. Polygraph tests may result in force confessions, either because suspects are going to believe that they have committed the crime ... or because they no longer see much opportunity to convince others of their innocence. (pp 205–7)

A British evaluation

The British Psychological Society (BPS) published a long, edited book (Gale 1988) called *The Polygraph Test: Lies, Truth and Science*. The conclusion, stated at the beginning of the book, is a good example of British scientific diffidence and caution. On page 2 the editor writes 'The truth is that we do not know the full truth about polygraphic lie-detection'. Gale (1988) notes a little later (p 9):

Advances in science and technology are unlikely to leave our lives untouched, and the polygraph is no exception. The polygraph is a scientific instrument used for research into bodily responses and their relationships with psychological processes. As an instrument, it is reliable in producing a record of bodily events. However, this does not imply that the uses to which the polygraph might be put are also reliable. Some members of The British Psychological Society have expressed concern that the use of the polygraph for lie detection might reflect badly on its use in basic research. Criticism has also been made of the term 'the polygraph test', a misnomer which is said to give lie detection procedures some respectability by their association with a scientific instrument.

The issues considered here are the vexed question of various procedures and their accuracy and validity; what we mean by truth and honesty and whether indeed the test measures it; what the test measures; whether the use of the test will actually be useful and cost-effective in national security vetting and the many legal and civil rights issues surrounding such tests.

Bull (1988) notes that the data is clear concerning the detection of lying just by observation. It's difficult, highly unreliable and not easily trained for. One can, as Ekman (2001) has shown never come to a final conclusion from lie detector data on whether a person is lying or telling the truth. Bull (1988) like all reviewers is worried about misclassification: particularly the innocent judged guilty. All sorts of issues come into play: is the person aware that they are lying; how valid do they believe the polygraph to be; how good is the polygrapher? He concludes:

> Until it is made absolutely clear on which forms of the testee's behaviours and responses, decisions about deceptions are based, there can be no proper scientific study of the validity of polygrapher's procedures. (pp 17–18)

Carroll (1988) did an early review on the accuracy of the polygraph based on reliability (agreement between examiners; subject consistency across time) and accuracy. He found both the reliability and the validity data unconvincing and concluded thus:

> If proponents wish to convince the scientific community of the merits of polygraph lie detection, I submit that they will have to develop a more convincing case than the one currently on offer. Their case must be founded on studies which include the necessary controls for non-polygraphic sources of information, that is, studies which compare the accuracy of assessments derived from case-file material and the subject's demeanour during questioning with that based on these sources plus the polygraph record. I strongly suspect that such studies would confirm what the available data suggest: that polygraph lie detection adds nothing positive to conventional approaches to interrogation and assessment. (p 28)

In a very British, BBC and balanced way the report allows the two famous US adversaries to describe and defend their position. In the pro-corner Raskin (1988), who addressed his essay thus 'Does science support polygraph testing?', set about marshalling the pro-evidence. He concludes:

> Careful consideration of the available evidence seems to indicate that there is scientific support for certain applications of polygraph techniques. Appropriate use of those techniques by qualified professionals in criminal investigation and forensic applications can achieve rates of accuracy that compare favourably with other forms of evidence, such as criminalistics, and are higher than common forms of evidence, such as eyewitness identification.

> Polygraph testing can have serious problems of inaccuracy in the most common application, commercial pre-employment screening. That application most likely produces such high rates of error that tremendous social and personal damage results from its widespread use. There seems to be little scientific support for such uses of polygraphs.

Polygraph examinations in the context of national security programmes raise the most complex issues. Assessments of lifestyle and prior history produce problems similar to those that arise in commercial employment screening. The problems associated with low base rates of espionage in counter-intelligence contexts must be balanced against the need to identify spies because of the great security and monetary costs of failing to do so. Often, national security needs are pitted against the social and ethical needs of protecting individuals. Only the most careful programmes and techniques, coupled with research and development to minimize the errors, can help to reduce those problems. Ultimately, the future of government uses of polygraph methods will be determined by political and social considerations, hopefully enlightened by objective and thorough scientific evaluations. (pp 109–10)

In the anticorner Lykken (1988), a long-time opponent of the polygraph, presented in equal measure his analysis of the issue. Note how different is his conclusion:

Unlike the fictional Pinnochio, we are not equipped with a distinctive physiological response that we emit involuntarily when, and only when, we lie. There are many reasons other than deception why a truthful person might show physiological disturbance in response to an accusatory question. Polygraphers cannot delude each innocent suspect into the belief that he or she has nothing to fear from the relevant questions but something important to fear from the 'controls'. The fact that one of several accusatory questions causes my heart to beat harder, my palms to sweat more, than the other questions do does not necessarily mean that I am guilty of that accusation. The assumptions on which the various forms of lie-detector test are based have only to be articulated to be seen to be implausible.

Many poorly designed badly controlled studies are to be found in the polygraph literature. The few relatively competent studies agree with each other and with what one might expect from the theory: polygraphic lie detection is wrong about one third of the time overall; it is seriously biased against the truthful subject; deceptive subjects with minimal coaching can deliberately produce augmented responses, undetected by the examiner, which will allow them to defeat at least one common type of lie test.

It seems to me that we must now acknowledge that this application of psychophysiology has been a failure; that polygraph lie detection does not and, in the foreseeable future, probably cannot work well enough to justify its continued use in the field. Polygraphic detection of guilty knowledge, based on entirely different and more plausible assumptions, has proved itself in the laboratory and deserves controlled study in the field of criminal investigation. (pp 124–5)

Can you beat the lie detector? Essentially there are two ways of doing this: physical or mental. Physical measures may involve self-inflicted pain (biting the tongue, keeping a drawing pin hidden in shoes; tensing and releasing muscles). Mental methods may include backward counting and fantasizing. The former are meant to give real, dramatic but misleading physiological responses picked up on the polygraph. The latter are meant to screen out the questions so making them indistinct. Studies have shown them to be equally effective and there seems to be some evidence that people in security jobs are taught to use them effectively. But there are limitations. First the person has to conceal carefully, precisely what they are doing. Second it is harder to fake in the guilty knowledge test than the control question test.

Gudjonnson (1988) addressed the problem of how (best) to defeat the polygraph. This was his conclusion:

> The use of different classes of counter-measures has been reported in the literature. The available evidence shows that mental counter-measures and the use of pharmacological substances (such as tranquillizers) are only moderately effective at best, whereas physical counter-measures can be highly effective under certain conditions. Two conditions appear important to the effective use of physical counter-measures. First, employing multiple counter-measures simultaneously improves the person's chances of defeating a polygraph test, at least as far as the control question technique is concerned. Second, physical counter-measures appear relatively ineffective unless people are given special training in their use. It is generally not sufficient merely to provide people with instructions about polygraph techniques and counter-measures.

> Although there are clear individual differences in the ability to apply counter-measures effectively, training by experts in the use of physical counter-measures poses a potentially serious threat to the validity of polygraph techniques. For this reason it becomes very important that the use of counter-measures is readily identified by polygraph examiners. Unfortunately subtle and effective physical counter-measures are not readily observable without special expertise and equipment which are not generally available to field examiners. (pp 135–6)

It would indeed be naive to believe there is a simple foolproof physiological method to detect deceit. Clearly, under certain circumstances the lie detector can be an extremely useful and impressive diagnostic. The worry however is the cost of misclassification – the innocent judged guilty and the guilty innocent. A reasonable question is that which asks for an alternative. In serious situations where other material can be brought to bare in the decision it seems reasonable at least to consider using the polygraph.

Conclusion

All people interested in selecting those whose integrity is fundamental to the job would like a simple, cheap, valid test that helped them select in those with integrity but select out those more likely to be compromised. They have an impressive choice ranging from simple questionnaires to new voice-stress analysers that may be used to analyse telephone calls.

The central issue for the researchers and the selector is validity. Any test that 'labels' the guilty innocent, the psychopath full of integrity or the thieving, deceiving employee a model worker has clearly failed in its primary duty. Equally, and perhaps more seriously from both a morality and a libellous point of view, so is a test that erroneously judges the innocent guilty or those who do have integrity as not having it.

There are good tests and bad tests: those which have been properly devised and tested and those which are 'quick-and-dirty' attempts to make publishers a lot of money. Certainly there are those who are implacably against tests and those who think they are useful. Looking at pen-and-paper tests it seems the reviewers conclude they can be useful. The test results can usefully *aid* decision making. That is, with test results and *other corroborative evidence* of guilt or innocence it is possible to significantly improve the probability of detecting those who have, or will commit, CWBs.

But note: tests improve the *probability* of detection. Tests should never be relied upon alone to do this. This situation is even more the case with the polygraph that has been very extensively tested. For some people the idea of psychological, as opposed to self-report, responses is very attractive. It seems much harder to 'beat the lie detector' then come up as convincing on a questionnaire.

Yet reviews have showed that whatever technique is used there are errors of classification. The optimist points to the overwhelming number of correct classifications, the pessimist to the errors, particularly those where the innocent are mislabelled. Again, used judiciously, and with supportive evidence it seems that there are incidences where the polygraph may be useful. But this is more likely to be in the law court than the office.

Many people who commit CWBs have no history of lack of integrity. They are often 'pushed over the edge' by their work situation: the bullying boss, team pressure, clear inequity. But there are also those with a long history of disregard for the law, others' rights, and company property. There are correlates of integrity and these we can measure and do so well. Those in the business of selection, then, need to consider carefully the issue of integrity testing and attempt a sensible route between rejection and naive acceptance, if they want to select out those individuals likely to commit CWBs.

8 The Psychology of Deception and Lying

Introduction

Cheating, sabotage, stealing and whistle-blowing at work, almost by definition, involve deception of one sort or another. This chapter will look at the difficult but important business of the detection of deception. How easy and reliable is it to spot people lying? Are some people simply better liars and liar-spotters than others? And what of the conscience-free, psychopathic liar – can they ever be detected?

Lying is, and will always be, a hot topic. It is at the centre of ethical and moral codes. It is essentially a false communication that benefits the communicator. It is deliberate and may or may not be successful. To be accused of being a liar, as opposed to occasionally telling lies, is a serious business. There is a bewildering array of words and concepts that deal with those who don't quite tell the full truth – the whole truth and nothing but the truth. Fibs, fabrications, falsehoods and fudgings. Politicians 'spin' the facts to the public. Organizations use public relations gurus to 'sex up' products, messages and services. Individuals, as part of daily intercourse and to save embarrassment and hurt, say things directly or indirectly (possibly through euphemism) to each other. Notice the way negative as opposed to positive feedback is dealt with at work.

One reason why the public is as well (or badly) informed about psychological issues is the number of popular articles on the topic. Some are based on reviews with authors, others on a sort of popularized precis of a book review.

Consider the following. In the November 2002 issue of *Men's Health*, a popular magazine, readers were given the following advice on how to lie:

1 Stay calm: Try not to fidget, twitch … things like sweating, rubbing hands together or bending paperclips completely out of shape all look like signs of guilt.
2 Plan: Have a good, well-prepared cover story.
3 Don't rehearse: Don't learn a speech with words you don't often use and be 'out of line'.
4 Look bored: Give the impression you don't have time for inane questions.
5 Appear distracted.
6 Do not cross your arms or legs.

7 Rebuttal: Answer probing and difficult questions with 'I don't know' rather than 'I don't recall'.
8 Be disagreeable: Appear outraged that someone gave you false information.
9 Don't touch any part of your face.
10 Neither stare nor avoid eye contact.
11 Have open palms and don't unconsciously give people the finger.
12 Cough or yawn to cover up the face when lying.
13 Try to reduce idiosyncratic quirks.
14 Don't brag about being a good liar.
15 Try to believe your own lies.

As we shall see some of the above is simplistic, wrong and misleading. Indeed, these articles reinforce ignorance and explain why people are such poor lie-catchers themselves.

Many professionals – doctors, the police, lawyers, teachers – have to deliver bad news. It is neither easy nor pleasant letting people know they are dying, a relative has died, they are going to prison or they have failed an exam. It requires skill, tact and timing. Still, some 'duck out' of their responsibilities and, in effect, lie.

But this book is not about this type of lying. It is about deliberate dissent, dissembling, dissimulation. Telling 'bare-faced' lies not to prevent hurt in others, but to prevent personally being caught. It is about self-serving untruths aimed at cover-up behaviour. It is about denying things that did happen (or are planned) and lying about those that did not. Frequently, a lie is morally, legally and ethically indefensible. Liars can choose not to lie. It is a deliberate act which may be done by a good or bad person, with or without good justification. Most liars prefer concealment to falsification which is easier.

Because to accuse another of being a liar is a serious social accusation, there are a range of synonyms and distinctions that are made either to refer to the motive of the person telling a lie or else to how they do so.

> It [a letter] contains a misleading impression, not a lie. It was being economical with the truth.
>
> Lord Robert Armstrong in Supreme Court, New South Wales, Australia 19 November 1986

The term 'deception' does not have to involve lying. Camouflage, be it on animals or on soldiers' tents is an attempt to deceive. It could be argued that make-up and plastic surgery are also attempts at deception. False hair, false teeth, false padding are used not only by actors, criminals and spies but by all sorts of ordinary people to attempt to disguise their real appearance. Many of these attempts at deception are considered to be socially acceptable, even necessary. There are essentially only two ways of lying: to conceal or to falsify.

At interviews, giving speeches and in viva-voce examinations people strive to 'hold their nerves': to appear more confident than they are. They may do this with the help of drugs, particular thought-patterns or other tricks that may or may not be successful. All this is considered normal, healthy – even desirable.

But there is, of course, another less acceptable, but no doubt equally common form of deception: telling lies. There are, as a result, all sorts of synonyms that somehow try to normalize the act and make it more acceptable. Psychologists may talk of dissimulation, dissembling, social desirability responding or idiosyncratic response bias. Business people may talk about impression management, presentation skills or business exaggerations, while ordinary people may refer to 'porky pies' or 'telling porkies' which is derived from cockney rhyming slang. A lie is quite simply a falsehood; an untruth.

But a broken promise, a failure to recall and a misinterpretation of an ambiguous statement are not really lies. Note what Ekman (2001) writes:

I have come to believe that examining how and when people lie and tell the truth can help in understanding many human relationships. There are few that do not involve deceit or at least the possibility of it. Parents lie to their children about sex to spare them knowledge they think their children are not ready for, just as their children, when they become adolescents, will conceal sexual adventures because the parents won't understand. Lies occur between friends (even your best won't tell you), teacher and student, doctor and patient, husband and wife, witness and jury, lawyer and client, salesperson and customer.

> *The true hypocrite is the one who ceases to perceive his deception, the one who lies with sincerity.*
>
> André Gide *The Counterfeiters*

Lying is such a central characteristic of life that better understanding of it is relevant to almost all human affairs. Some might shudder at that statement, because they view lying as reprehensible. I do not share that view. It is too simple to hold that no one in any relationship must ever lie; nor would I prescribe that every lie be unmasked. Advice columnist Ann Landers has a point when she advises her readers that truth can be used as a bludgeon, cruelly inflicting pain. Lies can be cruel too, but all lies aren't. Some lies, many fewer than liars will claim, are altruistic. Some social relationships are enjoyed because of the myths they preserve. But no liar should presume too easily that a victim desires to be misled. And no lie catcher should too easily presume the right to expose every lie. Some lies are harmless, even humane. Unmasking certain lies may humiliate the victim or a third party. (p 23)

There are a number of distinctions that can be made in this area:

▷ *Errors of omission vs. commission:* The former (omission) refers to leaving out (usually undesirable) facts. Thus a job applicant may choose not to mention his/her age, education, jail sentences or bankruptcy. People believe that failing to declare something is quite different (and more acceptable) than telling a deliberate lie. That, of course, depends on the situation and the ethical code of the judge. Errors of commission are quite simply telling lies. These may involve exaggeration or fabrication and are done consciously with a specific purpose in mind.

▷ *Self-deception vs. impression management:* Self-deception involves conscious deception that a person does not believe is a lie. It is people believing in their own positive reports. Thus a person may falsify an exam grade they felt they deserved or hoped for rather than the one they received. And they feel this to be a quite acceptable act: certainly not a lie. They may also – as they would say 'in all honesty' – report of their feelings, intentions and behaviours that are patently at odds with those of others.

They are in a sense deluded but they do not have to have a mental illness to be in this position. Impression management is about what is now called 'spin'. Reports may be 'sexed up' to make them more appealing.

Why do people lie?

According to Vrij (2000) people lie to make a positive impression on others; protect themselves from embarrassment/disapproval; obtain advantage; avoid punishment; to benefit others; and to facilitate social relationships.

Ekman believes there are essentially nine main reasons for lying (2001 pp 329–30):

1　*To avoid being punished.* This is the most frequently mentioned motive by either children or adults. The punishment may be for a misdeed or for an accidental mistake.
2　*To obtain reward not otherwise readily obtainable.* This is the second most commonly mentioned motive, by both children and adults.
3　*To protect another person from being punished.*
4　*To protect oneself from the threat of physical harm.* This is different from being punished, for the threat of harm is not for a misdeed. An example would be a child who is home alone telling a stranger at the door that his father is asleep now, to come back later.
5　*To win the admiration of others.*
6　*To get out of an awkward social situation.* Examples are claiming to have a babysitter problem to get out of a dull party, or ending a telephone conversation by saying there is someone at the door.
7　*To avoid embarrassment.* The child who claims the wet seat resulted from water spilling, not from wetting her pants, is an example of the child fearing not punishment but only embarrassment.
8　*To maintain privacy,* without giving notification of the intention to maintain some information as private.
9　*To exercise power over others,* by controlling the information the target has.

Clearly some people lie better than other. Actors and politicians are skilled at the task. Machiavellian manipulators are good too, as are adaptable and social people. Various factors, other than the liar's personality, increase their effectiveness and probability of not being caught. But the chances go up of catching liars if they are known to the lie-catcher; they are familiar with the topic; the liar is young, introverted or self-conscious and the liar is from the same ethic background as the lie-catcher.

Catching liars: why they fail

According to Ekman (2001) there are essentially five reasons why liars get caught in the act of lying. They leak cues to their deceit in their body, voice, or words. One reason is about thinking, the others are about feeling.

Lack of preparation: (bad lines)

A good lie requires preparation, rehearsal and memorization. A good liar should be able to anticipate when it is appropriate or necessary to lie; when to be inventive; that they must remain internally consistent; when the story must fit the known/revealed facts. The right words must be used but the liar must not take time thinking about it. Lies take rehearsal and being word-perfect. Curiously where people are overrehearsed, overconsistent and overwhelmingly convincing they too may be caught through their overpreparation. Conmen, used to telling the same series of well-prepared lies over and over again, succeed because of their preparation.

Lying about feelings

Lies that involve emotions are more difficult than lies about actions, facts, intentions, plans or thoughts. When a person is made angry, frightened or saddened, physiological changes (in the central nervous system) occur without the choice or selection. Strong emotions triggered by particular memories are hard to conceal and control. Trying to look angry when one is not or calm when frightened is not easy. Faking upset or anger takes considerable acting skill. Perhaps even harder is concealing strong emotions.

Feelings about lying

If a person feels guilty, silly or vulnerable about their deception (tax evasion, embezzlement, plagiarism) appropriate emotions are triggered which may be difficult to conceal.

Fear of being caught

This is also called *detection apprehension* and concerns being fearful about being caught and punished for the deception in the first place. The liar's fear is a function of a number of things. One factor is their belief in the aptitude and skill of the lie-detector. Some people are believed to be particularly good at detection: police officers, psychologists and psychiatrists, customs officers. They are likely to increase fear in the liar which may show up in a variety of emotional expressions. Some people seem natural liars and others are easily detected when telling any lies. Natural liars (excluding psychopaths) tend to be individualistic and competitive. Another factor of importance is how high the stakes are (what is involved for the liar). The more at stake the more the detection apprehension. There are two punishments for every lie: that for the lie failing and that of telling the lie. The latter is about losing trust and being labelled a liar.

According to Ekman (2001) apprehensiveness about being detected telling a lie is greatest under eight very specific circumstances (p 641):

▷ the target has a reputation for being tough to fool
▷ the target starts out being suspicious
▷ the liar has had little practice and no record of success
▷ the liar is specially vulnerable to the fear of being caught
▷ the stakes are high
▷ both rewards and punishments are at stake; or if it is only one or the other, punishment is at stake
▷ the punishment for being caught lying is great, or the punishment for what the lie is about is so great that there is no incentive to confess
▷ the target in no way benefits from the lie.

Deception guilt

This refers to feelings about lying not feelings about guilt. At extremes this guilt can induce shame and affects feelings of self-worth which can be very quickly physically manifested. People with a strict, moral upbringing naturally tend to be the most guilt-prone. The psychopath of course does not suffer from this problem.

There are a number of highly specific conditions which seem to either exacerbate or reduce deception guilt. Again, Ekman (2001) has specified eight of these (pp 75–6):

▷ The target is unwilling
▷ The deceit is totally selfish, and the target derives no benefit from being misled and loses as much as or more than the liar gains
▷ The deceit is unauthorized, and the situation is one in which honesty is authorized
▷ The liar has not been practising the deceit for a long time
▷ The liar and the target share social values
▷ The liar is personally acquainted with the target
▷ The target can't easily be faulted as mean or gullible

▷ There is reason for the target to expect to be misled; just the opposite, the liar has acted to win confidence in his trustworthiness.

Duping delight

Some liars get caught paradoxically because of the post-lie relief, pride and even smugness. Again, if these feelings are not concealed – and that can be difficult – it can lead to the liar getting caught. People can tempt fate, enjoy 'misleading others' and play games only to be caught by duping delight. This problem occurs particularly, according to Ekman (2001), under three circumstances (p 79):

▷ The target poses a challenge, having a reputation for being difficult to fool
▷ The lie is a challenge, because of either what must be concealed or the nature of what must be fabricated
▷ Others are watching or know about the lie and appreciate the liar's skilful performance.

Yet people remain bad at detecting lies for many reasons. Vrij (2000) lists seven:

1 People do not actually want to know the truth.
2 There are no typical deceptive behaviours for all people.
3 The differences between liars and truth tellers are very small.
4 Conversation rules prevent lie-detectors from carefully analysing an accused liar properly.
5 Observers' judgements are often affected by their personal bias, misbeliefs and systematic errors.
6 Nervous behaviour does not mean lying behaviour, though many believe that to be true.
7 Most observers fail to take individual differences into account.

Helpfully Vrij (2000 p 98) provides the following:

Guidelines for the detection of deception via behavioural cues.

1 Lies may only be detectable via non-verbal cues if the liar experiences fear, guilt or excitement (or any other emotion), or if the lie is difficult to fabricate.
2 It is important to pay attention to mismatches between speech content and non-verbal behaviour, and to try to explain these mismatches. Keep in mind the possibility that the person is lying, but consider this as only one of the possible reasons for this mismatch.
3 Attention should be directed towards deviations from a person's 'normal' or usual patterns of behaviour, if these are known. The explanation for such deviations should be established. Each deviation may indicate that the person is lying, but do not disregard other explanations for these deviations.

4 The judgement of untruthfulness should only be made when all other possible explanations have been negated.

5 A person suspected of deception should be encouraged to talk. This is necessary to negate the alternative options regarding a person's behaviour. Moreover, the more a liar talks, the more likely it is that they will finally give their lies away via verbal and/or non-verbal cues (as they continuously have to pay attention to both speech content and non-verbal behaviour). Bear in mind that probing in itself might elicit behavioural changes.

6 There are stereotyped ideas about cues to deception (such as gaze aversion, fidgeting, and so on), which research has shown to be unreliable indicators of deception. These can be a guide, but bear in mind that not everyone will exhibit these cues during deception and the presence of such cues may indicate deception, but does not do so in every case.

The clues to deceit

People communicate using verbal, vocal and visual cues. The words they choose, their voice quality and numerous body cues all provide information about their emotional and cognitive state and whether they may be lying. The lie-catcher needs to notice and interpret these manifold and subtle cues. The expert, professional, lie-catcher differs from the (often misguided) amateur by the cues he or she looks for, the trust he or she has in them, and the way they are interpreted.

Liars leak deceit. Most try hard to cover up their deceit but it is difficult trying to control your words, voice, face, feet and hands all at the same time. The voice and the face carry important cues. Vrij (2000 p 33) has identified 17 non-verbal behaviours that may be directly related to lying:

Vocal characteristics

1 *Speech hesitations:* use of the words 'ah', 'um', 'er', and so on.
2 *Speech errors:* word and/or sentence repetition, sentence change, sentence incompletions, slips of the tongue, and so on.
3 *Pitch of voice:* changes in pitch of voice, such as a rise or fall in pitch.
4 *Speech rate:* number of spoken words in a certain period of time.
5 *Latency period:* period of silence between question and answer.
6 *Frequency of pauses:* frequency of silent periods during speech.
7 *Pause durations:* length of silent periods during speech.

Facial Characteristics

8 *Gaze:* looking at the face of the conversation partner.
9 *Smile:* smiling and laughing.
10 *Blinking:* blinking of the eyes.

Movements

11 *Self-manipulations:* scratching the head, wrists, and so on.
12 *Illustrators:* functional hand and arm movements designed to modify and/or supplement what is being said verbally.

13 *Hand and finger movements:* non-functional movements of hands or fingers without moving the arms.

14 *Leg and foot movements:* movements of the feet and legs.

15 *Head movements:* head nods and head shakes.

16 *Trunk movements:* movements of the trunk (usually accompanied by head movements).

17 *Shifting position:* movements made to change the sitting position (usually accompanied by trunk and foot/leg movements).

Vrij has also given seven specifically verbal indicators that often relate to lying (Table 8.1).

There are some findings that are clearly true about lying. First, you can observe stress signals produced by the liar's autonomic nervous system: dry mouth, but sweaty palms, shallow uneven breathing, 'tickly' nose and throat, blushing or blanching. These are observable when someone is under stress whether they are lying or not. It is very easy to confuse the two. Most people in interviews are, initially at any rate, anxious. Also people are less conscious of their feet or legs: the further you are from the face the nearer you get to the truth. Sudden changes in foot tapping, pointing feet to the exit ('I want to get out of here') and simultaneous tight arm and foot crossing having been taken to indicate lying. Foot movements may be as reliable an index of boredom as they are of lying. The frequent crossing of legs may simply indicate an uncomfortable chair.

Posture is probably more sincere than gesture: it can be seen as more unnatural and forced when people lie. Because people seem less aware of their total posture they may secretly signal various desires (to leave) or are holding back the truth. However, the shape and comfort of furniture natu rally have something to do with it. Interestingly giveaway, expansive *gestures*

Table 8.1 Verbal indicators that relate to lying

Verbal characteristic	Description
1　Negative statements	Statements indicating aversion towards an object, person or opinion, such as denials and disparaging statements, and statements indicating a negative mood.
2　Plausible answers	Statements which make sense and which sound credible and reasonable.
3　Irrelevant information	Information which is irrelevant to the context, and which has not been asked for.
4　Overgeneralized statement	The use of words such as 'always', 'never', 'nobody', 'everybody', and so on.
5　Self-references	The use of words referring to the speaker himself or herself, such as 'I', 'me' or 'mine'.
6　Direct answers	To-the-point and straightforward statements (for example, 'I like John' is more direct than 'I like John's company').
7　Response length	Length of the answer or number of spoken words.

Source: Vrij 2000 p 104.

decline: because they feel they may be caught by excessive gestures people tend to sit on their hands, fold their arms, clap their hands together. The lack of spontaneity may be an index of lying – or fear – the fear of being caught. And of course some people are not simply as gesturally expressive as others.

Most people know about the *shifty gaze* of liars: when children are lying they look down or away. They look guilty but do not look you in the eye. Many an innocent person has been accused of lying through the avoidance of eye contact but people avoid eye contact for many different reasons – uncertainty about opinion, trying to remember facts, social embarrassment. Indeed it is impolite in some cultures to look one in the eye. And as we shall see some liars are caught because, knowing this 'rule', they state too much. In this sense they 'protesteth' too much and hence get caught.

Liars tend to be most careful, thoughtful and involved in their choice and use of words. They can rehearse, practice and become word perfect. They are also very conscious of their *facial expressions* during the lying episodes. But it is the voice and body that perhaps give most away – and are therefore the cues to watch to catch the naive and sophisticated. People are betrayed by their words if they are careless, if they make a (Freudian) slip of the tongue or the emotional tirade when words pour, rather than slip out. We also know that there are various vocal indexes of deceit relating to lying pauses, hesitations and tone and pitch of voice.

Finally there are a number of important, subtle body indexes of deceit including gestures, emblems, illustrations and manipulations. Emblems are well-known gestures with precise meanings: illustrations are movements that accentuate speech: manipulations are movements such as grooming, massaging, rubbing, holding, pinching, picking and scratching. The autonomic nervous system changes with emotional arousal. Certain body changes occur – sweating, blushing, pupil dilation, breathing pattern and frequency of swallowing, all of which are difficult to inhibit. They are the basis of the lie detectors/polygraph as we have seen.

Experts in the area, like Ekman (2001), have stressed facial clues to deceit and how facial expressions can serve a lie, but also provide manifold and very subtle cues to the truth. Ekman argues that the face can show which emotion is felt – anger, fear, sadness, disgust, distress, happiness, contentment, excitement, surprise and contempt can all be conveyed by distinctive expressions. The face can also show whether two emotions are blended together – often two emotions are felt and the face registers elements of each. The face also shows the strength of the felt emotion – each emotion can vary in intensity, from annoyance to rage, apprehension to terror, and so on (p 125).

People, through growing up, learn facial display rules. But to the skilled observer there are a range of micro-expressions which yield the emotions behind them. There are all sorts of technical terms that help describe expressions. For instance, a squelched expression is one where one (possibly natural) expression is masked or covered by another. Experts look for asymmetrical facial expressions, which show up on only one side of the face, the exact location of these expressions and the timing of the expression (with both words and other expressions).

To the expert like Ekman, the face really is the mirror of the soul. He believes one can distinguish between *eighteen* different types of smile from the contemptuous, dampened and miserable to the flirtatious, embarrassed and compliant smile. He also documents some of the characteristics which often accompany particular lies. False smiles are often inappropriate (that is, when they occur, how long they last); they are often asymmetrical, they are not accompanied by the involvement of the many muscles around the eye, and they only cover the actions of the lower face and lower eyelid.

Ekman (2001 p 161) concluded thus:

> The face may contain many different clues to deceit: micros, squelched expressions, leakage in the reliable facial muscles, blinking, pupil dilation, tearing, blushing and blanching, asymmetry, mistakes in timing, mistakes in location, and false smiles. Some of these clues provide leakage, betraying concealed information; others provide deception clues indicating that something is being concealed but not what; and others mark an expression to be false.

> These facial signs of deceit, like the clues to deceit in words, voice, and body described in the last chapter, vary in the precision of the information they convey. Some clues to deceit reveal exactly which emotion is actually felt, even though the liar tries to conceal that feeling. Other clues to deceit reveal only whether the emotion concealed is positive or negative and don't reveal exactly which negative emotion or which positive emotion the liar feels. Still other clues are even more undifferentiated, betraying only that the liar feels some emotion but not revealing whether the concealed feeling is positive or negative. That may be enough. Knowing that some emotion is felt sometimes can suggest that a person is lying, if the situation is one in which except for lying the person would not be likely to feel any emotion at all. Other times a lie won't be betrayed without more precise information about which concealed emotion is felt. It depends upon the lie, the line taken by the person suspected of lying, the situation, and the alternative explanations available, apart from lying, to account for why an emotion might be felt but concealed.

Furnham (1999) provided another, similar list of the following factors that help 'give away' liars:

Verbal cues (spoken language):

▷ *Response latency* or the time elapsing between the end of a question and the beginning of their response. Liars take longer. They hesitate more, than when not lying.

▷ *Linguistic distance* – not saying I, he, she, but talking in the abstract even when recalling incidents in which they were involved.

▷ *Slow but uneven speech* – as they try to think while speaking but get caught out. They might suddenly speak fast implying something is less significant. It is the change in pace as a function of a particular question that gives a clue that something is not right.

▷ *Too eager to fill silences* – to keep talking when it is unnecessary. Liars over-compensate and seem uncomfortable with what are often quite short pauses.

▷ *Too many 'pitch raises'* – that is, instead of the pitch dropping at the end of a reply it raises like a question. It may sound like 'Do you believe me now?'

Non-verbal:

▷ *Being too squirming/*shifting around too much in the chair.

▷ *Having too much* – rather than too little – eye contact as liars tend to over compensate. They know that liars avoid mutual gaze so they 'prove they are not lying' by a lot of looking … but 'a tad too much'.

▷ *Micro-expression* or flickers of expressions (of surprise, hurt, anger) difficult to see unless frames are frozen.

▷ *An increase in comfort gestures* – self-touching the face and upper body.

▷ *An increase in stuttering*, slurring and of course, Freudian slips. Generally an increase in speech errors.

▷ *A loss of resonance in the voice* – it becomes flatter, less deep, more monotonous.

For many observers the problem is distinguishing between lying and anxiety. The well-trained and arrogant liar may thus look innocent; the truthful but nervous witness the liar. The fast nervous ticks of the latter may be seen as classic signs of subordination – as if caught. There are not hard and fast practices about catching liars. At interview it is good to relax them (to get them off their guard) and then let them talk as much as possible. The more said the more opportunities to be caught.

Collett (2003) used the concept of 'tell' to specify signals or actions that 'tell you' what somebody is thinking even if that person does not know it themselves:

▷ *Detection tells:* Whereas most people believe they are good at detecting lies the opposite appears to be the case. They seem to fail at this all-important skill for five reasons. First, people prefer *blissful ignorance*, not wanting to admit that the other person is lying. Next, people set their *detection threshold very high* but highly suspicious people might set it very low. Third, people who rely on *intuition* and gut feelings do not do as well as those who look for clues to deception. Fourth, people forget that all behaviours have *multiple causes* and that there are few single, simple indicators of lying. Finally, people *look in the wrong places* and for the wrong cues – fidgeting as opposed to smiling. Collett then considered classic lying tells.

▷ *Eye tells:* People know about gaze patterns and control them but continuous rapid blinking and unusually intent staring may be signs of lying.

▷ *Body tells:* Despite popular beliefs, hand movements and fidgeting are under conscious control and therefore unreliable indexes of lying. However, other neglected things such as leg and feet movements and self-touching are better indicators. Further, just as many liars appear to freeze more rather than become increasingly animated when lying.

▷ *Nose tells:* Touching the nose really represents covering the mouth. The

'Pinocchio syndrome' may be simply due to anxiety and it remains unclear whether vasoconstriction (blood draining from the face/nose) or vasodilation (blood increasing in the face/nose) occurs when people lie.

▷ *Masking tells:* These are masks (often smiles) that people use to cover or mask their negative feelings about lying. The straight or crypto-relaxed face masks seem to work best.

▷ *Smiling tells:* Smiles are used extensively by experienced liars because they both make others feel positive and also less suspicious about them lying. But there are many types of smile – blended, miserable, counterfeit. Clues to the counterfeit smile lie in the duration (they last longer), assembly (they are put together and dismantled more quickly), location (confined to the lower part of the face), symmetry (less symmetrical).

▷ *Micro tells:* These are very fast, short-lived, micro-momentous expressions that are difficult to see live but can be seen on second-by-second videotape playback. They may relate to tension release or anger or a whole range of emotions associated with lying.

▷ *Talking tells:* Despite the fact that most people believe non-verbal cues are better than verbal cues to lying, it actually appears the opposite way around. Collett (2003) lists eleven of these:

1 *Circumlocution:* beating around the bush with long-winded digression.
2 *Outlining:* broadbrush, detail-less account. Liars rarely expand when asked, truth-tellers do.
3 *Smoke screens:* confusing, non-sensible statements.
4 *Negatives:* liars are more likely to use negative statements.
5 *Word-choice:* fewer self references (I, me) and more generalizations (everybody, always).
6 *Disclaimers:* excessive use of 'I know this sound strange', 'let me assure you', and 'You won't believe this but...'.
7 *Formality:* becoming more tense and formal, they say things like do not instead of don't.
8 *Tense:* liars use the past tense more to distance themselves from the event they are describing.
9 *Speed:* liars slow down because of the strain on their various capacities.
10 *Pause:* liars pause more with more traditional dysfluences like 'um' and 'er'.
11 *Pitch:* this rises with emotion.

Collett (2003 pp 239–40) provides the would-be lie-catcher with some good advice:

Although there is no guaranteed method of detecting lies, there are certain things that you can do to increase your chances of spotting a liar:

▷ To detect a lie successfully you need to set your criteria so that they're neither too high nor too low. That way you'll avoid coming to the conclusion that nobody ever tells a lie, or that everybody lies all the time.

▷ Where possible, the actions that someone performs while they are supposedly lying should be compared with how they behave when they are telling the truth.

▷ To be a good lie detector you should also concentrate on behaviour that falls outside conscious control or that people are likely to ignore.

▷ Given the opportunity, focus your attention on what people say and how they say it, rather than on what they do.

▷ It's important to work out whether the lie is likely to be spontaneous or rehearsed, and whether it's a high-stakes or a low-stakes lie. When the stakes are low or the lie has been rehearsed, the task of detecting the lie is much more difficult.

▷ To spot a lie you should always focus on a broad range of behavioural and speech clues. If you think you can spot a liar on the basis of a single clue, you're deceiving yourself.

Despite the fact there are numerous popular books and articles that seem to imply that you can 'read people like a book' and relatively easily catch liars, experts in the field say the precise opposite. One's ability to detect lies is multifaceted and problematic. In short, it depends on the nature of the lie, the personality and experience of both the liar and the person trying to detect the lie and the context/situation in which the lie is told.

Ekman (2001 p 8) notes:

Success in distinguishing when a person is lying and when a person is telling the truth is highest when:

▷ The lie is being told for the first time

▷ The person has not told this type of lie before

▷ The stakes are high – most importantly the threat of severe punishment

▷ The interviewer is truly open-minded, and does not jump to conclusions quickly

▷ The interviewer knows how to encourage the interviewee to tell his or her story (the more words spoken the better the chance of distinguishing lies from truthfulness)

▷ The interviewer and interviewee come from the same cultural background and speak the same language

▷ The interviewer regards the clues as hot spots, marking where it is important to get more information, rather than as proof of lying

▷ The interviewer is aware of the difficulties of identifying the truthful, innocent person who is under suspicion of having committed an offence.

From other research Furnham (1999) points out that there are both verbal and non-verbal cues to deceit and that, contrary to popular belief, verbal/vocal cues may be as accurate and sensitive an index as body language. Indeed it is precisely because liars believe there is more potential to catch them through their body than their voice that they concentrate too much on their body language and not on what they are saying or how they are saying it.

How do professional lie-catchers (that is, police, customs officers) go

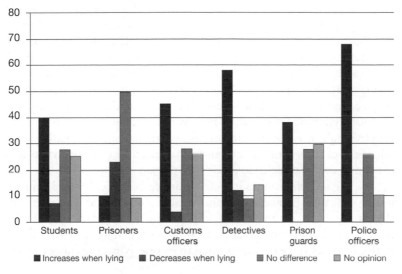

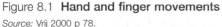

Figure 8.1 **Hand and finger movements**
Source: Vrij 2000 p 78.

about catching liars? Indeed are they better at it than non-professionals? Vrij (2000) reports on one study that showed large differences in the beliefs of different groups. Illustrated below is one behaviour: hand and finger movements. Note the difference between police officers and prisoners which no doubt relates to how they behave when either telling a lie or trying to detect lies (Figure 8.1).

Vrij also showed the cues police detectives typically use when trying to catch liars (Figure 8.2).

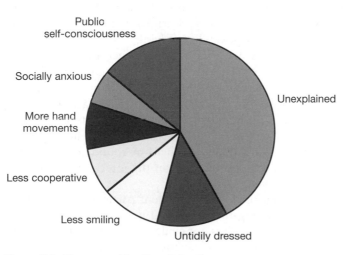

Figure 8.2 **Cues used by the detectives**
Source: Vrij 2000 p 80.

There are some simple but important strategies for everyone to bear in mind when trying to catch liars. First, one has to establish base-rate behaviour. This means in essence what people are like when they are normal, relaxed and telling the truth. Some always twitch others do not, some blink a lot, others rarely. Give people time to relax and see what they are like when it is unlikely that they are lying. Some people fidget more than others. Neurotics are more anxious than the stable most of the time. There are numerous idiosyncratic but stable non-verbal behavioural differences between individuals. It is too easy to mistake particular signs (sweating, eye-gaze avoidance) as a sign of anxiety and as a function of lying when it is perfectly normal everyday behaviour for that person.

Next, look for *sudden* changes in behaviour (verbal, vocal, visual), movements and so on. It is when behaviour noticeably alters that it is most meaningful. And it is particularly important when changes take place that are not restricted to a single modality (that is, face or voice). It is always better to interpret the changes in behaviour rather than one particular idiosyncratic feature.

Gradually one needs to note any mismatch between what is being said and how it is being said: differences in anxiety level as certain topics are raised. When the eyes, the voice and the words are not in emotional synchrony, it may well be a very good sign of lying. The forced smile or laugh to accompany the carefully prepared verbal line can be a powerful indicator that 'something interesting is going on'. In short, when the behaviour occurs when a particular topic is discussed this is a good cue.

Next for the scientist bit: formulate a hypothesis as to the cause? What are they lying about, what is the sensitive issue? Not everything is a lie. Why should they be lying about some issues and not others? It is important to consider the possibility of an alternative explanation that shows the person is *not* lying. Test the theory by bringing up a particular topic (the area of the lies) and see if the non-verbal pattern reoccurs. If there are persistent indicators of discomfort when particular topics are reintroduced into the conversation one may assume a stronger possibility of lying.

The bottom line, however, is that even for the trained expert it is often very difficult to detect liars. We have videotapes of famous spies lying; of murderers who pretend to be victims appealing for help; of politicians telling bare-faced lies in video close-ups. They succeed in fooling hundreds of people. Even the lie detector can be relatively easily fooled. Studies using it have shown that when misdiagnosis occurs it is much more likely that an innocent person is judged as guilty than the other way round. So beware the person who claims to be good at spotting liars in the interview. It could be true – or a self-delusional porkie!

But the experts caution against feeling confident particularly in the hard job of distinguishing, 'disbelieving-the-truth' and just as easily 'believing a lie'. Clearly absence of a sign of deceit is not evidence of truth. One problem as noted above are the ever-present idiosyncratic individual differences.

As Ekman (2001 p 166) notes:

The poker player in this example set up and exploited a disbelieving-the-truth mistake, profiting from being judged to be lying. More often when a lie-catcher makes a disbelieving-the-truth mistake, the person who is mistakenly identified as lying suffers. It is not deviousness that causes some people to be judged lying when they are truthful but a quirk in their behaviour, an idiosyncrasy in their expressive style. What for most people might be a clue to deceit is not for such a person. Some people:

▷ Are indirect and circumlocutious in their speech
▷ Speak with many or short or long pauses between words
▷ Make many speech errors
▷ Use few illustrators
▷ Make many body manipulators
▷ Often show signs of fear, distress, or anger in their facial expressions, regardless of how they actually feel
▷ Show asymmetrical facial expressions.

There are enormous differences among individuals in all of these behaviours; and these differences produce not only disbelieving-the-truth but also believing-a-lie mistakes. Calling the truthful person who characteristically speaks indirectly a liar is a disbelieving-the-truth mistake; calling the lying smooth-talker truthful is a believing-a-lie mistake. Even though such a talker's speech when lying may become more indirect and have more errors, it may escape notice because it still is so much smoother than speech usually is for most people.

How easy is it to determine whether somebody is lying? Which factors make it easier for the liar to avoid detection, and which for the detective to catch the liar? Essentially the hardest lies to tell are those when the liar has to try to conceal many strong emotions while telling the lie. Table 8.2 provides a checklist for detecting lies.

Table 8.2 Lying checklist

		Hard for the lie-catcher to detect	Easy for the lie-catcher to detect
Questions about the lie			
1	Can the liar anticipate exactly when he or she has to lie?	YES: line prepared and rehearsed.	NO: line not prepared
2	Does the lie involve concealment only, without any need to falsify?	YES	NO
3	Does the lie involve emotions felt at the moment?	NO	YES: specially difficult if: A. negative emotions such as anger, fear or distress must be concealed or falsified. B. Liar must appear emotionless and cannot use another emotion to mask felt emotions that have to be concealed.

cont'd

Table 8.2 continued

	Hard for the lie-catcher to detect	Easy for the lie-catcher to detect
Questions about the lie		
4 Would there be amnesty if liar confesses to lying?	NO: enhances liar's motive to succeed.	YES: chance to induce confession.
5 Are the stakes in terms of either rewards or punishments very high?	Difficult to predict; while high stakes may increase detection apprehension, it should also motivate the liar to try hard.	
6 Are there severe punishments for being caught lying?	NO: low detection apprehension; but may produce carelessness.	YES: enhances detection apprehension, but may also fear being disbelieved, producing false-positive errors.
7 Are there severe punishments for the very act of having lied, apart from the losses incurred from the deceit failing?	NO	YES: enhances detection apprehension: person may be dissuaded from embarking on lie if she or he knows that punishment for attempting to lie will be worse than the loss incurred by not lying.
8 Does the target suffer no loss or even benefit from the lie? Is the lie altruistic not benefiting the liar?	YES: less deception guilt if liar believes this to be so.	NO: increases deception guilt.
9 Is it a situation in which the target is likely to trust the liar, not suspecting that he or she may be misled.	YES	NO
10 Has liar successfully deceived the target before?	YES: decreases detection apprehension; and if target would be ashamed or otherwise suffer by having to acknowledge having been fooled, he or she may become a willing victim.	NO
11 Do liar and target share values?	NO: decreases deception guilt	YES: increases deception guilt.
12 Is the lie authorized?	YES: decreases deception guilt	NO: increases the deception guilt.
13 Is the target anonymous?	YES: decreases deception guilt.	NO
14 Are target and liar personally acquainted?	NO	YES: lie-catcher will be more able to avoid errors due to individual differences.
15 Must lie-catcher conceal his suspicions from the liar?	YES: lie-catcher may become enmeshed in his own need to conceal and fail to be as alert to the liar's behaviour	NO

cont'd

Table 8.2 continued

	Hard for the lie-catcher to detect	Easy for the lie-catcher to detect
Questions about the lie		
16 Does lie-catcher have information that only a guilty not an innocent person would also have?	NO	YES: can try to use the guilty knowledge test if the suspect can be interrogated.
17 Is there an audience who knows or suspects that the target is being deceived?	NO	YES: may enhance duping delight, detection apprehension, or deception guilt.
18 Do liar and lie-catcher come from similar language, national and cultural backgrounds?	NO: more errors in judging clues to deceit.	YES: better able to interpret clues to deceit.

Questions about the liar

19 Is the liar practised in lying?	YES: especially if practised in this type of lie.	NO
20 Is the liar inventive and clever in fabricating?	YES	NO
21 Does the liar have a good memory?	YES	NO
22 Is the liar a smooth talker with a convincing manner?	YES	NO
23 Does the liar use the reliable facial muscles as conversational emphasizers?	YES: better able to conceal or falsify facial expressions.	NO
24 Is the liar skilled as an actor, able to use the Stanislavski method?	YES	NO
25 Is the liar likely to convince himself of his lie believing that what he says is true?	YES	NO
26 Is she or he a 'natural liar' or psychopath?	YES	NO
27 Does the liar's personality make liar vulnerable either to fear, guilt, or duping delight?	NO	YES
28 Is liar ashamed of what liar is concealing?	Difficult to predict: while shame works to prevent confession, leakage of that shame may betray the lie.	
29 Might suspected liar feel fear, guilt, shame or duping delight even if suspect is innocent and not lying, or lying about something else?	YES: Can't interpret emotion clues.	NO: signs of these emotions are clues to deceit.

cont'd

Table 8.2 continued

	Hard for the lie-catcher to detect	Easy for the lie-catcher to detect
Questions about the lie-catcher		
30 Does the lie-catcher have a reputation for being tough to mislead?	NO: if liar has in the past been successful in fooling the lie-catcher.	YES: increases detection apprehension may also increase duping delight.
31 Does the lie-catcher have a reputation for being distrustful?	Difficult to predict: such a reputation might decrease deception guilt, it may also increase detection apprehension.	
32 Does the lie catcher have a reputation for being fair minded?	NO: liar less likely to feel guilt about deceiving the lie-catcher.	YES: increases deception guilt.
33 Is the lie-catcher a denier, who avoids problems, and tends to always think the best of people?	YES: probably will overlook clues to deceit, vulnerable to false negative errors.	NO
34 Is lie-catcher unusually able to accurately interpret expressive behaviours?	NO	YES
35 Does the lie-catcher have preconceptions which bias the lie-catcher against the liar?	NO	YES: although lie-catcher will be alert to clues to deceit, he/she will be liable to false positive errors.
36 Does the lie-catcher obtain any benefits from not detecting the lie?	YES: lie-catcher will ignore, deliberately or unwittingly, clues to deceit.	NO
37 Is lie-catcher unable to tolerate uncertainty about whether he/she is being deceived?	Difficult to predict: may cause either false-positive or false-negative errors.	
38 Is lie-catcher seized by an emotional wildfire?	NO	YES: liars will be caught, but innocents will be judged to be lying (false-positive error).

Source: Ekman 2001.

Some researchers and practitioners have begun to look carefully at the structured interview and a careful analysis of the content and qualities of statements. These are called criteria-based content analyses and look systematically at things such as the structure of the logic, the quantity of details, reproduction of conversations, details about the mental state of different parties involved, admitting lack of memory and so on. They also often look for the inappropriateness of language and knowledge, inconsistency in the statements and so on.

Conclusion

Training and experience does help in the business of lie detection. But it is by no means simple or foolproof. Because we are all used to lying it is an every-day occurrence and to a large extent socially acceptable. People have quite different beliefs about when one can, should and should not lie. And they have considerable personal experience to catch liars. However, many of us are not well informed and, as we have seen, either look for or misinterpret the lies (or truth) they observe. Hence the ability of many liars to get away with it!

There is considerable consistency and overlap between reviewers and researchers' conclusions in this area. They show that many 'lay theses' (that is, the theories of ordinary people) are wrong: almost dramatically opposed to popular belief. They also admit that it is not an easy business. Those who have made a lifetime research project to study the nature of lying admit that they can often get it wrong. But they also offer good advice.

Ekman (2001 pp 187–9) in fact offered ten specific suggestions that help people trying to detect lies to do a better, more reliable job. They are:

1   Try to make explicit the basis of any hunches and intuitions about whether or not someone is lying. By becoming more aware of how you interpret behavioural clues to deceit, you will learn to spot your mistakes and recognize when you don't have much chance to make a correct judgement.

2   Remember that there are two dangers in detecting deceit: disbelieving the truth (judging a truthful person to be lying) and believing-a-lie (judging a liar to be truthful). There is no way to completely avoid both mistakes. Consider the consequences of risking either mistake.

3   The absence of a sign of deceit is not evidence of truth; some people don't leak. The presence of a sign of deceit is not always evidence of lying; some people appear ill-at-ease or guilty even when they are truthful. You can decrease the Brokaw hazard, which is due to individual differences in expressive behaviour, by basing your judgements on a change in the suspect's behaviour.

4   Search your mind for any preconceptions you may have about the suspect. Consider whether your preconceptions will bias your chance of making a correct judgement. Don't try to judge whether or not someone is lying if you feel overcome by jealousy or in an emotional wildfire. Avoid the temptation to suspect lying because it explains otherwise inexplicable events.

5   Always consider the possibility that a sign of emotion is not a clue to deceit but a clue to how a truthful person feels about being suspected of lying. Discount the sign of an emotion as a clue to deceit if a truthful suspect might feel that emotion because of: the suspect's personality; the nature of your past relationship with the suspect; or the suspect's expectations.

6   Bear in mind that many clues to deceit are signs of more than one emotion, and that those that are must be discounted if one of those emotions could be felt if the suspect is truthful while another could be felt if the suspect is lying.

7   Consider whether or not the suspect knows he is under suspicion, and what the gains or losses in detecting deceit would be either way.

8   If you have knowledge that the suspect would also have only if he is lying, and you can afford to interrogate the suspect, construct a guilty knowledge test.

9   Never reach a final conclusion about whether a suspect is lying or not based solely on your interpretation of behavioural clues to deceit. Behavioural clues to deceit should only serve to alert you to the need for further information and investigation. Behavioural clues, like the polygraph, can never provide absolute evidence.

10 Use the checklist provided in the previous section to evaluate the lie, the liar, and you, the lie-catcher, to estimate the likelihood of making errors or correctly judging truthfulness.

9 Protecting Your Assets

Introduction

Staff disillusionment and defiance are probably at some time inevitable. A head of research may go to the press and expose an environmentally damaging aspect of the company's work; an exchange floor dealer may cream off millions of dollars of profits; a medical researcher may claim a piece of work as original when it was stolen from someone else; a poison pen letter-writer may disrupt and reduce morale in the workforce; an employee may put glass chips in baby food on sale on your shelves.

This chapter considers how first to handle such incidents and how to minimize the damage they can do. A positive attitude to security from all employees in a company helps to reduce the incidence and impact of disloyalty.

How a company protects its assets and secrets plays a significant part in creating its culture. Too heavy a hand, and productivity and loyalty will be significantly reduced. Excessive use of monitoring devices such as CCTV or physical searches and staff will begin to feel they are not trusted, resentment will set in and opportunities to get back at the employer will be taken.

Security rarely enjoys a good reputation in any organization. It is expensive and it generates no profit only substantial installation, maintenance and monitoring costs. Most companies recognize it can reduce the costs, but they would rather assign the subject to experts or consultants employed to conduct this rather seamy side of business. But it's a fact of business and corporate life.

If managers care about the fitness of the company, they can not ignore the hygiene factors (that is, quality of working environment) which contribute to a healthy corporate culture. Too much security or poorly applied rules stifle creativity and infect the atmosphere with suspiciousness, even paranoia.

This chapter answers the following questions: How much is 'enough security'? How to develop the right approach to security? Do strict security rules create the very distrust a company is seeking to avoid? Do all employees have to be treated in the same way? What specifically can a company do to protect its customers, investors, secrets and property? Will a company security policy document help and, if so, what should it consist of?

Issues around the security of property, computers and information will all be discussed in the context of creating a positive attitude to security amongst employees; removing opportunities for mischief; handling miscreants who are discovered.

The chapter does not however provide detailed advice on specific physical security measures, which might need to be deployed. Nor is it a comprehensive analysis of security measures needed to protect a company from all threats. Its focus is the people in the organization.

'Enough security'

It is much easier to put in a new security rule than it is to remove one. Creeping paralysis may well be choking the organization, but it takes a brave person to remove security rules. But the rules should be regularly reviewed, and with creativity as well as boldness. Further, it helps all the employees to be involved in making the rules and setting standards about security.

The objective should be to have 'enough security' to protect the assets, material and non-material of an organization, but no more. The process starts with a risk and threat assessment. Properly done this will identify those areas that need protection and the degree of protection required. Security experts and their consultants can do this, but the basic questions are very much the business of managers and the board as well as individual employees. They have to make the important judgements about what the critical areas are.

Table 9.1 Issues at risk

At risk	Internal threat or cause	The external threat or cause
Buildings and fixed fittings	Sabotage	Vandalism
Staff resignations	Disillusion, bullying, failed expectations; new challenges, better pay	Headhunters, seductive advertisements
Cash	Disaffected staff	Criminal individual or gangs breaking into property or taking advantage of absence
Company financial assets not held in cash	Criminal fraud with the advantage of insider information	Criminal fraud using insider information
Office consumables: for example stationery, print cartridges, telephone calls, photocopier	Virtually every member of staff has access to this and virtually everyone does it at some time in their career	Members of the public visiting and finding unprotected or easily stolen equipment
The company product itself: for example chocolates in a sweet factory, diamonds in a diamond mine	Employee theft	Retail shops suffer highly; criminals focus on small high-value products
Research data on the company's new products	Disaffected staff	Competitors
Information about customers or clients	Disaffected staff	Competitors
Company reputation	Disaffected staff	Competitors

The critical assets that need protection may include physical assets, including the property and offices. For many the retention of key staff will be important. Others will identify customers, company reputation and investors. This assessment also identifies the most likely threats to the assets. Table 9.1 illustrates the most common.

Each risk and threat will need different and proportionate measures. What follows will hopefully inform those who need to design a security policy which risks need attention and how they might be tackled. By the end of the chapter it will be possible to identify from a checklist how to introduce 'enough security' for each of the various risks and threats.

Recruiting the right people

The recruitment criteria for staff often refer to the need for integrity, honesty, 'impeccable character' and trustworthiness as essential qualities. Why do so many who fall short of these criteria get through the system? Is it possible to select out those who are inheritantly dishonest? Can recruiters *select* in the honest and reliable?

Those responsible for recruiting new staff, be they in human resources or the managers directly responsible for the job, can employ a number of measures to estimate a candidate's honesty (see Chapter 7). But sadly most rely on their instincts and how the candidate responds to some fairly obvious and rather naive questions: would you describe yourself as having integrity?

There are a number of options available to the recruiter, some more useful and deployable than others. None can offer 100% validity, but they can select out some of the more obvious problem employees and for that reason alone should not be dismissed. The list includes: rigorous interview techniques; assessment centres; lie-detector tests; references; personality tests; honesty tests; focused vetting interviews.

Some measures will seem more draconian than others and certainly more than 'enough'. All companies will however wish to assure themselves of their employees' reliability to some extent and therefore will need to deploy a number of the measures suggested above. If companies have a need for absolute trust of their staff then they will need to consider all of the above. Most companies will need to apply such rigour to a relatively small number of employees.

Interviewing

Trying to discover someone's reliability and integrity in an interview is beset with dangers. This surprisingly rarely puts off the recruiters or managers, who are invariably confident in their abilities to spot the 'bad egg'. Research sadly shows that their confidence is seriously misplaced (see Chapter 8).

The validity of interviews is disputed by many researchers, which applies particularly to the unstructured interview that characterizes most recruitment procedures. Structuring questions that reveal something about a candidate's honesty and commitment needs considerable thought beforehand.

An interviewer might prepare an integrity question by identifying an incident when an employee had in the past not lived up to the standards of the organization: for example the use of company credit cards. A question could be structured on the following basis.

The rules state that employees may use a credit card for personal use but must pay to the company outstanding personal balances in full at the end of every month. The company pays the credit card company independently. It is known that the accounts department does not check card repayments rigorously.

It is December and you are short of cash for buying Christmas presents. You use the company card to pay for them. At the end of the month when you get your pay cheque you have insufficient funds to repay the debt and have no other credit cards available. What would you do in this situation?

(a) I would never use the company card for personal reasons – end of story (good)

(b) I would speak to my line manager and seek his or her advice on how I could repay the debt and interest later (good)

(c) I would go to the bank (or family or friends) and ask for a loan to pay the money I owed the company (average)

(d) I would save and pay the company at the end of January (poor)

(e) I would hope the debt would not be noticed, but if challenged would claim it was an oversight and pay as soon as possible (very poor).

A more subtle style of question would be to put the same situation to a candidate but ask what he would do if he were the line manager who received the subordinate's admission that he could not pay the credit card debt. The responses of the line manager might be:

(a) The problem is a personal one for you to sort out. It's not my concern as your boss (average – the manager is effectively covering up a problem which might lead to dishonesty)

(b) How much is it – I will lend you the money to cover the debt (average)

(c) Don't worry – pay it next month, together with the interest – no one will ever notice (poor – condoning dishonesty)

(d) Speak to accounts department and ask what can be done. Here is the number, let me know if you have any problems (average – the manager needs to ensure that the subordinate does report the incident)

(e) I would speak to accounts department and seek a solution (good).

The use of critical incidents in a structured interview needs training and diligence in preparation. Few staff are trained adequately in interviewing skills – a theme that is repeated often in this book.

Personality and integrity tests

The use of integrity (sometimes known as honesty) tests is surrounded in controversy (see Chapter 7). Yet as we have noted, reviewers seem, overall, to be positive. Mark Cook (1998 p 434) asserts:

1 Honesty tests work; they predict counterproductive behaviours very well.
2 Honesty tests also predict general job proficiency very well.
3 Main stream psychological tests are no more successful than specialist honesty tests.

Kline, a dissenting voice, on the other hand concludes:

it is difficult to recommend tests of honesty in occupational selection. To use them is to pretend a validity which they do not have. This is, indeed, a spurious science. (2000 p 434)

For instance one approach is to measure personality because it has been established that traits are consistently related to CWBs. Two traits are particularly implicated: conscientiousness and agreeableness. Conscientious people value dutifulness, diligence and hard work. Agreeable people are empathetic, kind and altruistic. Disagreeable people with a low conscientiousness score are likely to be inefficient, disorganized, unreliable, unself-disciplined, unforgiving and sceptical. Further, neurotic individuals are touchy, thin-skinned and self-conscious and may react very badly to setbacks at work.

Personality test scores give one an idea of an individual's approach to their work and their resilience when faced by stress. They may well be able to pinpoint those individuals more in danger of, or likely to commit CWBs than others.

Referees

Those who provide references are not, as some still assume, exempt from the law of libel. For that reason and to avoid other problems with departing employees, referees are often unwilling to say anything negative about a candidate. Candidates are also smart enough only to offer up referees who will report positively on them.

Research in the US suggests that references are unreliable; in the UK references are considered more reliable (Cook 1998 p 69). Occupational psychologists in general tend to dismiss them. There is, however, some consensus that references can be useful if focused on factual information rather than seeking general comments. For the purposes of verifying someone's honesty a reference can help, but more to select out people rather than selecting in.

Reference questionnaires or letters should be properly structured, asking, where appropriate, direct questions, as well as seeking to confirm factual data necessary for the rest of the recruitment process. Questions such as the following can elicit useful information:

▷ Has this person to your knowledge ever been found guilty of theft or a serious breach of office rules?
▷ Was this person the subject of an incomplete disciplinary investigation at the time of his/her departure?
▷ On a scale of 1 to 10 (10 being high), how would you assess this person's integrity?
▷ Would you employ this person again?

It is particularly valuable to follow up a reference with a telephone call. People are often more willing to be frank on the phone than they are in writing. Be sure when phoning to check that you know to whom you are speaking in the company and that you have independently verified the number you are ringing.

David Davies gives a number of chilling examples in his book *Fraud Watch* (2000 pp 46–7) demonstrating how companies could have avoided substantial losses by being more rigorous in their pursuit of referees. The message is that referees can provide useful information, but to be effective recruiters have to be proactive, asking specific questions, of specific individuals who have been targeted.

Focused vetting interviews

Those involved in the recruitment process have many criteria to judge; honesty is only one. Integrity might not therefore receive all the attention it deserves in occupations where personal security is held to be essential.

Civil services around the world require their senior staff who work in sensitive departments, such as the Ministry of Defence or the Foreign Ministry, to undergo a vetting interview designed to explore their integrity and reliability. This typically will involve a credit check, interviews with referees, including school and university, as well as an in-depth interview with the candidate. The vetters may also seek access to medical records (with the candidate's permission) to confirm the absence of serious psychological disorders.

The practice is not however exclusive to the civil service. Companies are increasingly using this to ensure the integrity of their key staff. Usually the process is contracted out. Entering 'personnel vetting' on an internet search engine produces a mass of results. There are also companies online that will carry out criminal checks for a relatively small fee (£30/$40 per enquiry). All of this can be handled by specially trained people whose sole task is to check out the honesty and integrity of prospective recruits or indeed current employees.

There is no panacea – no single test or combination of tests that can give the employer complete confidence that their new staff are entirely reliable.

The recruitment processes are probably best at selecting out those who are potentially dishonest and unreliable. Even if someone could at the moment of recruitment be assessed as reliable and honest, the subsequent influences may well tempt him or her to consider resignation or some more pernicious form of retribution.

Induction

The first few days in the office make a big impression on staff. They are usually apprehensive, excited and emotionally charged up. This is the moment that all trainers look for, when staff are at their most receptive. It is a great opportunity to put over your messages. If however there is no clear message and the new staff member is met by an indifferent attitude to security by their line manager, that impression will carry forward, and be difficult to change.

Content

What should an induction programme say about security? There is a difficult balance to achieve. On the one hand there are some rules that need to be followed but, for security to be effective, employees have to accept personal responsibility for security and be able to make judgement calls that rules cannot always predict. Employees need therefore to understand the security policy and what the organization is trying to protect.

Trainers and security personnel should think carefully about their objectives and how to achieve them.

Some dos:

▶ *Encourage staff to see those in security as friendly and approachable*

▶ *Trainers, managers and leaders should demonstrate support for the security policy*

▶ *Explain the company's security policy openly. If there are areas that are more secret than others and where access is restricted then say so openly*

▶ *Train your security section on how to make presentations. All too often they come over as defensive or they overplay their hand by making their briefing sound threatening*

▶ *Establish good practices at the beginning – see below for more details*

▶ *Give a realistic picture of the threats to the company*

▶ *Tell staff what to do if they see or are responsible for a breach*

▶ *Encourage a non-blame culture*

Some don'ts:

▶ *Trainers and facilitators running the induction course should not abandon the speaker(s) on security implying that they come from a specialist section – security is for all*

▶ *Frighten people or make claims about security department's abilities which are untrue*

▶ *Impose everything from above*

Need-to-know principle (NTK)

This principle is one of the pillars of many civil service departments around the world and increasingly in companies. Where it applies it should be introduced on day one of the induction course. It comes as no surprise therefore and employees' natural curiosity is to some extent controlled.

A senior member of the UK civil service visited his daughter at her work. She was a secretary in a stockbroking firm. Having met the chairman and discussed business, and once the chairman had gone, the civil servant asked if (as a proud and interested father) he could see his daughter's office. She turned round and with great assurance and some aplomb said that would not be possible as he did not have clearance and it was the most sensitive area in the building. 'But I have the highest clearance in the land' he protested, 'Tough' she said, 'that doesn't count here!'

Of course she was right – there was no need for him to see or know anything about the business of the City.

The beauty of NTK is that it limits the information that has to be kept confidential, leaving most information to be freely exchanged. People can therefore have access to it if they need it in their work. The onus is on management to identify and justify why some information must be limited to only a few. If properly explained, particularly in the early days of their employment, staff will understand this readily enough and apply it. Many people do not want the burden of secrets and this principle releases them from the responsibility.

However, a need-to-know principle applied insensitively can worsen the very problem it is trying to reduce (Davies 2000 p 56). If an employee needs to hide a problem he could do so under the guise of need-to-know. Fewer people see the big picture and therefore fraud becomes easier to conceal. NTK has a place in some organizations, but it should be applied in a balanced manner.

Password security

Passwords are everywhere: cash cards, email accounts, internet banking, combination locks, computer log-on procedures and many more. It is inevitable that people will take short cuts. It is impossible to remember them all especially when one has to change them every six months.

In the induction course, help people by giving them acceptable methods to remember letters or numbers. Explain how to hide the password using secure clues or codes in their diaries. Stories of people sharing computer passwords or writing them on pads near their PC are all too frequent. By being trained in such methods, staff have more chance of following the security rules. Just explaining the rules and telling people to follow them has little effect if people are being asked to do something unreasonable.

In the workplace

Good security means that standards have to be kept up throughout a working career. It will usually be respected if employees feel it is reasonable and that it does not unnecessarily get in the way of their work or social lives. The following sections cover the main issues, but not all, that employers need to consider.

Computers

The electronic age has brought many great advances and made many lives better. But it has also created a vast new set of problems for those with information to protect. For the paranoid the PC represents unbounded opportunities to work out their condition. Even for the sensible but concerned managing director, the potential damage can seem overwhelming. Many find it too difficult to comprehend and give up or, ostrich like, hope that it won't happen to them. Computer specialists are not always good at explaining the situation – some may do it deliberately to ensure their own indispensability or just to increase the size of their contract.

Examples of staff using company computers for nefarious purposes abound. In 1991 San Francisco staff in a company called Charles Schwab used their intranet to buy cocaine; a worker in a hospital allowed a rapist access to the password and he was then able to leaf through patient records and make obscene phone calls. It is not however too difficult to hold on to a few basic facts and to take appropriate action to protect the business.

> *Everyone basically told us: 'Software is a stupid thing to invest in because the assets walk out of the door at night.'*
>
> Ann Winblad *Fortune* October 1999

The bad news:

▷ You can take vast quantities of information away on a CD or floppy disc.
▷ Discs are easy to hide in a pocket or a bag.
▷ Information on laptops is particularly vulnerable if the machine can be taken outside the office.
▷ Passwords provide comfort but little security unless properly administered and even then can often be broken by an internal hacker – your system administrator will almost certainly be able to access all the company's information in the memory.
▷ If a PC is connected in any way to the internet or other external information data machines, staff can send information outside without having to carry it away in their pocket or bag.
▷ Staff can inadvertently send information to others not in the information loop.

The good news:

▷ Disc drives can easily be removed from a PC. This takes away one of the simplest methods of stealing information. An alternative method of backing up information may have to be provided.
▷ You can buy PCs that have removable hard discs (memory banks). These can be locked away so securing the information under lock and key.
▷ Laptops can easily be locked away to provide that extra protection and their issue can be controlled.
▷ Passwords can be secure if staff change them regularly and know how to create them; better still they are given them and are trained to remember them or not to write them down in obvious places.

The bad outweighs the good, but it is not all doom and gloom. There will come a time when you will need to bring in a consultant or computer company to develop sophisticated IT and security systems. But before calling in the consultant consider the following: identify who in your company has the sensitive information and who needs access to it; ask whether their PCs really need to be linked to everyone else's in the company; do all the PCs need disc drives? If not they can be removed from the PC or immobilized. Train staff in the use of passwords; they can provide some protection against the average computer user, but only if they are kept secret. Training should include how to memorize words, letters and numbers.

Where information can be held on a limited number of computers consider using removable hard disc drives so that they can be kept under lock and key. If the whole company has to have access to the same intranet and the information is really sensitive, consider buying a bespoke security package from a reputable software manufacturer. This limits access only to those who need the information and it can also allow you to monitor who does access it. But training becomes even more important.

The extent of the problem in IT

In fact, in the most recent survey on cybercrime by the FBI and the San Francisco-based Computer Security Institute, 81% of corporate respondents said the most likely source of attack was from inside the company.

ComputerWorld – Nov 2001

It's clear that internal security is the No. 1 threat.

The biggest security threat? *Insiders* ZDNet June 2001

Only 15% of listed activity comes from outside ... 60% comes from the inside.

Employees Are the Security Risk – ZDNet Sept 2000

Attacks by insiders cost an average of $2.7 million per incident, reports the 1998 survey conducted by the Computer Security Institute and the FBI's Computer Intrusion Squad ... an increase of 533% in just four years.

Overall, it is estimated that businesses lost $1.6 trillion last year in computer down time resulting from security breaches and virus attacks from hackers ... the majority of security problems in the United States happen from within (companies).

Accounting Web – Feb 2001

It is however all too easy to get carried away and to worst case the threat. A degree of proportionality is needed. Staff expect access to the internet at work; indeed managers expect them to use it. PCs are vulnerable, but the principles are not hard to understand. Managers should be able to influence what is needed and that is – enough, but no more.

Physical security

There are not many employers who can go to the lengths of searching staff as they leave their premises, though it may be done with those working with highly valuable objects such as jewels. The London and East India Dock Company at the beginning of the twentieth century had no shortage of labour and could and did treat its workforce, most of which was casual anyway, without the consideration of today. The same is still true in diamond mining companies.

Less intrusive methods are becoming acceptable. Many government departments ask visitors to leave their mobile phones at the front desk and some have random checks of staff bags. The purpose seems more to remind honest staff that they should not take classified things home with them or to worry would-be wrongdoers, than to prevent them carrying anything out. More and more this is seen as an act of security: what one is bringing into rather than what one is taking out of an organization.

We are more accustomed to it in the modern age of the aircraft hijacker. Anyone travelling by air is used to having their luggage checked and quite often opened for inspection, and to being physically frisked. We accept that, but would we also accept similar treatment leaving the building in which we worked? It is unlikely.

There may be some places where a physical check is acceptable, but to be effective in a normal office environment, it would have to be an intimate search. Floppy discs are easy to hide and papers, while less efficient, can be carried off easily enough.

Where then does an intrusive protection policy help an employer with staff, who might physically remove company assets secrets? How far can an employer go and is it effective? There are three things that an employer might want to prevent a member of staff from stealing: material items; cash and, thirdly, information held on paper or in some electronic form. There is little that the employer can do to stop someone systematically taking information away in their memory.

The larger the material item, the more difficult it is to hide and the easier it is to detect. Diamond miners have an easier task of stealing than workers in a car manufacturer. Neither is impossible to perpetrate; neither is impossible to prevent. The problem for the employer becomes more difficult when the items leave the premises on company transport and they are therefore under the control of the employee and not the employer.

Money can be easily removed from the petty cash or transferred to someone else's account, electronically or through the accounting and banking systems used by the company. Various methods have to be deployed to counter staff intent on such action. Some will be appropriate for you others will not. Much depends on the threat assessment you made at the beginning.

Security officers at all exits

Security officers have the company's authority to stop people and ask them to open their bags, car boot or whatever. Their success relies largely on staff fearing a spot check and being caught. Most people are not criminally minded and while they might want to take out a half-used laser print cartridge, they are likely to be discouraged by the fear of a search. The security officer must therefore do some unpredictable spot searches. The number of exit points needs to be limited. This funnels staff through places where you can watch them more efficiently.

Security officers need training. To search quickly and effectively is a skilled job; they also need to do it politely and with sensitivity. Too often do you see officious security officers who create anger among staff because of the way they do their business: 'I'm only doing my job' is not sufficient as a response. They may also get bored: they stop and search more to amuse themselves than to catch others.

Companies are in the business of keeping staff happy. If spot searches are necessary then those being searched have to be treated with courtesy. The company needs to make it clear at recruitment that this happens and remind staff regularly why it is necessary.

But we should be quite clear of the limitations of using searches at the exit points. At best it is only going to find the casual and not very clever thief and even then only a few of them. Their main purpose is to deter those who might be thinking about pinching stuff and who would do so if there were no checks. The truly determined pilferer will find a way around the security guard whose presence, in any case, may be becoming an expensive option.

Electronic methods: closed circuit TV (CCTV) and so on

Video cameras are now so sophisticated and so common that many of us have stopped noticing them. They peer at us in blatant forms in stores with their winking red lights and some follow us round as we walk up and down the aisles. They can be used effectively inside the building as well as at the exits. There is advantage to having them outside and obviously so. Staff feel they are being watched and therefore are reluctant to do anything wrong in front of them. The screens in the monitoring room do not of course have to be monitored all of the time. It is the fear of being caught, and not knowing whether the CCTV cameras are on, which is usually sufficient. Again they are only likely to catch the amateur thief and to push the hardcore criminals into ever more sophisticated methods, which will make your job that much more difficult.

CCTV *inside* the office is there principally for one reason and that is to monitor staff. This does not give an impression of trust; and that in itself generates feelings of resentment and undermines loyalty. If management does not trust its staff then why should they show loyalty to the company. The argument can be taken too far and with a proper communication policy to explain what you are doing use of CCTV is possible. If not properly handled the effect on staff of internal monitoring through CCTV can be negative.

It is possible to install more discreet cameras. These are more likely to catch people because they will assume they are not being watched, but come the day when you do catch someone you will have to reveal your evidence and that means staff will find out and that could cause even more problems for you.

Whether or not your CCTV is discreet you have the problem of monitoring the screens. This means employing enough security officers to watch the TV screens and training them so they know what to look for and what to do, particularly if you are monitoring the screens in real time, that is, as the action happens. Watching them afterwards is a real bore and catching the thief is unlikely. There may be some advantage in catching, say, a saboteur after the event but luck will have to play its part as well.

X-ray machines can also be deployed at the exits to look for hardware items in bags leaving the building. If they are efficient and do not lead to the all too familiar queue one finds at airports, they might just become part of the scenery and acceptable; but they are expensive and intrusive.

The gadget market is full of other electronic means to deploy. They include sophisticated software to track what employees are doing on their computers or telephones, using security cards not only to give people access to their office, but also to check their times in and out (a more sophisticated clocking-in system, but useful if staff are coming in and out at times when no one else will observe them in the office). It is possible to reduce the size of CCTV cameras so that they will not be spotted by employees. Locks can be fitted with devices to monitor how many times they have been opened.

Policing the police

Security officers have a hard job and checking on staff is among the most thankless. Security staff are not high in a company's pecking order. Employers expect a lot of them but give them limited status; they tend to be at the bottom of the pay scales and yet they are in charge of protecting valuable assets. The formula is not one that is likely to work out in the company's favour.

Security staff often feel they are undervalued. If so, they will not do their job well, will cause resentment in other staff because they may anger other employees or they will join the forces of evil and actually facilitate the misdemeanors. The answer is to ensure they are well trained, properly managed and have adequate terms and conditions.

Employing physical methods to prevent the loss of material items can have a deterrent effect and may catch a few perpetrators. They are probably essential where the company has a high-value product and employs relatively large numbers of staff who do not stay long with the company. The level of work the staff do is largely irrelevant; this can apply to rapidly changing staff in highly paid sectors just as much as in the lower paid areas.

Throughout, management has to communicate properly what it is doing and why it is necessary. The objective is to avoid innocent individuals feeling that they are not trusted. The measures are an unfortunate byproduct of society and most staff will understand that – so long as their own privacy is not invaded *unreasonably*. Proportionality and communication are the principles to guide managers.

Exit policy

How a company treats staff who leave, for whatever reason, speaks volumes about that company's attitudes to its employees. An overriding principle for employers is summed up in one word 'dignity'.

If someone leaves and they feel badly treated, ignored or unappreciated their already negative feelings are going to be compounded. There will be no restraints on what they say about the company nor will they feel guilty about giving away what they can remember of the company's clients, research programmes or other secrets. It is perhaps too much to expect staff who leave to remain loyal to their former employer, but with the right handling and aftercare their propensity to be disloyal can be limited.

Jeffrey Wigand (the head of research at the tobacco company Brown and Williamson, who blew the whistle on their inclusion of narcotic substances into cigarettes, see separate case study in Chapter 3) felt that he was reasonably well paid-off and his first thoughts were not to 'blow the whistle'. It was only after he was called back, made to sign another confidentiality agreement and threatened, that he became seriously disillusioned – with some encouragement from Lowell Bergman, the journalist from the US TV company CBS.

Wigand felt badly treated by the tobacco company and resentment began to set in, leading him to break his confidentiality agreement and therefore to lose his benefits. There was of course also a real desire to reveal what was happening in the tobacco company. If he had been treated more sympathetically, it is quite possible Wigand would not have gone through with the whistle-blowing.

Whenever someone leaves, whether through resignation or enforced, the rest of the organization is watching how that person is treated. If the organization is perceived to have treated them fairly, then staff feel comfortable and are that much more ready to remain loyal to the company. If however they see someone treated badly the seeds for trouble will have been sown.

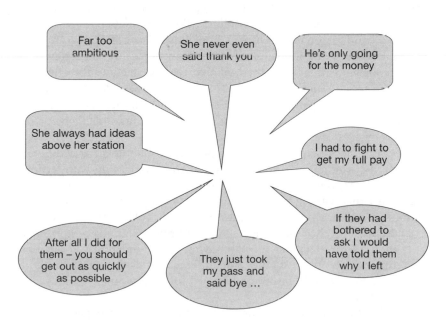

Figure 9.1 **Negative comments following a mishandled staff departure**

Handling resignations

However important the person is or however critical he or she is to the organization's work, the principles of handling their departure are the same:

▷ An expression of genuine (if appropriate) sorrow
▷ Check conditions of employment and respond to any requests for exceptions with sympathy and, where possible, flexibility
▷ Ask and listen to their reasons for leaving, particularly to any comment on how the organization might have been responsible for their decision
▷ Make time to be with them for their last few hours in the office
▷ Make best use of the exit questionnaire and interview
▷ Maintain contact after they leave. Ensure they feel welcome when they return.

The overall aim is to make the individual feel that their departure is a loss and that their work in the company has been valued. The purpose is twofold. Whatever the professed reason for leaving, there is a reasonable chance that their departure has something to do with failed expectations. They may be feeling disillusioned or unhappy with the company or their current boss.

Assuming the decision is final, the departure procedures should do nothing to reinforce any negative feelings. If possible they should reverse them. Having left the company, the individual will speak about the company to prospective investors, customers, clients and possibly competitors. They may have useful information for others. It is possible for people to remain loyal to previous employers; if they depart with dignity the chances of them not bad-mouthing the company and not passing on confidentialities are higher.

The second reason is even more compelling. Those staff who are left will be watching how the individual is treated on departure. That person will have friends who are left and they will express their feelings forcefully. How people are treated on departure sends a strong message to those remaining about how the company manages its staff. Everyone leaves at some stage even if it is retirement. Figure 9.1 shows how staff might feel when a resignation is mishandled.

Circumstances may well cause employers to handle people differently. Staff may be working in a sensitive area. If they are leaving with feelings of resentment, access to their office should be immediately controlled. It is not easy to do this without compounding the feelings of resentment. Before taking this action, employers need to be sure that the individual is likely to take advantage of their continued access and remove goods or information.

If an employer does this they are saying to the individual in unambiguous terms 'we do not trust you'. The individual is likely to respond 'in that case I have no reason to respect your goods or secrets and I shall say and do what I like now'.

The Public Interest Disclosure Act in the UK protects people in some cases when they have information which it is in the public interest to release.

But staff have a duty of confidentiality and this can be written into their terms and conditions of service. If confidentiality agreements are employed, staff leaving should be reminded of the terms of the agreement.

Enforced departures

Is there any hope for those forced to leave? The answer is yes, but there is a greater price put on the professionalism of your managers and personnel department. Staff are forced to leave for one of four reasons: retirement, redundancy, inefficiency or disciplinary.

Retirement

This is the least threatening to organizations. Neither party need feel guilty. Both have (usually) honoured their part of the deal and the retiree may well be going off to do nothing more threatening than sailing round the world or retiring to the country and living off the company pension.

But there are some threats. Employees may still need to earn money to bolster their pension and their biggest asset could be the knowledge they have accumulated over the years working for your company. Their value as a consultant to the industry could be considerable. Your competitors, be they business or institutional, will be only too happy to learn from their experiences in your company.

Staff retiring deserve the same minimum treatment defined above for staff resigning. They are more likely to appreciate some kind of contact after they have gone. Retirement is a shock to the system and many feel lonely. Company support systems are appreciated. Where they are absent, retirees may feel cross and abandoned.

Retirees need help to adjust. Many companies now run retirement courses and offer counselling to help them find new occupations, not necessarily in business, but something to fill the void of a hitherto active working life. If they are likely to go into alternative employment, then an outplacement agency will be able to monitor and indeed influence where they go.

Some organizations employ someone specifically to help staff thinking of leaving find new jobs. The strategic value of this person outweighs the cost of employing him or her. The advantages are: staff who are leaving feel the company is still interested in them; the company can influence where ex-employees go when they leave and therefore deter them from going to the opposition; the outplacement agency/individual can maintain contact with those leaving and organize any further contacts.

Redundancy

The early and unexpected sacking of people, because the company no longer needs those staff, is one of the cruellest turns of the employment hand of fate.

Sometimes it is predictable and staff will have some warning, but either way it is uncomfortable for all concerned. The numbers involved may affect the precise details of how you manage the news, but the principles are the same whether for 20 or 1000 (the law in the UK defines redundancy as 20 or more over a six-month period). The principles here apply equally for any number of staff being asked to leave a company for structural reasons.

Above all else, management needs to communicate well and fully to those who are leaving and to those staying. Sackings can be one of the most disruptive influences on productivity. People fear they may be next and will be looking even more carefully at the way the company treats those affected. The trade union, where it exists, will need consulting at some stage.

Whoever gives the information must be sure they know how to deliver bad news. Managers, in particular, often need help and advice. They feel the need to sugar the pill with initial explanations about how the individual concerned has many qualities and is a good person. If people are treated properly and with respect the company is more likely to receive respect and loyalty in return.

Sacking because of inefficiency, incompetence or indiscipline

It is a major part of a manager's job to maximize the output of those working for him or her. 'Managing poor performance' is a management competency that is frequently found wanting. Failing to act should not be an option. Staff in the section will become disgruntled because they have to carry the person who is not pulling his or her weight. Alternatively they will see that misdemeanours or poor performance are condoned and might follow that example. Sacking is the final option.

To avoid resentment, staff who are not up to the job need to be told in clear terms how they are underperforming and be given the opportunity either through training or through coaching to improve. The processes have to be gone through and each company should have clear standards about how to manage inefficiencies. This may not mean written regulations but managers should explain what they are doing and be consistent. Written procedures can often help to ensure consistency and that staff know what to expect. ACAS in the UK produces useful guidelines on what to do and how (ACAS 2000).

If the rules are not clear and are imposed inconsistently staff will have cause for complaint. Once the procedures have been exhausted and there is no alternative to sacking, managers need again to adhere to the minimum standards already outlined. Who does what may vary. The personnel manager might need to administer some procedures, the line manager others. More senior people might have to be involved. But a plan of action needs to be drawn up and followed.

A well-administered sacking need not lead to any resentment; sadness probably, but not a feeling that the individual has been hard done by. When handled professionally, staff can leave expressing gratitude for the way they have been treated and expressing the view that this is the best option for both parties.

Delivering bad news

An action plan should contain at least the following:

▶ Preparation time. *Ensure top management and unions are all saying the same things; the reasons for the redundancies are known; the reasons for choosing these particularly people are clear; details of the redundancy package are already settled and can be passed on.*

▶ The interview. *Think about the timing, Fridays are not good as those concerned have no one at work to turn to over the weekend; allow sufficient time, choose a quiet location with a separate exit if possible, so if upset they can leave without contact with others; make sure the room is laid out in a non-confrontational way. Be clear and unambiguous. Get straight to the point, chatty preliminaries are inappropriate on this occasion.*

▶ Afterwards. *Be sure there is a plan of action for those leaving, such as employment advice, a retraining package or counselling. Be prepared for some people to take time for the information to sink in. They may want to come back and discuss again on another day.*

Anticipating trouble: a manager's checklist

A company can spend enormous sums of money putting in expensive electronic surveillance equipment and employing the best security guards, but it will be of little value if the managers are not sensitive to the causes and manifestations of problems in the first place. A manager's job is to maximize productivity by inspiring and supporting staff to greater efforts and by finding ever more efficient methods of 'delivering the goods'. But this effort will be undermined if he or she is not able at the same time to spot the losses through pilfering, cheating or fraud. Nor will he/she be maximizing profits if staff are turning over at an unacceptable rate. The manager will have significantly failed if he or she does not identify that someone in the department is so unhappy that they are about to tell the rest of the world about all that is bad about the company and the story will not be spoilt for a ha'p'orth of tar.

What then should the company and its managers be doing? There are five key elements: leaders and managers setting a good example; managers who know their staff; managers who know what to look for; managers who are skilled in interviewing; and clear and well-understood procedures for handling misdemeanours and those leaving.

If CEOs want their staff to behave honestly then the bosses must be seen to be honest and fair in their dealings. Not only do they have to show that they themselves are not fiddling, but they have to be seen to be earning their money. This can be demonstrated by increased profits, productivity and hard work. Many will see their managers working long hours. The very large earnings of some CEOs does raise questions in some staff minds but it becomes a real problem when the company performs poorly under their stewardship.

Companies that pay off staff who have behaved dishonestly, or performed poorly, run the danger of losing the confidence of their existing staff. It is in a sense condoning bad behaviour. The management will have weighed this up and can justify it in their own minds but their reasoning is rarely communicated to staff. They are left with the facts: a member of staff breaks the rules, resulting in a large pay-off. It becomes a joke in the canteen that that is the way to get rich. It is a joke, but while no one really would contemplate similar action, it gnaws away at the company's stated values of the need for honesty. Where misdemeanours are discovered they have to be dealt with through a proper, open disciplinary and grievance procedure. ACAS publishes good advice on how to establish this in the UK.

Managers need to know enough about their staff to be able to identify when their behaviour changes, which might indicate a problem. We discuss below what to look for but these are only indicators and will vary for each individual.

Nor should managers be unduly suspicious. If someone starts taking telephone calls and sounding embarrassed and putting the phone down quickly, it does not mean they are talking to a headhunter or recruitment agency; they may be in the middle of a divorce, chatting to a new girlfriend or asking for medical results.

Managers need at the very minimum to be observant and to recognize the normal behaviour patterns of their staff. Many can and like to go further not for purely managerial reasons but also because they are naturally interested in people and enjoy social contact at work. The problem can then become one of overfamiliarity. It is much harder to take disciplinary action against those who are our friends. But that is a classic dilemma for the boss.

What then are the telltale signs which manifest themselves in staff whose loyalty is beginning to be transferred elsewhere? The most commonly recognized are:

▷ Unusual absences or time keeping such as frequent sick days, or unexpected half-days taken because of some minor crisis at home can indicate that the staff member has something else on the mind.
▷ Longer lunch hours, coming in late and leaving early can also indicate a distraction.
▷ A refusal to let others share work or determination to keep an aspect of work exclusively to themselves might mean that they have something to hide or that they want to keep this valuable access to information exclusively to them.
▷ A change in personal habits or appearing permanently tired can show that the individual has a problem.
▷ A change in their telephone habits or a long time spent with friends in the office can indicate a lessening of commitment.

In all the above the emphasis is on *change* in behaviours. There may be those who come in and who are already cheats. In which case other methods of detection will be necessary, but the manager still has a responsibility. He or she has to show they are dealing with the problem.

And dealing with the problem is the hardest thing. We often suspect there is something wrong, particularly when we are not responsible for running the department. Confronting problems is easy to talk about and to admire in others when we see it. How do we achieve it?

There are two essentials: the manager's ability through discussion and interviewing to find out what is happening or what has caused the change of behaviour and secondly that he or she follows the procedures for handling suspected misdemeanours.

Interviewing skills is a much-overlooked quality in managers. Most of us seem to reach positions of seniority in a company through impressing others. This puts a premium on talking and influencing. Of course people listen to their bosses and they are adept at picking up what the company wants from them. But they seem able to leap from an ability in those skills to an assumption that they are good at listening and elicitation that is, interviewing; even assuming they believe it has any relevance at all in their work. But managers have to do it all the time, whether it is at the recruitment stage or during an appraisal interview, however formal the system employed by the company. The authors posit the view that most managers think they are good interviewers but that most are not. They ask low-yield questions, seem lacking in insight and rarely correctly process the answers. Hence the data that shows interviews have very poor reliability.

An interview is held for one or more of three reasons: to pass on information, to extract information or to influence an individual. In a good appraisal interview all three motives are usually there. Bosses need to be able to find out how the employee feels about his or her performance, they need to tell the individual how they think he or she is performing and they need to encourage the employee to continue to work at the same level or how to change his or her behaviour in order to perform better.

When dealing with the early stages of handling a potential problem the manager should mostly be in listening mode – and that is where so many managers fail. Without giving the person a chance to explain properly what is happening there is no chance of progress. The manager has to do more however; he/she has to probe further and find out what else might lie behind the manifestations of the problem. The real skill is about listening.

Such a practical skill is hard to teach through reading and it is beyond the scope of this book. There are many good courses available to help develop good interviewing skills. The good news is that they are not hard to learn nor do they take much time to acquire. A few days spent learning how to interview properly is an investment well worth making.

Finally managers should consider the following:

▷ Ensure everybody in the organization takes at least two weeks' leave in one break. Many fraud cases are discovered when the perpetrators are away and someone else *has* to do their work.

▷ Meet the family. Include wives, husbands and children in some company social gatherings. It is in any case a good thing in order to further loyalty. If family feel they are included and can benefit from some of the company's largesse they will encourage the breadwinner to stay. But it also gives the manager a chance to see if there are any seeds of discontent amongst close relatives.

▷ Find ways to encourage staff to report to managers when they see wrong-doings amongst their colleagues. This may mean establishing a confidential or anonymous reporting procedure.

▷ A good exit policy has a number of features. Although there are some common elements there are differences depending on whether you are asking the individual(s) to leave or they are resigning of their own accord.

The law

The law gives employees the opportunity to ensure they are treated properly and fairly. It also puts a number of obligations on the employee. This extends to performing competently as well as to duties of maintaining confidentiality, let alone providing employers with protection against fraud or pilfering.

The law can do little to stop people leaving and it should be clear what to do when someone is found misappropriating property or money. The question of confidential information is much less easy to define. There can be no substitute for proper legal advice. There is however a clear obligation on staff not to disclose company secrets or confidential information, except where it is in the public interest (see below for more on what the Public Interest Disclosure Act 1998 requires of employers).

Slade's *Employment Handbook* (1998 p 409) summarizes the law as follows:

> Breach of confidence is an independent equitable wrong, not confined to the employment relationship or indeed to cases where there is a contract between the parties. Both current and former employees are under an implied obligation not to use or disclose information if it amounts to a trade secret or is so highly confidential that it requires the same protection as a trade secret. Trade secrets are not confined to technical information. The duty of fidelity upon current employees goes further, so as to prevent them from disclosing or using information which falls into a secondary category, being confidential, but not to such an extent as to amount to a trade secret.

Confidentiality contracts may be an added protection, but the law is adequate for most cases. The problem is of course enforcing it. How do you know if that ex-employee has approached some of his ex-clients? The law is not a whole answer but we should know it and be willing to use it when feasible.

The Public Interest Disclosure Act 1998 is complex, but its basic purpose is to protect workers who having seen a wrong in the workplace can report it to someone outside the organization without being discriminated against. In the context of this book it is of interest because it provides many with the excuse to whistle-blow. They justify their action using the PIDA. Where there is something to be disclosed then of course the company deserves to be shown up. The situation is rarely simple. The company may be in the wrong. Few organizations will be without fault of some kind. Few whistle-blowers will not feel encouraged or vindicated by some act of poor management.

Most managers have a respect for the law and some knowledge of it. This is important for them to do their job. It is also important for them to know where and when to seek advice.

Response to a breach of security

There are two aspects to consider: whether and, if so, how to discipline the person committing the breach; and how to handle the press should the breach come to their attention, for example through a whistle-blower or the discovery of major fraud.

Disciplining staff

The possible sanctions range from doing nothing to sacking, together with legal proceedings. As far as the latter are concerned, the organization may not have any choice; the law simply takes over, but there are times when the organization may, if it wishes, press charges.

Larger organizations will have established disciplinary proceedings written into their contracts, staff regulations or other official documents which will be issued to new employees and be available to all. Disciplinary proceedings are designed to cover a number of issues (including many that are the subject of this book such as theft and absenteeism)(Armstrong 2001 p 461).

> The approach to handling disciplinary cases should follow three principles of natural justice:
>
> 1   Individuals should know the standards of performance they are expected to achieve and the rules to which they are expected to conform.
> 2   They should be given a clear indication of where they are failing or what rules have been broken.
> 3   Except in cases of gross misconduct, they should be given an opportunity to improve before disciplinary action is taken.

Security breaches are no different. Security rules may not be properly described in the official documents and they may not cover all the eventualities. Companies are now sensitive to the need, where appropriate, for confidentiality agreements, but care needs to be taken in drafting these. The legal issues can be complex and advice is needed. In any event the performance standards should be clearly set out and easily available. If they are to be obeyed, they also need to be reasonable.

Where a breach has occurred, the manager, security department or HR should not just assume the worst and put the infringement down to carelessness or wilful wrongdoing. There may be other reasons which need to be investigated. One of the most common causes of security breaches is lack of time or work pressure.

Another may be that while the individual recognizes there is a rule and that it has been broken, he or she does not really understand why it is important. The reason for obscuring passwords, particularly from other members of staff, is often not understood. The need to know principle is not intuitive in an organization which encourages teamwork and friendliness.

A sympathetic initial response is important not only to acquire a full picture, but because in the area of security, more than any other, employers need to encourage staff to come forward and admit their mistakes. If they see the procedures are fair and considerate, they will be more willing to come forward.

If however employees fear the consequences of their security breach they will try to hide it. This means that the organization will never know that their information has been compromised. Imagine that an employee loses their wallet containing not only their money and cards, but a business card with the company website and the passwords. The individual may well report that to the police but will think twice about reporting it to their boss if they work in an office with a blame culture or which is known to treat such cases harshly. The wallet might be picked up by a hacker or a competitor who could make malevolent use of the information inside.

Handling the press

When news of a security calamity (fraud, whistle-blowing, sabotage) breaks, the two most common responses are to blame the culprit or say nothing. The former approach involves a company spokesperson saying that the company can hardly be held responsible for the problem as it was the culprit's either malicious or illegal activity. Some may be tempted to assign a cause such as revenge or greed. This approach, however, is guaranteed to goad the individual into becoming more determined and possibly more litigious. It will also paint a picture of the organization as being hard, unsympathetic and uncaring; the precise opposite of the 'we care about our employees' image that most like to portray. Observers may also be tempted to ask whether there might be a problem inside the organization.

The second approach is to preserve a determined silence: the 'no comments' option. The company lawyer, fearful of admitting any responsibility, may advise the PR department to stay quiet. This strategy may seriously backfire. Imagine what the investigative media do when faced with silent PR people and senior management. They hunt for a talkative secretary or a garrulous security guard, flattered by media attention, and more than happy to comment. The media may simply interview staff leaving the plant or office, and finding the angry, alienated employee who slates the company's management practices is an easy task. The media like to unroll a crisis, to keep a 'human interest' story alive for as long as possible. These creeping crises are often more damaging than a 'one-off' disaster. Seeing a company duck and dive, refuse to admit responsibility and appear callous about its victims, leads to a true PR disaster.

Burrell: Further secrets are on the way

AN UNREPENTANT Paul Burrell, whose controversial curtsy-and-tell book goes on sale today, rode out the deepening row over his 'betrayal' of his former employer, Diana, Princess of Wales by going on the offensive against the Royal Family.

Diana's former butler ... claimed Princes William and Harry's minds were being 'poisoned' by the palace.

In a newspaper interview which will be of great concern to a Royal Family already devastated by the damaging revelations serialized in the Mirror *last week, Mr Burrell suggested his claims had merely been 'the tip of the iceberg' and threatened to reveal further Royal secrets ...*

The extraordinary and unprecedented war of words between the palace and the former Royal servant of 21 years' standing – which began on Friday when the princes accused him of a 'cold and overt betrayal' of their mother – continued unabated yesterday.

http://www.news.scotsman.com 27 October 2003

Organizations must learn they can only control that which they manage. They need to be prepared for what follows. What the public want to know is what happened and why; whose fault it was; when the company first thought it might happen; what they did immediately it did happen, and what they are doing now. In other words, they want to know the full story of the incident. They also want to know that it won't happen again. Finally, they need to be convinced why they should trust the company again.

What all organizations, particularly those in manufacturing, need to do is essentially the following. First, when news of the crisis breaks, assume the worst-case scenario. This is not unduly pessimistic, but focuses the effect clearly. Second, be prepared to survive the media gaze. Choose articulate, intelligent people and keep them. Next, make sure you are communicating directly with your most important audience, whether customers, shareholders or staff. Centralize the flow of information, ensuring it all goes to, and leaves from, one specified point. Create a good crisis team and empower them to make the crucial decisions. They will always have to attempt to define the real problem and desired outcome throughout the crisis. The problem must be contained, even if it leads to short-term costs or loss of face. It is far too easy to escalate a relatively minor problem by dealing with it badly.

Lastly, and perhaps most important, resist the combative instinct. An exasperated research and development scientist, harassed by journalists, gives in to his emotions and shouts on camera. This is just not good. What the public wants to know is what is being done to prevent the crisis recurring. They are not a naive, gullible, litigious mass, baying for the destruction of your company. They would prefer you to say you are doing your best, are truly sorry, and will endeavour to stop this kind of thing ever happening again. In short, you must demonstrate that you are a responsive and responsible company.

Conclusion

Security is one of the Cinderella's of any organization. But to be effective it has to be embraced by all and respected by all. This is an area where there are no separate rules for those in top management. If anything, it is more important for them to follow the rules as they have more sensitive information or access to assets than anyone else in the company.

The following checklist provides a basis for organizations to make a security health check:

Security policy

▷ The starting point is a risk assessment: what really needs protection and who has access to it. Limit sensitive information to those who need to know.

Induction

▷ Reinforce messages of security standards during first few days of a newcomer's time in the office when they are at their most receptive.

Computers

▷ Does everyone need access to disc drives?
▷ Does every computer have to be connected to the intranet/internet?
▷ Train staff in use of memory for passwords
▷ Consider locking up the most sensitive hard drives/PCs
▷ Consider a reputable software company who could provide a system for you. But remember proportionality.

Physical security

▷ Deploy staff at exits, but train them in how to do their job
▷ Funnel staff through a limited number of exits
▷ Train security officers in courtesy
▷ Be aware of its limited value – largely deterrence
▷ Police the police – treat the security officers well
▷ Communicate to staff why it is necessary.

Exit policy

▷ Consider
  ▶ Exit interviews after they leave
  ▶ Confidentiality clause and the law
  ▶ Alumni or contact after they have left
▷ For staff forced to leave through retirement
  ▶ Outplacement facilities
  ▶ Contact after they leave tends to be more important
▷ For staff being made redundant
  ▶ Communication policy
  ▶ Clarity of package
  ▶ Delivering bad news principles
▷ For staff leaving because of incompetence, inefficiency or indiscipline
  ▶ Ensure processes and rules are clearly understood and consistently applied
  ▶ Consider if they should go immediately or work out their notice period.

Management awareness

▷ Set a good example and model desired behaviours
▷ Know staff and use the appraisal process to understanding their needs and concerns
▷ Know what to look for when considering CWBs
▷ Train managers in interviewing techniques
▷ Have clear procedures for handling misdemeanours.

The law

▷ Employees have a duty of confidentiality to their employers
▷ Consider confidentiality agreements
▷ Be aware of the Public Interest Disclosure Act.

10 Fostering Loyalty

Introduction

The moral of our story is positive: loyalty can be fostered and maintained, even grown over the working life. A garden left untended quickly grows into a wilderness, with brambles, bindweed and thorns dominating the ground and threatening to strangle the flowers and vegetables. But with some attention and knowledge plants, flowers and vegetables will grow. In this sense managers may need to build an agricultural or horticultural model on how to develop and sustain employee loyalty.

The influences of personality of employees and the outside world can lead to a reduction in loyalty. The good news is that the level of knowledge to produce a reasonable level of commitment and loyalty is no more than that needed to produce a garden that blooms with fine flowers and luscious shrubs.

There are many things employers will want to encourage in their staff apart from loyalty: efficiency, enthusiasm, commitment, new ideas and more productivity to name only a few. But this book, and this chapter in particular, concerns issues around loyalty. There are many books on good management practices designed to maximize productivity. This chapter does not attempt to replicate or go over that ground. The focus is on increasing loyalty and commitment.

News Corporation, the US media group led by Rupert Murdoch, has defended the controversial candidacy of James Murdoch the media mogul's 30-year-old son, as the next chief executive of British Sky Broadcasting in spite of misgivings among institutional shareholders.

Financial Times 13 October 2003
www.FT.co.uk

Loyalty comes in two versions: emotional and cognitive. The emotional variety comes from the heart and is associated with instincts such as family loyalties, old friends and tribal or religious origins. Some may think this kind of loyalty plays no part in a business, but even the most hard-headed businessmen (perhaps women as well, but the evidence is sparse) have often favoured their offspring. James Murdoch may well have been an excellent candidate for the post of CEO of BskyB (see the box above), but it is hard to believe that he would have got the job had his father not been chairman of BSkyB and News Corp, which controls 35.4% of the pay-TV company. Parents will argue, and the authors do not doubt that their children are well qualified and may have come up the 'hard way', but blood ties do matter and there are many examples of family loyalties taking priority over those who come from outside. There is a thin line between loyalty and nepotism: the latter tends to foster powerful disloyalty in non-family members.

Despite the law outlawing racial or religious prejudice, people of the same nationality, religion or race do tend to come together in business. People feel more comfortable with people 'of the same kind' even though there may be others more qualified or better suited to the job. They instinctively see things in the same way; share the same values.

Cognitive loyalty on the other hand comes with time, experience and a logical assessment: 'If the company is loyal to me then I shall be loyal to it.' No matter that the employee is thinking about an institution that has no feelings, feelings of loyalty do exist.

Why do people become loyal to their organization? The simple answer is that an organization provides its employees with some of their fundamental needs: security (through pay cheques), social contact, identity, relationships with other people and a challenge to use personal skills and talents. People are also not usually fickle and when something goes wrong they forgive; unless of course things frequently go wrong. They will stay the course until the situation becomes intolerable.

> *I walk into all these organizations, and I'm always puzzled when I realize that people still want to be there. Most people really want to love their organizations. We need that level of commitment ... Yet organizations have done very little to deserve that kind of staying power.*
>
> Walter Wriston (*b* 1919), US banker to Scott London, US national public radio

In other words, an organization is not an impersonal thing: it is the sum of the people who work there; people who share common objectives, interests and values. Employees are therefore loyal to the other people in the organization; to behavioural patterns and rituals. People tend to be loyal to their small work group and department rather than to the whole organization.

Conflicts can easily arise. Top management can get it wrong but staff will maintain their loyalty to their day-to-day managers and of course vice versa. That is the nature of the psychological contract.

The distinction between emotional and cognitive loyalty is blurred but there is a more rational approach to colleagues in the workplace, particularly in a large company where the top managers are rarely seen or are at some distance geographically. Procedures for promotion have to be fair and be seen to be fair. Trust works only when those in a position of responsibility are accessible. When they are not, trust does not count and suspicion will take over. Loyalty comes from contact; consistent contact over time.

For most employers therefore loyalty is not a given; it has to be earnt and it has to be nurtured. Every organization that wants a loyal workforce has to select the right people, ensure they know what to do from the beginning, nurture their expectations, through any number of changes, and allow staff who are no longer producing efficiently to leave with dignity. The gardening metaphor works well. It is the opposite of the Darwinian approach which encourages a fight to survive.

Good gardeners will know their soil, climate and other environmental conditions and will choose their plants accordingly. Rhododendrons will not grow in sandy soil; orchids need warmth. They will plant them and spend comparatively more time with their new plants than those that are already established. The potting shed or greenhouse is where the gardener spends much time in a carefully controlled environment when plants are at their most vulnerable. Thereafter the gardener ensures the plant is properly fed and watered and that the more exotic are pruned and trained into shapes or encouraged by other means to maximize their productivity or beauty. Gardeners will also try to protect the plant from disease and other external damage. If they do not, the plant will become diseased and may well infect other plants. Finally, a plant will outlive its usefulness and either die or need to be removed. A good gardener will ensure that this is done properly so that diseases are not left behind to harm what is left.

In the remainder of this chapter we look at how organizations, in order to foster loyalty, should:

▷ Recruit the right people knowing the job they are going to do (select the plants, knowing the soil and other environment constraints)
▷ Induct staff so they know what to do and how to do it, and understand the company values (nurturing seedlings and new plants as they settle into their different environment)
▷ Manage staff during their careers so that they maintain commitment (watering, feeding, pruning and protecting plants from disease)
▷ Ensure staff leave with dignity and at the appropriate time, often before retirement age (removing dead wood, plants when dying or of no further cosmetic or food value).

Recruitment

Too many employers or HR professionals seek staff who are perhaps too well qualified. They are impressed by first-class honours degrees from the top universities, when in reality they are selecting for jobs that are, maybe, not sufficiently demanding for a top graduate. Management qualifications also appear attractive. Qualifications are only good if the new recruit knows how to apply the theoretical knowledge and skills learnt at college. A proven track record may be much more important than the latest MBA, though the degree may indicate an ability to learn new things.

The skills and qualities of the ideal candidate need to be properly defined. Tests and interviews have to be run to discover which candidate fits the requirements best. But is that enough to be sure the new intake will remain loyal?

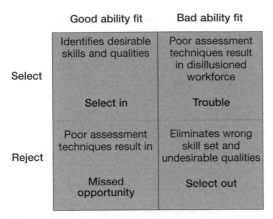

Figure 10.1 **Consequences of good and bad selection procedures**

A misfit will not stay in the organization or if he or she does will quickly become disillusioned and disruptive. To be certain of someone's loyalty it is important to ensure not only that the job description and competencies are properly established, but also that the right personality is employed with a set of clear values that complements that of the organization.

Figure 10.1 shows both the consequences of a misfit and how recruiters might ensure they are recruiting people with all the qualities required for the job.

The boxes which spell trouble or a missed opportunity are straightforward enough. Most recruiters look for the skill sets and select in, not out. That is, they look for the qualities they want rather than looking for the qualities they definitely do not want. For those who want to recruit and select people who are going to be loyal, equal attention needs to be paid to those who should be selected out. It is relatively easy to eliminate those who do not have the skills set, but little attention is paid to the undesirable qualities. It seems that only organizations interested in security are concerned with the all-important bonuses of selecting *out* undesirable candidates.

Are these qualities universal? If someone has a particular personality trait is he or she effectively unemployable? Are some people more prone to disloyalty than others? The answers to these and other similar questions are not a firm yes or no. Each job has its own demands and requirements and somewhere there is a job for everyone – the trick is to be sure that the recruiters know which qualities are needed and which are not. Chapter 7 discusses the value of integrity tests in this context.

The selection process

There are alas no quick or cheap solutions to recruiting staff who are likely to remain loyal. Identifying the right skills set is hard enough, but the qualities of integrity and commitment are even more difficult to operationalize.

The investment might be high, but the returns are higher for getting it right.

There are however organizations that enjoy high levels of loyalty and that do not suffer much employee revenge. There are none that have not had some manifestation of disloyalty. A study of those in the UK that have a good record shows that the recruitment process is taken seriously, but with some surprising characteristics.

The full menu of options for recruiting loyal and committed staff involves a variety of different stages. They complement the requirement for the right skills as well. The basic requirement is an assessment centre of some sort. For many, this is no more than an interview, but there are numerous variations on this theme. What happens before and after the assessment centre is also instructive.

The process described below is a good model, taken from those companies and organizations that have a good retention and loyalty record. None do it all but all do most.

At the start, care is taken in drafting the job advertisements. Prospective candidates of course need to be attracted to the post. This does not mean however that the advert has to present only the most attractive aspects of a job or the employers. Candidates need to be able to judge whether this is the employer for them. For this to happen they need some evidence about whether they would be happy and fulfilled working there. An advertisement such as this says something about what is needed but little about the company:

We are seeking an experienced Aeronautical and Environmental Data Processing engineer to work within a highly respected and interesting Air Traffic Control Environment.

The role demands someone with considerable experience of Air Traffic Management (ATM) systems particularly in the field of Environmental and Flight Data Processing (FDP). You will ideally have some experience supporting the Safety team and also have knowledge of ATM system Architecture.

Taken from the Internet Oct 2003

All the candidate can take from this is what is needed in him- or herself. It makes no reference to what he or she might need in an employer. The application might attract plenty of applicants, but many will be from people who would not come to the company if additional information was added such as:

The job requires staff to work on a rota basis including some evenings and weekends when overtime is paid. There are periods of intense activity which require concentration and accuracy and other periods when the pace is slower. Employees need to be able to communicate effectively orally and remain calm in times of crisis. The working environment is supportive and friendly and teamwork is highly valued.

The above is illustrative and employers could add much more to give the candidate a feel for what the work will be like. If people are put off by an accurate description of the job, they are probably not the sort of people who should be considered and time (and money) can be saved.

More importantly the danger of such candidates getting into the expensive assessment centre process is considerably increased. And once in the system most try to do their best which means they will present what the employer appears to want.

A better example from the situations vacant pages:

> We also like to differentiate ourselves from other pharmaceutical companies. We are enhancing the benefits package next year by rolling out a series of pioneering reward/recognition schemes that will really motivate and retain. Our representatives enjoy high levels of autonomy in broad-ranging roles that are unique in the industry covering both GP surgeries *and* hospitals. You will not be a 'small cog', if you have creativity and initiative, you can make a real difference and help shape the future of the organization.
>
> We will provide you with a comprehensive induction training programme, then continue to develop your skills throughout your career. We welcome applications from experienced sales representatives and new entrants to the industry. You must be able to demonstrate graduate-level intellect, a proven track record of achievement in any field and a real determination to succeed.
>
> We value achievement, customer orientation and integrity. We dare to be different and we go for it.
>
> If you share these values, please forward your CV together with a covering letter highlighting your personal values to ...

Before candidates are called in to an assessment centre, the application forms can be studied and judgements made on the suitability of the applicants. The application form should be designed to extract the most useful information. Biographical data can provide useful indicators to someone's suitability and possibly their loyalty record to other institutions. At the same time written references are followed up. Ideally there should be a number of these (3 to 6). They are a cheap and efficient method of signalling important issues in a prospective employee's behaviour pattern. Following them up with a call is important as people will often say things over the phone which they would not be prepared to do in writing.

At this stage candidates with the right skills can be selected in and out. Depending on the number of positions vacant for the particular job and the number of apparently suitable applicants, the recruiters might want to proceed further with those who are in the grey area. Where someone is needed with proven scientific or engineering skills, a combination of qualifications acquired, work history and references will inform the sifters.

Many companies rely on agencies, headhunters or referrals from staff or others to identify potential candidates. This may produce good results, but only if the talent-spotters know exactly what they are looking for. Regular, detailed, explicit briefings are an absolute prerequisite; but good feedback on the referrals is also important. When they have put up someone who has fallen significantly below the standards required, the referrers need to know. Where they get it right, they should also be told.

It is also possible at this stage to call candidates in to complete some preliminary tests. These might be cognitive tests; are they bright enough? Or personality tests; are they sufficiently stable or open to creativity? Or integrity tests? We have seen these have predictive validity.

Where the company is large and there are many applicants, the above procedures can safely be outsourced to a properly briefed agency or consultancy. There is sufficient evidence to produce a reliable short list of suitable candidates, with most of those who might be disloyal sifted out. But from here on employers need to involve people from the company; and not just those in HR.

Staff who are working in the areas where a new recruit might be working or with whom he/she can identify, are an important asset at this stage of the recruitment process. These are the people who know what is required in the job and the sorts of people who best fit in. They are also the people whom the candidate needs to meet if he/she is to make an informed judgement about the company and whether it is the sort of place he/she wants to work.

The administration of any interviews can still be outsourced or monitored by HR to ensure appropriate recruitment standards are maintained, but the interviewing skills required are not hard to acquire. The advantages are considerable and worth the investment. Interviewing skills are an essential part of any manager's job and training in them is rarely money wasted – if done properly.

The next stage of the model is to conduct some *preliminary* interviews. Views vary on whether the candidates should be interviewed by two people or one. Interviewers need to be conscious of each other and the candidate may be distracted by the differing styles of the interviewers. At this stage the process is still about information gathering and hypothesis forming and not so much about testing. That should come later. These are still important stages for both parties to discover more: effectively this is an 'inter–view' where both have an active role.

There should however, ideally, be two sequential interviews and both should be written up. This means about 800 words from the first interviewer of his or her impression of the candidate, any issues, the ratings and judgements about the candidate's abilities, traits, values and the potential fit with the organization. This informs not only the second interviewer but also is essential evidence for those at the assessment centre, which is the next stage.

Cook (1998 p 3) records that:

> in the USA *realistic job previews* are increasingly used to tell applicants what being, for example, a telephone operator is *really* like – fast paced, closely supervised, routine to the point of being boring, and solitary. The more carefully worded the advertisement and the job description, the fewer unsuitable candidates apply. (emphases in original)

There are many models for assessment centres. One of the best and most widely used for graduate candidates is the UK's Civil Service Selection Board known as CSSB (pronounced 'sisbi'). This was established shortly after the Second World War and has been developed over the years. It is a two-day assessment centre (AC), which assesses five candidates at a time. The AC consists of a variety of cognitive and other tests, a taxing analytical exercise and group activities to assess candidates' abilities to analyse, communicate and negotiate, together with interviews with each of the assessors. On the third day the three assessors – a senior civil servant, a psychologist and a younger member of the civil service – analyse the evidence, including the application form and written references and make their recommendations, which are then fully written up and used for feedback to the candidates as well as to pass on to receiving departments.

It is expensive and takes time, but the civil service does enjoy a relatively high rate of graduate retention and, while it has been evaluated many times it survives as one of the most powerful, effective and cost-sensitive selection procedures in the UK and worldwide.

After the assessment centre, employers might ask successful candidates from the AC to come for the final interview at which a member of the top management team (not the HR director, who may be the final arbiter) is usually present. He or she sits with two or three others, including a psychologist or HR professional and probes any areas that remain unclear or about which there are questions.

The final interview ensures that standards are maintained, and top management is involved in an important part of the company's work – selecting the right people – as well as allowing those candidates who may be borderline a chance to redeem themselves.

At this stage a provisional letter offering a post can be sent out. The provision is there for those companies which set some store by the loyalty and integrity of their employees. *This is the time when employers should conduct an in-depth background investigation of their candidates.* Referees, claimed qualifications and previous employers (at this stage candidates should be prepared to admit to a current employer that they have another job offer and therefore allow previous employers to be contacted) are interviewed, credit ratings checked and an extended interview conducted with the candidate by an experienced investigator into the individual's integrity and commitment.

In the civil service in the UK this is done for those posts which work with confidential or secret material such as the Foreign and Commonwealth Office, Cabinet Office and the Ministry of Defence. In the US a similar system exists for its civil servants but because numbers are so great it includes a lie detector test as well.

There are however an increasing number of companies and consultancies that provide a similar service. A search on 'Google.com' for employee check produced the names of eight companies in the US and UK who would, for example, 'Take the risk out of recruitment. Use the CV validation specialists' or claim they could 'Learn anything about anyone. It's easy, inexpensive and legal'.

Table 10.1 Loyalty checklist

Essential loyalty checklist – how well does your company do?
1 Does the advert reflect the real values and actual work of the company?
2 Does the application form seek salient information which will inform the recruiters about all aspects of the candidate?
3 Are referees followed up by phone?
4 Are qualifications and other claims on the application form checked?
5 Where the recruitment process is outsourced, are these organizations properly and regularly briefed in detail?
6 Are line managers introduced into the recruitment process early enough?
7 Are all recruiters properly trained/skilled for the purposes of the job?
8 Do candidates have enough opportunity to assess the company – does the 'inter–view' really tell candidates the full picture of the job?
9 Is the assessment centre designed to probe candidates' skills, motives and qualities in the areas important to your company or is it off-the-shelf?
10 How rigorous are the checks on candidates' history and personality?

For some companies a medical test is also appropriate and usually happens at this stage. Mostly this concerns an individual's physical health but where mental stability is important it might also cover subjects such as depression or previous mental illnesses.

The array of options for employers considering their selection procedures is daunting. But where companies or organizations have invested in the recruitment process the returns in staff retention have been high. The costs and consequences of making a mistake at the recruitment stage are much greater. Most of the examples and case histories given throughout this book could have been avoided by more rigorous recruitment procedures. The checklist in Table 10.1 should help employers assess how vulnerable they are to making similar mistakes.

Induction

Every new employee goes through an implicit or explicit induction process as they get to experience the new job. At the very least someone shows them to the desk or machine and tells them to get on with it. The question is how effective is it and can it help the employer who wants to create a loyal and committed workforce? There are many who claim, and who provide data to suggest, that a good induction programme helps staff retention in the early months of a job. Graham and Bennett (1995 pp 190, 216) recommend a two-stage induction course for new employees to reduce staff turnover.

There are it seems five implicit models for induction courses:

1 The 'dog's body' or general factotum model
2 The wonderfully welcoming but 'let down' model
3 The 'deep end' version, with or without training

4   The 'apprenticeship' with structured and osmotic variations
5   The 'moratorium'.

In the first, the 'dog's body' version, the new entrant is brought to the person responsible for HR or their first boss, who spends an hour or two with the individual and explains the company and work. They are then taken round the section or if a small company the whole workforce, and then shown where they work and what to do. Someone is asked to help them out during their first few days.

The boss or HR representative might put in an appearance a few times during the first week and encourage the new recruit to come and discuss any problems directly. Those expressions are often well meant but not often convincing. The new entrant often feels nervous and unsure about what they can ask and they do not want to make a fool of themselves. This last emotion is not exclusive to those who go through the 'dog's body' induction course. New entrants often feel inhibited from asking important questions or approaching others in the organization. Employers or colleagues have to make a real effort to encourage new staff to ask seemingly ignorant or unwise questions without making too harsh a judgement on the questioner. This is a time for answers. It is the beginning of expectation management and the start of the real psychological contract.

The wonderfully welcoming but 'let down' model provides new entrants with an uplifting few days when they are introduced to charismatic top managers and other key personnel, receive good presentations and are shown around the offices. Often these events are accompanied by wine and delicatessen-provided sandwiches in a party celebration-like atmosphere. They finish up feeling elated and happy to be part of such a lively fun company.

Sadly the feelings do not last long as they arrive at their desk or workstation and the reality is very different. Colleagues may be disillusioned, managers not as responsive as suggested, the work is dull, the canteen food is not the same 'deli' quality, in short the work looks very different to the impressions created during the first days.

In the 'deep end' model, new entrants may literally be told no more than this is your desk, you have the qualifications otherwise you wouldn't be here, now just get on with it: Darwinian swim or sink. More often the employers using this version spend quality time training the new entrants so they can perform effectively when they reach the desk. This happens most often when the skills used in the organization cannot be 'bought' in. Companies producing high tech, state-of-the-art products cannot expect new staff to know the systems and have to train them up. In other organizations such as army or air-force officer corps, new entrants will also be given intensive training in the first few months before being sent to their new posts.

For many new entrants this is a welcome challenge and the trust shown in them as they take on their new roles largely unsupervised is much appreciated. For others it can be threatening, but if the recruiters have got it right the majority will be in the first category.

'Apprenticeship' is the classic model which produced over the years many highly skilled craftsmen and professionals. It applied to trades such as carpentry, gardening and butlers as well as professions such as accountancy and the law. In the best work environments new recruits would be groomed by an already skilled worker and gradually shown the tricks of the trade. They are assigned to a master-craftsman, an expert in the field. The relationship between the two develops over time and while it might be characterized by gruffness and authoritarianism there would be great respect and even affection. It is the *master–student* relationship often seen in the music world. Indeed there is currently a great fad for the master class.

Loyalty would be bred into the new person as an essential ingredient given that the employer was known by the standards of the day to be good. It was not, and where it exists today is not, always so. The process might be more osmotic than planned. The instructor might not take his or her responsibilities seriously and leave the recruit to learn on their own. At its best, apprenticeship is an excellent system, fostering high standards not only of the skills of the trade but also of values such as loyalty and hard work. The loyalty however may only be to the master. At its worst, it institutionalizes feelings of distrust, a poor work ethic and standards as well as feelings of resentment towards management.

The 'moratorium' model allows the new entrant to move around the new business experiencing how each section or department works and their relevance to the overall core objectives of the company. During this period, which might last three or four months (even a year), the new entrant is not productive and adds little to the business, but once they emerge they have acquired a wide knowledge of the workings of the company which will ensure they are able to put their own work into a proper context. Such programmes are accompanied by regular sessions in the induction centre where more general company policies and values can be explained.

Induction in its many forms has some practical benefits and provides solutions to some legal issues about due care and attention. It should be designed to help a new recruit feel less disoriented and nervous and so promote greater productivity. According to Marchington and Wilkinson (1996 pp 138–9), the primary purposes of an induction programme cover:

▷ Terms of employment
▷ Housekeeping and security issues
▷ Health and safety regulations
▷ Wages and benefits
▷ Company rules and policies
▷ Employee development opportunities
▷ Information about the company and the industry
▷ Job performance issues.

It is also an opportunity to instil in the recruit feelings of loyalty and commitment and to begin to establish the psychological contract (see Chapter 2). Skeats (1991) contends that induction can engender:

> a feeling of belonging to a company [which] develops a commitment to organisational goals. The employer then maximises the contribution of the workforce and gets a faster return on investment. (p 18)

This is not to be confused with indoctrination: the blind or uncritical acceptance of company policies and instructions. To be fully committed and loyal staff need to feel they can contribute to the debate and question procedures. They are not clones of top management.

Induction should prepare staff for the downs as well as the ups of work. Not all line managers will be saints, there will be issues and problems that will frustrate the employee over the years to come, but a properly conducted induction process will prove an effective inoculation for the rough times ahead.

Maintaining commitment

Having found the right staff and given them their inoculations how can the organization maintain their commitment? There are any number of books and courses to help the hapless manager who is charged with looking after employees, whether potentially difficult or full of energy and self-starting. The managers charged with maximizing productivity will acquire a number of skills as they progress.

Management is often a difficult, thankless if (on occasion) well remunerated task. Managers have a variety of different tasks from budgeting to PR. And most crucially they have to be good people managers. Management, like politics, is the art of getting things done. But what is the essence of good man management? What skills are required? And if it is all so easy why do managers get it wrong so often?

Good management lies in five things: giving people clear definable goals; continuous and helpful support; hopeful feedback; advice for managing change and continuous good communication.

Goal setting

Whether it is called management by objectives or performance management, step one is about individual, as well as team and function, goal setting. These may be called different things: individual goals, strategic objectives, key performance indicators, key result areas, measurable outcomes.

The above are usually simply terminological differences favoured by different organizations for historical reasons. The task however is always the same. The individual needs to know clearly and explicitly what he or she should achieve and, equally importantly, how it should be measured. He or she should know what is expected of them and precisely what outcomes are effectively performance targets.

In the context of creating loyalty and commitment, goal setting both ensures employees have jobs that are sufficiently stretching and avoids any potential confusion about what might or might not be expected of the individual.

Support

It is all very well to give clear instructions and set explicit objectives but it then, of necessity, becomes the manager's job to help their report staff obtain these objectives. There are different types of support:

▷ *Technical support:* People often need equipment and technology that is appropriate, up-to-date and functional to do the job. It is the manager's role to identify, source and maintain this equipment.

▷ *Training support:* As jobs change and new equipment becomes necessary, staff need training. They also benefit from training in the soft skills such as selling, counselling, negotiation. Managers need to provide timely, effective and appropriate training.

▷ *Financial support:* This means more than paying the wages. Most managers have a budget which may be linked to departmental efficacy. Managers, like their staff, need money to buy, fix and up-grade technology and perhaps hire in staff during very busy periods, as well as to use for performance-related pay.

▷ *Informational support:* All staff need to be kept up-to-date with information about changes in trends, products, customer wishes, company plans and so on. People are worried about change and need help understanding it. Information is power: and it can empower staff.

▷ *Emotional support:* Managers are responsible for morale which should never be underestimated. Morale is both a cause and a consequence of work productivity. It is easy to sink down in a *vicious cycle* where poor business results lower morale which in turn leads to further lack of success. It is partly a function of management to create *virtuous cycles*. That is to help foster a spirit of optimism, commitment and loyalty which helps productivity. Loyalty is two-way and the manager is the embodiment of the organization.

It is said that people join organizations but leave individual managers. Exit interviews demonstrate how some managers are almost exclusively the cause of stress. They refuse to do those management things which are the essence of management. They can be bullies, control-freaks or absentee landlords – the very opposite of the supportive manager – and these qualities are bound to undermine loyalty amongst staff (see Chapter 5).

Feedback

Every coach, every psychotherapist and every teacher knows that learning occurs fastest with accurate, regular feedback. People quite simply need to know 'how they are doing'. They need to know the criteria upon which they are being evaluated, who is doing those evaluations and, most importantly, how to improve their performance.

To live in a feedbackless world is to live without any knowledge of what one is doing, right or wrong. To live in a world of distorted, erratic or biased feedback creates tension and undermines commitment.

Giving reliable, specific (based on evidence), timely, regular and useful feedback is the essence of good people management. It also provides the manager with an opportunity to listen to any issues or problems the employee might have. Should the employee be failing in any way, then this provides the time to inform and correct.

The role of the manager, like that of the coach, is to 'shape' the behaviour of those they look after. They do so by giving pertinent, helpful, regular feedback and advice.

Managing change

Change is inevitable – it is welcomed, indeed encouraged by many. For others it brings nothing but problems and has to be avoided. Consider the following quotations (Bloomsbury Reference Books, 2003):

▷ Faced with change, employees have one question: 'what's going to happen to me?' A successful change management communication programme will avoid that question? (Scott Adams, b 1957, *The Dilbert Principle*)
▷ Change means movement; movement means friction. (Saul Alinsky, US activist 1909–72)
▷ When the winds of change blow, some build walls, others build windmills. (Anonymous)
▷ Better, never means better for everyone … It always means worse, for some. (Margaret Attwood, b. 1939, *The Handmaid's Tale* 1985)
▷ I never think of the future. It comes soon enough. (Albert Einstein, interview 1930)
▷ Don't wrap the flag of Coca-Cola around you to prevent change taking place. (Roberto Goizueta, 1931–97, US CEO of Coca-Cola, speech 1995)
▷ Change is inevitable in a progressive country. Change is constant. (Benjamin Disraeli, 1804–81, British Prime Minister, speech 1867)

An interesting indicator of people's attitude (positive and negative) to change is that of all the chapters in *Talking Shop, Over 5000 business quotes to help you through your working day* from Bloomsbury Reference Books, the one on 'change' has the most entries: 134 compared, for example, with 97 on 'money'.

As far as the employee is concerned, the impetus for change comes from four sources: the individual, the job, the organization and society. Individuals grow older and, as they do, any or all of the following may happen:

▷ Acquiring close friends, acquaintances, even spouses
▷ New responsibilities at home with marriage and children
▷ House moves, perhaps involving a better or worse journey to work
▷ Health deterioration, temporary or permanent
▷ Promotion or job moves involving new responsibilities
▷ Training courses which give them new ideas
▷ Life-changing events of many sorts.

Managers have to be aware of these changes and make necessary adjustments to the goals and support offered. Where the change comes from an external source, where employees are being changed by others, they tend to be more accepting of change when:

▷ It is understood
▷ It does not threaten security
▷ Those affected have helped create it
▷ It follows other successful changes
▷ It genuinely reduces a work burden
▷ The outcome is reasonably certain
▷ The implementation has been mutually planned
▷ Top management support is strongly evident.

It is also important for managers to understand the forces that generate change and to anticipate change. Some of the factors for change are as follows:

▷ Repealed or revised laws or regulations (often government based) that lead to new opportunities, markets, or ways of operating
▷ Rapidly changing environment (geographic market or political situation that makes old methods, processes or products redundant)
▷ Improved technology or technology that can do things faster, cheaper, more reliable new product development or selection by consumers
▷ Changing workforce (for example more educated, more women) with different demands and skills
▷ More technically trained management who appreciate the possibilities of, and for, the new technology
▷ Organizational crisis (for example impending bankruptcy, purchase) that requires change of necessity
▷ Reduced productivity, product quality that leads to a change
▷ Reduced satisfaction, commitment by staff which forces ultimately a crisis of morale and reduced productivity
▷ Increased turnover, absenteeism and other signs of organizational stress.

Communication skills

A manager is responsible for production, managing other people, customer relations, analysis, alerting senior people or investors to potential problems, giving good news, negotiating – the list could go on. But in every single function one or other form of communication is needed.

There are at least four elements to communication: writing, speaking, reading and listening. The spoken and written words provide the hard evidence which people will use to feel comforted, gruntled and happy or to turn against the speaker or writer to claim an injustice. To be convincing, the body language has to be consistent with the words.

Harvey Thomas and Roy Lilley are both experts in the spoken word and have advised prime ministers and CEOs on communicating skills. Their golden rule is: 'If they haven't heard it – you haven't said it!' (Thomas and Lilley 1995). People do not take on board everything that is said or written and they have an alarming tendency to hear things that have not been said or to interpret it in other ways.

There are four basic rules to any communication, written or spoken (Gower 1987 pp 12, 24):

1 *Simplicity.* Unusual words may show the writer or speaker to be clever and well educated, or more often a show-off, but simpler words have more impact and are therefore easily understood.
2 *Brevity.* Any person can only absorb a finite amount of information. Only a small part of a long text or statement will therefore be remembered. Murphy's law will ensure that the important parts are the ones not committed to memory.
3 *Humanity.* Style is a contentious issue and people will hold on to their views. In office communications a degree of humanity helps the reader or listener relate to the messenger and the message. It should be friendly, sympathetic and natural.
4 *Accuracy.* An obvious statement, perhaps, but all too easily shaded or, in the modern idiom, spun out of recognition.

> *If language is not correct, then what is said is not what is meant; if what is said is not what is meant, then what ought to be done remains undone.*
>
> Confucius

The one factor that improves everyone's ability to read and absorb the plethora of material available is time. The spread of computers, the internet and ease of email have put so much more information on our screens or in newspapers, pamphlets or books that no one can read everything in their field. The burden then falls even more on the writer to ensure that what is written follows Gower's rules quoted above.

The communication skill that is still the Cinderella of communication is listening. It is also perhaps the most important when it comes to building and maintaining loyalty. There are two levels of listening:

1 *Effective listening* – understanding and remembering what others say and
2 *Active listening* – the listener demonstrates sympathetically that they are listening and therefore encourages the other to reveal more. The active listener also interprets all the signals, verbal and non-verbal.

The key elements to active listening are:

> *Listening is a magnetic and strange thing, a creative force. The friends who listen to us are the ones we move toward. When we are listened to, it creates us, makes us unfold and expand.*
>
> Karl Menninger

▷ Time, that most elusive of commodities for a manager, but unless people are able to have sufficient time to collect and order their thoughts important details will be missed. Many interviewers find that the nugget which reveals the real problem comes just as the person is leaving the room.

▷ Demonstrate you are listening through your responses, sometimes called the grunt factor – the occasional 'umm' or 'yes', nods of the head, paraphrasing of what has just been said all help to encourage a speaker because they believe they are being listened to.

▷ Avoidance of critical judgements. If someone feels their views are being challenged they will shut up, rather than argue or become defensive.

▷ The interviewer's body language. While it should be open and relaxed to encourage discussion it should not be completely at odds with the other person. To some extent the body language should 'mirror' that of the other, but avoid mimicry.

Management reluctance

There is nothing new, surprising or counterintuitive in all this. It is plain common sense. But it is surprisingly infrequently done.

Perhaps the two types of support that are most often conspicuous by their absence are informational and emotional support. There are three reasons why people at work are not really given the information they require. First, managers themselves are kept in the dark and so they do not have the salient information to pass on. Second, they do not know what information people need: that is, they are unable to distinguish between signal and noise and give staff useful information. Third, and most ominously, managers have information of crucial importance to their staff, such as a change of computer system or an M&A, but will not give it because they fear it will undermine their power and authority and lead to staff morale dropping.

Ask the average manager if they believe that their boss has some important 'secret' information which they have not passed on to them and 90% say yes. They might or might not be right but it indicates their need to be kept informed.

Managers do not provide emotional support primarily because they do not know when or how to do it. A manager is responsible for strategy *and* morale. They need to know how to 'lift' flagging morale as well as do individual counselling for those in need. Managers need to 'look out for' the task, the group and individuals. Managers don't have to be caring-and-sharing training counsellors. But they do need to support their reports emotionally in time of need.

Sometimes people do not receive feedback on their performance because manager's have no good data on their performance. There is, in a sense, nothing to feedback, except perhaps rather vague impressionable data. Most people don't get feedback, however, because pusillanimous, conflict-averse managers fear giving negative feedback. Note how successful candidates are phoned up; unsuccessful candidates sent letters. It is easy to give good news; much less so bad.

Most managers have been burnt by the experience of trying to give a below-par individual some honest feedback about their performance. The scenario goes like this. The manager prepares his/her case with 'documentary evidence' and examples about the type of behaviour he or she is unsatisfied with. The poorly performing employee is told their performance is weak; they demand evidence/an example. The manager provides it. The poorly performing employee disputes it. A long argument about specific incidents in the past ensues. Both parties become emotional: angry, bitter, hurt. The experience is a failure. The manager resolves that this never happens again. They do this by avoiding the feedback activity or simply faking average for bad.

People can hear negative feedback under two conditions. First, if it is based on reliable evidence. But second, and perhaps more importantly, the person needs to know what to do to avoid this sort of feedback in the future. If you know what to do differently to receive good feedback it is possible to hear bad feedback. Feedback is supposed to be rewarding or correcting. Its aim is to give useful information about how one works (comparatively) and the outcomes of work.

All people in the change business know it is imperative to find ways of letting people access data on their performance. The bathroom scales give feedback on diet; the speedometer feedback on speeding. Olympic judges give feedback to divers as do judges at dog shows.

People can be taught to describe and choose tea and wine such that tasters are interchangeable and the product up to standard. This is achieved by training. Judging means learning the language for subtle phenomena and applying it.

At work, managers need to know both how to rate/judge/score but also how to give that information back to individuals. It is a very important aspect of their jobs and is often underplayed. The ability to, and necessity of, evaluating others' performance and using this information to shape it is one of the central functions of management.

The characteristics of competent managers

There are lots of lists of this nature: the six (or so) habits (traits) of highly successful people. Some are based on research, others not. Some use technical language, others everyday terms. The trouble with these lists is that it is unclear:

▷ If the list is rank-ordered from most to least important traits?
▷ How the traits of highly effective managers are related to each other. Are they all essentially independent or statistically related?
▷ When the list ends. Some people want to split, others combine various traits and there seems no rationale for doing either.
▷ Most importantly, where these traits come from: nature vs. nurture; heredity vs. environment. Inevitably, the answer is both, but it is most important because it is an indication of how much the characteristic can be changed. That is, can it be taught/trained or has it to be selected?

The following list is not arbitrary. It is based on research though it is constantly being revised:

1 *Intelligence:* People have to be *bright enough* for the job they have to do. The more complex and varied the tasks, the brighter they have to be. The more they have to learn to keep up-to-date, the brighter they have to be. At the senior level, intelligence may be the single best predictor of success at work. And it is, alas, not trainable. Surprisingly perhaps, given the data on intelligence, it is so infrequently measured at work. Intelligence predicts both knowledge and attitude to learning.

2 *Emotional stability:* Stress at work is a given. The question is how vulnerable we are to experiencing it and how we cope with it. Less emotionally stable people are prone to anxiety, depression, hypochondria and absenteeism. Hardy robust people are able to withstand the inevitable stresses at work. Less stable people cope poorly and have little time or energy for others.

3 *Conscientiousness:* You need to work hard to be successful at work. At times one has to come in early, stay late and take work home to complete the job on time. Some people struggle in adverse conditions and always give their best. Others give up. The work ethic is a must.

4 *Integrity:* The single feature people most want in their bosses is not competence, vision or emotional intelligence but honesty. People admire the leaders with a clear oral code and the courage to live by it. This is not a matter of zealotry

> *Leadership above all consists of telling the truth, unpalatable though it may be. It is better to go down with the truth on one's lips than to rise high by innuendo and doubletalk.*
>
> Alfred Robens (1909–99)
> Chairman of National Coal
> Board, speech 1974

but a matter of weighing up various options and acting in a way that is not dishonest.

5 *Engaging:* Great leaders work by inspiring and getting the best out of others. Some can get their staff to do almost anything through their charisma, their charm and their insight into others. They are able to be sociable and approachable. They need to know how, when and why to engage others, be they customers, staff or shareholders.

6 *Courageousness:* Good managers need courage to fail and the courage to be different. Real innovators are courageous: they have to be. It is about taking appropriate risks.

Honesty and transparency

If the culture of the organization is one where deception is the norm, where top managers are known to be taking money not properly earnt, then the rest of the workforce will follow that example. Similarly if employees cannot see or understand how decisions affecting their livelihood are being made, they will think the worst if things go against them.

Paternalistic management styles suggest that the decision-makers know best what is in the interests of the worker. They may be right but in recent times this view is constantly challenged by younger generations who believe they should be given insights into the process if not the actual discussions. They want to see the evidence for decisions. References to personal gut feeling or instincts do not carry much weight for the modern graduate. They are more likely to see this, at best, as lazy thinking – there should be evidence and a good mind will be able to identify the reasons for a decision rather than rely on the equivalent of reading tea leaves. At worst, they will believe decisions were taken based on the basis of bias, prejudice or old-fashioned thinking.

Johnson and Phillips in *Absolute Honesty* (2003 pp 49–51) show how to build a culture rooted in six laws of honesty:

1 *Tell the truth.* When the news is good this is rarely a problem but when there is something unpalatable managers avoid the issue or try to sugar the pill to the extent that the real truth is obscured. In the long run telling the truth will earn managers respect and trust and encourage others to do likewise.

2 *Tackle the problem.* Where there is disagreement people often take the apparently easy path and just go along with the idea and cooperate. This does not help and people should be encouraged to deal with the issues with constructive confrontation.

3 *Disagree and commit.* The culture should allow people to disagree. Too often people attend meetings where consensus is reached but then go back to their colleagues or staff and lobby against the decision. People should feel free to disagree with policies they believe to be wrong, partic-ularly if they concern ethics, morals or the law.

4 *Welcome the truth.* If a manager is justly criticized they should not become defensive, but accept they are in the wrong.
5 *Reward the messenger.* Unpalatable information is never easy to pass on. When a subordinate does so to a senior manager the difficulties are much greater.
6 *Build a platform of integrity.* Lead by example; even when things get tough, stick to the principles and values that matter.

Exit policies

The issue of departures was discussed in detail in Chapter 9 on 'Protecting Your Assets'. There are two reasons why it is important to have an exit policy as far as this chapter is concerned:

1 The person or persons leaving should feel they have been treated fairly. If they do not there is no quicker way to create a possible long-term enemy. Once out of the organization and with few if any reasons to constrain their actions, they will lash out. They will at the very least bad-mouth the company and some of that mud will stick. At the worst they will seek more violent forms of revenge. Done properly the person will feel the organization is good and that the decision to leave was a joint one and best for all concerned. The best personnel officers and managers will aim to have employees who are leaving come to them on their last day saying 'thank you very much' and meaning it.
2 Others in the organization will note how the person leaving is being treated. Even if his departure is welcomed by colleagues, they are unlikely to want to see him humiliated in the process. They will want to see that he has been treated fairly and above all with dignity. Why – because everyone at some stage will leave and they will want to think they will be treated in the same way. When they see people leave with their self-esteem intact they will feel safe and that when their turn comes – as it surely will – those who are left behind are still friends and not speaking ill of them. Their commitment to the company will be that much greater.

> *In the end we are all sacked and it's always awful. It is as inevitable as death following life. If you are elevated there comes a day when you are demoted.*
>
> Alan Clarke (1928–99) British politician and diarist (diary 21 June 1983)

> *To downsize effectively you have to have empathy with the people who are losing their jobs … What you say to them has a lot to do with the attitude of the survivors: whether they see the company as a money machine or keep their respect for it.*
>
> Percy Barnevik (b 1941) Swedish former CEO of ABB, interview 1995

> *If you have made someone redundant it is your responsibility to help them ... You have removed the certainties from their life and your personal support and help is the least you can provide in return.*
>
> John Harvey-Jones (b 1924) former chairman ICI *All Together Now* 1994

The consequences of getting it wrong can be dramatic or, as the following examples show, disastrous.

A man who held up a bank just outside Paris on Saturday, killing three people, was a former employee, it has been revealed. He has told investigators he was taking revenge on the branch manager for sacking him.

13 August 2001 www.bbc.co.uk

SEVEN people are dead after a sacked employee returned to an auto parts warehouse on Chicago's south side and opened fire on former co-workers before being shot dead by a policeman, a police official said.

14 October 2003 www.news.com.au

'The hackers came to light last summer when thousands of e-mails were scattered across the Net offering access to pictures of underage Japanese girls.

To cover their tracks, the Japanese group sent its pornographic invitation through a San Francisco computer specialist, Quick Print. *They were able to do this because a sacked employee gave them the passwords.* The message invited people offended by the lewd invitation to send back an e-mail asking to be removed from the pornographer's mailing list so they would not be troubled again.

According to Wood, the offer to be removed from the list was a trap. 'They had no idea whether they had the right e-mail addresses so they needed people to get disgusted with the offer of illicit material,' he says. 'As soon as they answered and asked to be removed, the hackers had their e-mail address and the address of their host server.' (Authors' italic)

28 May 1998 http://www.attrition.org

On the other hand, where departures are handled well the results can be surprisingly different:

A major confectionery manufacturer in the UK decided to close its two southern manufacturing units over an 18-month period, employing approx 500 staff. The initial announcement was made by the Managing Director personally at each of the sites involved. Counsellors were on hand from Coutts Consulting to provide individual support to employees that were either upset or concerned by the announcement. A company was also employed to manage the media.

Neither of the sites recognized a union so all consultation was done through a body of elected employee representatives on each site. The attitude of the employee representatives was a key factor in the success of the process. Each employee also had a series of one to one consultations with their line manager.

Three months prior to the first member of staff leaving a full outplacement centre was set up on each site by Coutts Consulting to provide advice across all shifts, on writing CVs, attending interviews and job search techniques, a range of jobs were also advertised. The service was full time and operated until the closure.

On top of the training provided by Coutts, employees were offered training to improve their skill base. A range of courses were provided from basic computer skills and fork lift truck training through to basic literacy and numeracy.

The company recognized that some staff may want the opportunity to relocate to the manufacturing units in the North so those who were interested were taken by coach to visit the units and the local area to help them decide if they would like to relocate. Two or three staff subsequently emigrated with financial support from the company to units in Canada.

To mark the closure of both sites each employee received a gift from the company engraved with the name of the company and the opening and closing dates of the site. The company also funded a closing party for each site which was arranged by the employee representatives.

As a result of this policy:

► There were no incidents of product sabotage

► The staff were all cooperative: some staff went to train colleagues at other sites on how to use the machinery being transferred to them

► In all areas production levels were maintained and in some production increased

► Although the majority of the staff were made redundant at the end of the process there was not one claim for unfair dismissal

► The remaining staff recognized that the company was a fair and reasonable employer and even in tough times treated its staff well.

October 2003 www.yourpartnerinhr.co.uk

Conclusion

It is appropriate, and by design that this book ends on an optimistic note. While most of the preceding chapters have dwelt on the dark side of behaviour, the purpose has always been to help CEOs, senior executives, managers and human resource specialists avoid low retention rates, theft, fraud, deceit, information leakage or sabotage.

The aim has been to explain the motives of those who commit counter-productive acts and so contribute to creating a loyal and committed workforce, willing to go the extra mile. Many organizations achieve it in both the public and the private sectors, in the Americas, Europe, Asia, Africa and the Middle East.

Most people would prefer to work in an environment of trust, where there is a culture of honesty and integrity amongst all employers and employees. Just as important are the consequences on the bottom line – the costs, the productivity and the profits. Counterproductive behaviour directly affects the core business of any organization. This book is dedicated to reducing its prevalence and promoting loyalty and commitment in all employees.

Bibliography

ACAS (2000) Code of Practice 1: *Disciplinary and Grievance Procedures* London: Advisory, Conciliation and Arbitration Service.

Aiken, M. and Hage, J. (1966) Organizational alienation: A comparative analysis. *Journal of Applied Psychology,* **65,** 497–501.

Ambrose, M., Seabright, M. and Schminke, M. (2002) Sabotage in the work place: The role of organizational injustice. *Organizational Behaviour and Human Decision Processes,* **89,** 947–65.

Analoui, F. and Kakabadse, A. (2000) *Sabotage* Chalford: Management Books.

Armstrong, M. (2001) *Human Resource Management Practice* London: Kogan Page.

Babiak, P. (1995) When psychopaths go to work: A case study of an industrial psychopath. *Applied Psychology,* **44,** 171–88.

Bennett, R. and Robinson, S. (2000) Development of a measure of workplace deviance. *Journal of Applied Psychology,* **85,** 349–60.

Billsberry, J. (2000) *Finding and Keeping the Right People* London: Prentice Hall.

Blackman, M. and Funder, D. (2002) Effective interview practices for accurately assessing counter-productive traits. *International Journal of Selection and Assessment,* **10,** 109–16.

Bloomsbury Reference Books, (2003) *Talking Shop* London: Bloomsbury Publishing.

Bobocel, D., McCline, R. and Folger, R. (1997) Letting them down gently: conceptual advances in explaining controversial organizational policies. In C. Cooper and D. Rousseau (eds) *Trends in Organizational Behaviour,* **4,** 73–88.

Broad, W. and Wade, N. (1985) *Betrayers of the Truth: Fraud and Deceit in Science* Oxford: OUP.

Brockway, J., Carlson, K., Jones, S. and Bryant, F. (2002) Development and validation of a scale for measuring cynical attitudes towards college. *Journal of Educational Psychology,* **94,** 1–15.

Brown, R. and Colthern, C. (2002) Individual differences in faking integrity tests. *Psychological Reports,* **91,** 691–702.

Buchanan, B. (1974) Building organizational commitment. *Administrative Science Quarterly,* **19,** 533–46.

Buitenen, P. van (2000) *Blowing the Whistle* London: Politico's Publishing.

Bull, R. (1988) What is the lie-detector test? In A. Gale (ed.) *The Polygraph Test.* London: Sage, pp 10–18.

Burrell, P. (2003) *A Royal Duty* London: The Penguin Group.

Butler, T. and Waldroop, J. (1999) Job Sculpting. *Harvard Business Review,* September/October.

Camara, W.E. and Schneider, D. (1995) Questions of construct breadth and openness of research in integrity testing. *American Psychologist,* **50,** 459–60.

Carnegie, D. (1998) *How to Win Friends and Influence People* London; Vermillion.

Carroll, D. (1988) How accurate is polygraph lie detection? In A. Gale (ed.) *The Polygraph Test.* London: Sage, pp 19–28.

Casal, J. and Zalkind, S. (1995) Consequences of whistle-blowing. *Psychological Reports,* 77, 795–802.

Centre for Retail Research (2003) *The European Retail Theft Barometer* 3rd report.

Cizek, G. (1999) *Cheating on Tests* Mahway, NJ: LEA.

Cleckley, H. (1976) *The Mask of Sanity* (5th edn) St Louis, MO: Mosby.

Collett, P. (2003) *The Book of Tells* London: Doubleday.

Connolly, C. (1988) *Enemies of Promise* London: Andre Deutsch.

Cook, M. (1998) *Personnel Selection* Chichester: John Wiley.

Crino, M. (1994) Employee sabotage: a random or preventable phenomenon. *Journal of Managerial Issues,* 6, 311–30.

Cropanzano, R. and Greenberg, J. (1997) Progress in organizational justice. In C. Cooper and I. Robertson (eds) *International Review of Industrial and Organizational Psychology,* 12, pp 317–72. New York: Wiley.

Crowne, D. and Marlowe, D. (1964) *The Approval Motive* New York: Wiley.

Dailey, R. and Kirk, D. (1992) Distributive and procedural justice as antecedents of job dissatisfaction and intent to turnover. *Human Relations,* **45,** 305–17.

Davies, D. (2000) *Fraud Watch* London: ABG.

Di Battista, R. (1991) Creating new approaches to recognise and deter sabotage. *Public Personnel Management,* **20,** 347–53.

Di Battista, R. (1996) Forecasting sabotage events in the workplace. *Public Personnel Management,* **25,** 41–52.

Douglas, M. (1986) *How Institutions Think* New York: Syracuse University Press.

Earley, P. (1997) *Confessions of a Spy* London: Hodder & Stoughton.

Ekman, P. (2001) *Telling Lies* London: W.W. Norton.

Eoyang, C. (1994) Models of Espionage. In T. Sarbin (ed.) *Citizen Sabotage*, New York: Praeger, pp 69–92.

Eysenck, S., Eysenck, H. and Barrett, P. (1985) A revised version of the psychoticism scale. *Personality and Individual Differences*, 6, 21–9.

Fallon, J., Avis, J., Kudish, J., Gornet, T. and Frost, A. (2000) Conscientiousness as a predictor of productive and counterproductive behaviours. *Journal of Business and Psychology*, 15, 339–50.

Fortmann, K., Leslie, C. and Cunningham, M. (2002) Cross-cultural comparison of the Reid Integrity Scale in Latin America and South Africa. *International Journal of Selection and Assessment*, 10, 98–108.

Franklin, J. (1975) Power and commitment. *Human Relations*, 28, 737–53.

Furnham, A. (1990a) The fakability of the 16PF, Myers-Briggs and Firo-B personality measures. *Personality and Individual Differences*, 11, 711–16.

Furnham, A. (1990b) Faking personality questionnaires: fabricating different profiles for different purposes. *Current Psychology*, 9, 46–55.

Furnham, A. (1999) *The Psychology of Behaviour at Work* Hove: Psychology Press.

Furnham, A. (1999) *Body Language at Work* London: CIPD.

Furnham, A. (2003) *Mad, Sad and Bad Management* Cirencester: Management Books.

Furnham, A. and Argyle, M. (1998) *The Psychology of Money* London: Routledge.

Gale, A. (1988) (ed.) *The Polygraph Test: Lies, Truth and Science* London: Sage.

Gillespie, I. (1996) From the head of department's point of view. In S. Lock and F. Wells (eds) *Fraud and Misconduct in Medical Research*. London: BMJ Publishing Group.

Goldberg, H. and Lewis, R. (1978) *Money Madness* London: Springwood.

Gordievsky, O. (1995) *Next Stop Execution* London: Macmillan – now Palgrave Macmillan.

Gower, Sir E. (1987) *The Complete Plain Words* London: Penguin Books.

Graham, H.T. and Bennett, R. (1995) *Human Resources Management* London: Pitman.

Greenberg, J. (1998) The cognitive geometry of employee theft: negotiating 'the line' between taking and theft. In R.W. Griffin, A. O'Leary-Kelly and J. Collins (eds) *Non-violent behaviors in organizations (Vol. 2). Dysfunctional behaviors in organizations*, pp 147–93. Greenwich, CT: JAI.

Greenberg, J. (2002) Who stole the money, and when? Individual and situational determinants of employee theft. *Organizational Behaviour and Human Decision Processes*, 89, 985–1003.

Greenberg. J. and Scott, K. (1996) Why do workers bite the hands that feed them? *Research in Organizational Behaviour*, **18**, 111–56.

Greenberg, L. and Barling, J. (1996) Employee theft. In C. Cooper and D. Rousseau (eds) *Trends in Organizational Behaviour*, **3**, 49–67. Chichester: Wiley.

Griffeth, R., Hom. and Gaertner, S. (2000) A meta-analysis of antecedents and correlates of employee turnover. *Journal of Management*, **26**, 463–88.

Grover, S. (1993) Lying, deceit and subterfuge: A model of dishonesty in the workplace. *Organizational Science*, **4**, 478–95.

Gudjonnson, G. (1988) How to defeat the polygraph tests. In A. Gale (1988) *The Polygraph Test*. London: Sage, pp 126–36.

Hackett, R., Lapierre, L. and Hausdorf, P. (2001) Understanding the links between work commitment constructs. *Journal of Vocational Behaviour*, **58**, 392–413.

Hakstian, A., Farrell, S. and Tweed, R. (2002) The assessment of counterproduction tendencies by means of the California Psychological Inventory. *International Journal of Selection and Assessment*, **10**, 58–86.

Harris, J. and Brannick, J. (1999) *Finding and Keeping Great Employees* New York: Amacom.

Hay Group (2001) *The Retention Dilemma* www.haygroup.com.

Herriot, P., Manning, W. and Kidd, J. (1999) The content of the psycho logical contract. *British Journal of Management*, **8**, 151–62.

Herzberg, F. (1993) *The Motivation to Work* New York: Wiley.

Hogan, J. and Hogan, R. (1989) How to measure employee reliability. *Journal of Applied Psychology*, **94**, 273–9.

Hogan, R. and Hogan, J. (1994) The mask of integrity. In T. Sarbin (ed.). *Citizen Espionage*. New York: Praeger, pp 93–105.

Holder, R. (1998) Detecting fakers on a personnel test. *Journal of Social Behaviour and Personality*, **13**, 387–98.

Holder, R. and Hibbs, N. (1995) Incremental validity of response latencies for detecting fakes on a personality test. *Journal of Research and Personality*, **29**, 362–72.

Hollinger, R. (2002) *National Retail Security Survey Final Report* University of Florida.

Hollyforde, S. and Whiddett, S. (2002) *The Motivation Handbook*, London: CIPD.

Hough, L. (1996) Can integrity tests be trusted? *Employment Testing*, **5**, 97–111.

Hovorka-Mead, A., Ross, W., Whipple, T. and Renchin, M. (2002) Watching the detectives. *Personnel Psychology*, **55**, 329–62.

Howard, S. (2002) The Missing £7 Billion. *People Management,* 21 March 2001.

Husson, J.M., Bugaievsky, J., Huidberg, E., Schwarz, J. and Chadha, D. (1996) Fraud in clinical research on medicines in the European Union: facts and proposals. In Lock and Wells (eds).

Jackson, C., Levine, S., Furnham, A. and Burr, N. (2002) Predictors of cheating behaviour at university. *Journal of Applied Social Psychology,* **32,** 1–18.

Jahoda, M. (1982) *Employment and Unemployment* Cambridge: CUP.

Johnson, L. and Phillips, B. (2003) *Absolute Honesty* New York: Amacom.

Jones, J. (1991) *Pre-employment Honesty Testing* Westport: Conn-Quorun Books.

Jones, J., Brasher, E. and Huff, J. (2002) Innovations in integrity-based personnel selection. *International Journal of Selection and Assessment,* **10,** 87–97.

Keenan, J. (1990) Upper-level managers and whistle blowing. *Journal of Business and Psychology,* **5,** 223–35.

Keenan, T. (1997) Selection for potential: the case for graduate recruitment. In N. Anderson and P. Herriot (eds) *International Handbook of Selection and Appraisal* Chichester: Wiley.

Kelloway, E., Loughlin, C., Barling, J. and Nault, A. (2002) Self-reported counter-productive behaviours and organizational citizenship behaviours. *International Journal of Selection and Assessment,* **10,** 143–51.

Kibling, T. and Lewis, T. (2000) *Employment Law* London: Legal Aid Group.

Killick, M. (1999) *The Fraudbusters* London: Indigo.

Klein, R., Leong, G. and Silva, J. (1996) Employee sabotage in the workplace: A biopsychosocial model. *Journal of Forensic Sciences,* **41,** 52–5.

Kline, P. (2000) *Handbook of Psychological Testing* New York: Routledge.

Koch, J. and Steers, R. (1978) Job attachment, satisfaction and turnover among public sector employees. *Journal of Vocational Behaviour,* **12,** 119–28.

Lacono, W. and Lykken, D. (1997) The validity of the lie detector: Two surveys of scientific opinion. *Journal of Applied Psychology,* **82,** 426–33.

Leeson, N. (1996) *Rogue Trader* London: Warner Books.

Lilienfeld, S., Alliger, G. and Mitchell, K. (1995) Why integrity testing remains controversial. *American Psychologist,* **50,** 457–8.

Lind, E., Greenberg, J., Scott, K. and Welchans, T. (2000) The winding road from employee to complainant: situational and psychological determinants of wrongful termination claims. *Administrative Science Quarterly,* **45,** 557–90.

Lock, S. and Wells, F. (1996) (eds) *Fraud and Misconduct in Medical Research* London: BMJ Publishing Group.

Logan, B. (1993) Product tampering crime: A review. *Journal of Forensic Sciences,* **38**, 918–27.

Lykken, D. (1988) The case against polygraph testing. In A. Gale (ed.) *The Polygraph Test.* London: Sage, pp 111–23.

McCall, M. (1998) *High Flyers* Boston: Harvard Business School Press.

Marchington, M. and Wilkinson, A. (1997) *Core Personnel and Development* London: CIPD.

Marcus, B. (2000) Towards a more comprehensive understanding of counterproductive behavior in organizations. Paper presented at the EAPP in Germany.

Marcus, B., Schuler, H., Quell, P. and Humpfner, G. (2002) Measuring counter productivity. *International Journal of Selection and Assessment,* **10**, 18–35.

Marcus, N., Hoft, S., Riediger, M. and Schuler, H. (2000) Integrity tests and the five-factor model of personality. Paper given at APA conference, Washington.

Mars, G. (1984) *Cheats at Work* London: Unwin.

Mars, G. (2000) Culture and crime. In D. Carter and L. Alison (eds) *The Social Psychology of Crime.* Dartmouth and Ashgate, pp 23–49.

Martinko, M., Gundlach, M. and Douglas, S. (2002) Towards an integrative theory of counter productive workplace behaviour. *International Journal of Selection and Assessment,* **10**, 36–50.

Maslow, A. (1970) *Motivation and Personality* New York: Longman.

Maslow, A. (1998) *Maslow on Management* New York: John Wiley.

Miceli, M., Dozier, J. and Near, J. (1991) Blowing the whistle on data fudging. *Journal of Applied Social Psychology,* **21**, 271–95.

Miles, D., Borman, W., Spector, P. and Fox, S. (2002) Building an integrative model of extra role work behaviours. *International Journal of Selection and Assessment,* **10**, 51–7.

Miller, D. (2001) Disrespect and the experience of injustice. *Annual Review of Psychology,* **52**, 527–53.

Miner, J. and Capps, M. (1996) *How Honesty Testing Works* London: Quorun Books.

Mitnick, K. (2002) *The Art of Deception* Indianapolis: Wiley.

Morris, J. and Moberg, D. (1994) Work organization as contexts for trust and betrayal. In T. Sarbin (ed.) *Citizen Espionage.* New York: Praeger, pp 189–202.

Morrison, E. (1994) Role definitions and organizational citizenship behaviour. *Academy of Management Journal,* **37**, 1543–67.

Murphy, K. (1993) *Honesty in the Workplace* Pacific Grove, LA: Brooks.

Murphy, K. and Lee, S. (1994) Personality variables related to integrity test scores. *Journal of Business and Psychology,* **8**, 413–24.

Murray, H. (1938) *Explorations in Personality* New York: Oxford University Press.

Near, J. and Miceli, M. (1995) Effective whistle-blowing. *Academy of Management Review,* **20**, 679–706.

Near, J. and Miceli, M. (1996) Whistle-blowing: Myth and reality. *Journal of Management,* **22**, 507–26.

Nicehoff, B. and Paul, R. (2000) Causes of employment theft and strategies that HR managers can use for prevention. *Human Resources Management,* **39**, 51–69.

Oldham, J. and Morris, R. (1991) *Personality Self-portrait* New York: Bantam Books.

O'Malley, M. (2000) *Creating Commitment* New York: Wiley.

Ones, D. (2002) Introduction to the special issue, 'Counterproductive Behaviours at Work'. *International Journal of Selection and Assessment,* **10**, 1–4.

Ones, D. and Viswesvaran, C. (1998) Integrity testing in organizations. In R. Griffin, A. O'Leary-Kelly and J. Collins (eds) *Dysfunctional Behaviour in Organizations. Vol. 23B. Non-violent Dysfunctional Behaviour.* Greenwich, CT: JAI Press.

Ones, D.S., Viswesvaran, C. and Schmidt, F.L. (1995) Integrity tests – overlooked facts, resolved issues, and remaining questions. *American Psychologist,* **50**, 456–7.

Ones, D.S., Viswesvaran, C. and Reiss, A. (1996) Roles of social desirability in personality testing for personnel selection: The red herring. *Journal of Applied Psychology,* **81**, 660–79.

Organ, D. and Lingl, A. (1995) Personality, satisfaction, and organizational citizenship behaviour. *Journal of Social Psychology,* **135**, 339–50.

Pearce, J. and Henderson, G. (2000) Understanding Acts of Betrayal. In C. Cooper and I. Robertson (eds) *International Review of Industrial and Organizational Psychology,* **15**, 163–87. New York: Wiley.

Penney, L. and Spector, P. (2002) Narcissism and counterproductive work behaviour. Do bigger egos mean bigger problems? *International Journal of Selection and Assessment,* **10**, 126–33.

Ponting, C. (1985) *The Right to Know* Reading: Cox and Wayman.

Poole-Robb, S. and Bailey, A. (2002) *Risky Business* London: Kogan Page.

Porter, L. and Smith, F. (1970) The etiology of organizational commitment. Unpublished paper. University of California: Irvine.

PricewaterhouseCoopers (2003) *Economic Crime Survey* London: PricewaterhouseCoopers.

Punch, M. (1996) *Dirty Business* London: Sage.

Raskin, D. (1988) Does science support polygraph testing? In A. Gale (ed.) *The Polygraph Test*. London: Sage, pp 96–110.

Reichheld, F. (2001) *The Loyalty Effect* Boston: Harvard Business School Press.

Rieke, M. and Guastello, S. (1994) Unresolved issues in honesty and integrity testing. *American Psychologist*, **50**, 458–9.

Rimington, S. (2001) *Open Secret, The autobiography of the former Director General of MI5* London: Hutchinson.

Robinson, S. and Bennett, R. (1997a) A typology of deviant work-place behaviours. *Academy of Management Journal*, **38**, 555–72.

Robinson, S. and Bennett, R. (1997b) Workplace deviance: its definition, its manifestations and its causes. *Research on Negotiations in Organizations*, **6**, 3–27.

Rokeach, M. (1973) *The Nature of Human Values* New York: Free Press.

Rosse, J., Miller, J. and Ringer, R. (1996) The deterrent value of drug and integrity testing. *Journal of Business and Psychology*, **10**, 477–85.

Rothschild, J. and Miethe, T. (1999) Whistle-blower and management retaliation. *Work and Occupations*, **26**, 107–25.

Ryan, A. and Sackett, P. (1987) Pre-employment honesty testing. *Journal of Business and Psychology*, 248–56.

Sackett, P. (1994) Integrity testing for personnel selection. *Current Directions in Psychological Science*, **3**, 73–6.

Sackett, P. (2002) The structure of counterproductive work behaviours. *International Journal of Selection and Assessment*, **10**, 5–11.

Salgado, J. (2002) The big five personality dimensions and counter-productive behaviours. *International Journal of Selection and Assessment*, **10**, 117–25.

Schein, E. (1980) *Organizational Psychology* Englewood Cliffs, NJ: Prentice Hall.

Schmitt, M. and Dorfel, M. (1999) Procedural injustice at work, justice sensitivity, job satisfaction and psychosomatic well-being. *European Journal of Social Psychology*, **29**, 443–53.

Schneier, B. (2000) *Secrets and Lies* New York: John Wiley.

Seeman, M. (1959) On the meaning of alienation. *American Sociological Review*, **24**, 783–91.

Serious Fraud Office (2003) *Annual Report* London: The Stationery Office.

Shepherd, J. (1972) Alienation as a process. *Sociological Quarterly*, **13**, 161–73.

Shore, L. and Tetrick, L. (1994) The psychological contract as an explanatory framework in the employment relationship. In C. Cooper and D.

Rousseau (ed.) *Trends in Organizational Behavior*, 1, 91–109, Chichester: Wiley.

Sibbald, B., Bojke, C. and Gravelle, H. (2003) Primary Care: National survey of job satisfaction and retirement intentions amongst general Practitioners in England. *British Medical Journal*, 1 January 2003.

Singer, T. (1996) Stop thief! Are new employees robbing you blind? *Entrepreneur*, January: 144–53.

Skeats, J. (1991) *Successful Induction: How to get the best from your employees* London: Kogan Page.

Slade, E. (1998), *Employment Handbook* Croydon: Tolley's Employment Service.

Somers, M. and Casal, J. (1994) Organizational commitment and whistle-blowing. *Group and Organizational Management*, 19, 270–84.

Sprouse, M. (1992) *Sabotage in the American Workplace* San Francisco: Pressure Drop Press.

Thomas, H. and Lilley, R. (1995) *If They Haven't Heard It, You Haven't Said It! A Guide to Better Communication* Potters Bar: Progress Press.

Vrij, A. (2000) *Detecting Lies and Deceit* Chichester: Wiley.

Warek, J. (1999) Integrity and honesty testing: what do we know? How do we use it? *International Journal of Selection and Assessment*, 7, 183–95.

Warr, P. (1987) *Work, Unemployment and Mental Health* Cambridge: CUP.

Weiner, T., Johnston, D. and Lewis, N. (1995) *Betrayal* New York: Random House.

Zickar, M. (2001) Using personality inventories to identify things and agitators. *Journal of Vocational Behaviour*, 59, 149–64.

Zweig, D. and Webster, J. (2002) Where is the line between benign and invasive? An examination of psychological barriers to the acceptance of awareness monitoring systems. *Journal of Organizational Behaviour*, 23, 605–33.

Index